# WHAT ARE YOU AFRAID OF?

FROM THE *NEW YORK TIMES* BESTSELLING AUTHOR

# DR. DAVID JEREMIAH

# WHAT ARE YOU AFRAID OF?

## FACING DOWN YOUR FEARS WITH FAITH

Tyndale House Publishers, Inc., Carol Stream, Illinois

Visit Tyndale online at www.tyndale.com.

*TYNDALE* and Tyndale's quill logo are registered trademarks of Tyndale House Publishers, Inc.

*What Are You Afraid Of?: Facing Down Your Fears with Faith*

Designed by Dean H. Renninger

Edited by Stephanie Rische

Published in association with Yates & Yates (www.yates2.com).

**Library of Congress Cataloging-in-Publication Data**

Jeremiah, David, date.
  What are you afraid of? : facing down your fears with faith / Dr. David Jeremiah.
    pages cm
  Includes bibliographical references.
  ISBN 978-1-4143-8046-9 (hc)
  1. Fear—Religious aspects—Christianity. 2. Faith. I. Title.
  BV4908.5.J47 2013
  248.8´6—dc23                                                    2013026928

Printed in the United States of America

ISBN 978-1-4143-8947-9 (International Trade Paper Edition)

19   18   17   16   15   14   13
8    7    6    5    4    3    2

*Dr. Ken Nichols is a biblical counselor and communicator whose friendship and partnership in ministry reach back more than thirty-five years. Wherever he has been, you will find people whose lives have been healed because of his ministry. Over the last several years, we have talked often about the subject of fear, and he was the first to suggest that I write a book on the topic. Here it is, Ken. It is dedicated to you. Thank you for your encouragement!*

# Contents

# Introduction

You are asleep in your bed when your clock radio shocks you awake, blaring into the beginning of the day with news of traffic tie-ups, approaching thunderstorms, overnight killings, fires, stock-market plunges, government scandals, and car wrecks. Instead of jumping out of bed, you pull the covers up over your head. You know what a fearful world we live in, and you dread facing all the challenges of the day.

But maybe your morning fears are not in the news; they're about your job. You live in constant fear of getting caught in the downsizing trend. Or you're apprehensive about a business deal that has your career on the line.

Maybe your deepest fears lie at home. Can you meet this month's mortgage payment? Does your marriage seem shaky? Are your kids worrying you? After a recent service at the church I pastor in Southern California, a young soldier who had just returned from Afghanistan wept as he asked me to pray for him. He feared that he might be losing his family.

*Might*. That's the word that's haunting him. Our greatest fear is the conditional might—the threat of what *might* happen. Fear trades in the market of possibility. Or even impossibility—for fear is the tyrant of the imagination. It imposes itself upon us from the shadows, from its hazy mirror of maybe.

My friend Don Wyrtzen has been there:

> The illusive monster of fear lurks in the shadows, waiting to claw my soul to shreds. As one prone to melancholia, I see its ugly face often: when I'm struggling with the emotional stress of a difficult relationship, when I'm afraid failure is just around the corner, when success seems too hard to handle, and on days when free-floating anxiety is getting the best of me.[1]

That last phrase captures it for me: "free-floating anxiety." That's the worst one—the foreboding fear that something is wrong, but you don't know what. It envelops you like a cloud.

If you have struggled with fear, you are not alone. Fear is no respecter of people or of ages. It strikes the weak and the powerful. It haunts the young and the old, the rich and the poor. Even those who seem to have it all, including celebrities and heroes and "fearless" leaders, confess to a wide array of phobias.

Jennifer Aniston, Cher, and Whoopi Goldberg are all aviophobes. They are afraid of flying. Barbra Streisand is xenophobic—she is uncomfortable around strangers. Michael Jackson was haunted by the fear of contamination, infections, and diseases. He was mysophobic. But the celebrity with the most phobias is Woody Allen. He's afraid of insects, sunshine, dogs, deer, bright colors, children, heights, small rooms, crowds, and cancer.

Famous people of the past were no different. George Washington was scared to death of being buried alive. Richard Nixon was terrified of hospitals, and Napoleon Bonaparte, the military and political genius, feared cats.

Phobias: a circus parade of mental enslavement.

Some fears attack us only momentarily, but others can stay with us for a lifetime. A person with a fear of heights might feel her pulse shoot up when she steps into a glass-walled elevator and ascends twenty stories over a hotel lobby. But her fear is over the moment she steps out of the elevator into the hotel hallway.

On the other hand, our fears of failure, loneliness, rejection, impending disaster, or contracting a major illness never seem to go away. They are lifetime fears that simmer on the mind's back burner. They are fears that prey on life itself. Those are the fears I address in this book.

These fears can be described with what linguists call a "semantic range" of words: *fear, worry, anxiety, intimidation, unsettledness, dread, unease, alarm, distress, apprehensiveness,* and others. Sometimes it's hard to know exactly which of those words best describes what we're feeling, and it really doesn't matter. Whatever term we use, these feelings can all trigger toxic responses: immobilization, paralysis, withdrawal, passivity, depression, and psychosomatic disorders—physical maladies with no discernible physical cause.

When I ask, "What are you afraid of?" I'm asking, "What is it that immobilizes you? What is stealing your joy and destroying your hope? What is robbing you of sleep, night after night? What keeps you from living by faith and being a risk taker? What keeps you from giving your life wholly to a loving God who wants nothing but the best for you?"

I think I know the answers to these questions, at least in part, because I've lived shoulder to shoulder with a lot of mature Christian people my entire life. And I've been a pastor to thousands for nearly five decades. I've discovered that everybody—including me—is afraid of something. Our challenge is to discover and analyze our fears and find a godly (biblical) response to them.

When the apostle Paul was giving counsel to Timothy, his young protégé, he knew Timothy was afraid of something—probably of his assignment to lead the large church in Ephesus. Timothy was raised in a small town in Asia Minor, and Ephesus was the big city. Paul himself had spent three years in Ephesus, building up the church there. It was led by a strong group of elders, yet false teachers were causing trouble. And Timothy was supposed to go in and be the leader of the whole thing. What young pastor wouldn't have felt fear at the prospect?

So what did Paul tell Timothy? "Your fear is not from God. What do come from God are power, love, and a stable mental attitude" (2 Timothy 1:7, my paraphrase).

Paul knew that when we get God's perspective on the source of our fear, we can set aside what is not from Him and embrace what is. In all my years of following Christ, studying the Bible, and pastoring well-intentioned Christians, I have yet to find a fear for which God does not have an answer. And the reason is simple: God Himself is the answer to all our fears.

Think about it—fear is almost always based on the future. Sometimes we're afraid because we know what's coming in the future. But more commonly, we're afraid of what we don't know about the future. We're afraid of what might happen. For instance, the Gallup organization asked thirteen- to seventeen-year-olds what they were most afraid of. In descending order, the top ten fears of these teens were terrorist attacks, spiders, death/being killed, not succeeding in life/being a failure, war, heights, crime/violence, being alone, the future, and nuclear war.[2]

Notice that all these fears are future focused, and all are merely "maybes." These teens may encounter none of them. Whether the future is just a minute from now (you're waiting on a doctor's diagnosis) or five years from now (you worry about having enough money for retirement), fear's home office is the future.

But what is the future to God? To Him the future is now! We live inside time while God, who made it, lives outside it. We know relatively little about the future, while God knows everything about it. All the events in our lives occur in two time frames: past and future. (The present is a continuously fleeing, infinitesimal moment that becomes past even before we can define it.) God, on the other hand, has only one frame of reference: the eternal now, in which He sees and knows everything, including the future.

That's why God is the answer to all our fears. If God is good and loving (and He is), and if God is all-powerful (and He is), and if God has a purpose and a plan that include His children (and He does), and if we are His children (as I hope you are), then there is no reason to fear anything, for God is in control of everything.

I know—that's good theology, and you probably believe it. But you still have fears and apprehensions and a hollow place in the pit of your stomach, either sometimes or all the time. The great author Edith Wharton once said that she didn't believe in ghosts, but she was afraid of them. It's one thing to know something with the mind, and another to believe it with the heart.

How do you help a little child face her fear of the darkness? First you appeal to the mind. You turn on the light and show her there's nothing scary in the room. Then you help her attune her heart to what her mind has accepted. This is the process of faith, for all of us. We accept that God is in control, and on that basis, we shift our burdens to His perfect shoulders.

But what about our shaky future? Pessimism doesn't work, because it's another form of mental enslavement. Optimism may have no basis in reality. The one way to walk boldly and confidently into an unknown future is to stake everything on the power and goodness and faithfulness of God.

To understand why God is the answer to all our fears, we must understand what the Bible says about fear. And it says a lot. It tells us more than three hundred times not to fear. "Fear not" is its most frequently repeated command. The word *afraid* occurs more than two hundred times, and *fear* more than four hundred. And lest you think our Bible heroes were fearless, more than two hundred individuals in Scripture are said to have been afraid. And not all these were the "bad guys"; many were the main characters—David, Paul, Timothy, and others.

Biblical heroes were regular people who had to learn the same things you and I have to learn—to drive out fear by increasing their knowledge of God, to shift their focus from their present fear to the eternal God, to replace what they didn't know about the future with what they did know about Him. They had to put away childish things (being afraid of everything) and grow up in their faith and understanding.

I wrote this book because I see fear as a real and present danger in the body of Christ. Many Christians are not living lives free of fear, and there can be serious consequences when fear is not removed. Author and educator Neil T. Anderson writes,

> Fear is a thief. It erodes our faith, plunders our hope, steals our freedom, and takes away our joy of living the abundant life in Christ. Phobias are like the coils of a snake—the more we give in to them, the tighter they squeeze. Tired of fighting, we succumb to the temptation and surrender to our fears. But what seemed like an easy way out becomes, in reality, a prison of unbelief— a fortress of fear that holds us captive.[3]

Jesus came to "proclaim liberty to the captives," and I believe that includes those held captive by fear (Luke 4:18). He also says that truth is the key to freedom (John 8:32). And here is the truth: God is good (Psalm 119:68), God is love (1 John 4:8, 16), and God has a future filled with hope for His children (Jeremiah 29:11; Romans 8:28-29). God is a refuge and a fortress, a shield and a defender for those who trust in Him (Psalm 91:2-4). For those reasons, and more . . .

> You shall not be afraid of the terror by night,
> Nor of the arrow that flies by day,
> Nor of the pestilence that walks in darkness,
> Nor of the destruction that lays waste at noonday.
> A thousand may fall at your side,
> And ten thousand at your right hand;
> But it shall not come near you.
>
> PSALM 91:5-7

As you read this book, my prayers are that you will grow in your conviction that God is the answer to all your fears, that as you look to the future you will see nothing except His power and love guarding your every step, and that you will find the truth that sets you free to live the fearless life God created you to enjoy.

*Dr. David Jeremiah*
JUNE 2013

# CHAPTER 1

# DISASTER:
## *The Fear of Natural Calamity*

*We will not fear, even though the earth be removed, and though*
*the mountains be carried into the midst of the sea.*

PSALM 46:2

At least the Trowbridges had a place to hide—a neighbor's cellar. Kelcy, her husband, and their three children filed into its cool darkness, huddled beneath a blanket, and listened to the warning sirens howling through a Monday afternoon in May of 2013. The Trowbridges lived in the suburbs of Oklahoma City, and a deadly tornado was on its way.

The family could only sit, holding hands and listening as the sirens were drowned out by sounds that were louder and far more terrible. Shrieking winds converged upon the house, and there was a violent pounding on the cellar door. The children began to cry. "Shhh, it's just debris," Kelcy said. "Loose things blowing around, hitting the walls."

Then, after about forty minutes, an eerie silence fell. The

Trowbridges emerged into the light of a world they didn't recognize. The neighborhood was a shambles. Where was their home? It lay flattened to the earth, like rows of other houses on their street. Where was the family car? They eventually discovered that it had been lifted into the air, carried down the street, and then thrown on its roof.

One by one, the neighbors emerged, all speechless. Where there should have been birds singing, there was only the sound of muffled sobs. Here were the remains of their lives and the loss of comfortable illusions—illusions of stability and security in a rational world.

Mr. Trowbridge wasn't one to stand around. He went to work salvaging, sorting. But after a moment, he pulled back abruptly.

"Call the police," he said in a flat tone.

There, amid the bricks and pipes and rubble, was a little child—a girl no more than two or three years old. She was dead. Mr. Trowbridge was stoic until the police arrived, and then he lost it—weeping for the girl, for his family, for the violence of the earth.

Meanwhile, near Plaza Towers Elementary, Stuart Earnest Jr. saw and heard things that he knew would haunt him for the rest of his life. The school was directly hit by the tornado. Seven children lost their lives, and Earnest couldn't block out the sounds of the tragedy. He heard the voices of those screaming for help and the equally heartrending screams of those trying to come to their assistance.

A fourth grader named Damian Britton was among the Plaza Towers survivors, thanks to a courageous teacher who had saved his life. It seemed to Damian that all the horrors occurred in a five-minute period before the students came out of their hiding places. It was much the same everywhere—five short minutes for little ones, or anyone else, to learn such profound lessons of life and loss.

I have to tell you that it is difficult to recount those stories. It would be so much easier to keep the tone pleasant and comfortable, even in a book about fear. The problem, of course, is that the stories are true, and we know it. And they can happen again in another five minutes or tomorrow or the next day. Every year the news brings us yet another reminder that the natural forces governing this planet are troubled and unstable.

We live in a kind of necessary denial. We proceed with our daily lives as if we have guarantees of security that simply aren't possible in this life. We congratulate ourselves for our impressive advances in technology, and we pretend we've conquered every challenge to life and health. But it's not so. Nature is gorgeous and inspiring—and also monstrous and inhuman.

In 2004 the big tragedy was the Indian Ocean tsunami, which killed 230,000 people. I can't get past those numbers. In 2005 we encountered Hurricane Katrina. And who can forget 2010–11? The earthquake in Haiti cost another 220,000 people their lives; the tsunami in Japan, at least 15,000.

But those are merely the headline weather events. There are too many earthquakes, fires, floods, hurricanes, tornadoes, famines, storms, and tsunamis for us to even keep a running tally. Natural calamities rage on in our world, costing us countless billions of dollars and, more significantly, hundreds of thousands of lives.

Natural disaster raises many questions about the nature of our security, about our fear of the uncontrollable, and especially about the character of God. These questions need answers. But I'd like to open the discussion by sharing about a biblical character who experienced two natural disasters in the space of twenty-four hours. His name, of course, was Job.

## NATURAL DISASTERS IN THE LIFE OF JOB

Job has become the quintessential model for enduring disaster, and if ever there was someone we'd think didn't deserve it, it was Job. The first few verses of his book give testimony concerning Job in four areas. We learn first of all about his *faith*—that he was a man who was "blameless and upright, and one who feared God and shunned evil" (Job 1:1). Job was not sinless, but he was mature in character and a man of righteousness.

Job is also distinguished because of his *fortune*: "His possessions were seven thousand sheep, three thousand camels, five hundred yoke of oxen, five hundred female donkeys, and a very large household, so that this man was the greatest of all the people of the East" (Job 1:3).

In Job's day, wealth was calculated in terms of land, animals, and servants, and Job had all three in abundance. He was the wealthiest man of his time.

He wasn't just a man of fortune but also of *family*. The first chapter tells us that he raised sons and daughters who were close knit. They held great birthday feasts for one another, after which their father would make burnt offerings to God on their behalf. He said, "It may be that my sons have sinned and cursed God in their hearts" (Job 1:5). Faith and family were intertwined for him.

Finally, he had many *friends*. Some are famous for their role in Job's book, but there were no doubt many others who weren't mentioned. Job 2:11 recounts how a group of his closest friends arrived to mourn with him after the great losses he sustained. If you know anything about Job's narrative, you remember that these friends ended up letting him down. But still, they were his friends, and they came from distant parts to minister to him in his time of need.

They were right to sit with him to help him bear the load of mourning. Where they went wrong was when they attempted to give pat explanations and solutions for a situation that was anything but simple. In the end, they brought out the worst rather than the best in Job. Yet we're told that he forgave them and there was reconciliation (Job 42:9-11).

What those friends couldn't know—what Job himself couldn't know—was that spiritual forces were in play far beyond their reckoning. The details are recounted in Job 1:8-12:

> The LORD said to Satan, "Have you considered My servant Job, that there is none like him on the earth, a blameless and upright man, one who fears God and shuns evil?"
>
> So Satan answered the LORD and said, "Does Job fear God for nothing? Have You not made a hedge around him, around his household, and around all that he has on every side? You have blessed the work of his hands, and his possessions have increased in the land. But now, stretch out Your hand and touch all that he has, and he will surely curse You to Your face!"
>
> And the LORD said to Satan, "Behold, all that he has is in your power; only do not lay a hand on his person." So Satan went out from the presence of the LORD.

Armed with God's permission, Satan went to work, and Job's ruin came rapidly, with four calamities occurring in one day. These were the terms: Satan could come after Job's possessions, but not his person. And so the great experiment began. But what we see already is that it's clear who is in charge of this world. The devil can test Job, but not without God's permission.

Our God reigns, and we can't afford to forget it during a discussion of disaster—or any other time.

What do you give the man who has everything? Disaster—that was something Job had yet to experience. It begins during one of those feasts, with the sons and daughters all gathered together, laughing and enjoying one another's company.

A messenger approaches Job with disturbing news. Sabean raiders have descended on his estate, hijacked Job's cattle, and killed his servants. This messenger alone has survived to tell the tale (Job 1:13-15).

Yet even before the servant has finished his account, before Job has taken it all in, the door opens and another messenger stands there. He is pale, his eyes wide, as he whispers, "The fire of God fell from heaven and burned up the sheep and the servants" (Job 1:16).

At this point it seems that Job's day can't get any worse. But a third messenger is right behind. The phrase "while he was still speaking" is used three times in this passage. For Job, at least, the old adage is true: calamities often come in bunches.

The third messenger brings news that there has been a raid by the Chaldeans. They have stolen the camels, killed the servants, and yes, left one distressed messenger (Job 1:17).

A lot has gone wrong for Job—calamity piled upon calamity. But before he can make sense of any of this, let alone form any kind of recovery plan, the coup de grâce falls:

While he was still speaking, another also came and said, "Your sons and daughters were eating and drinking wine in their oldest brother's house, and suddenly a great wind came from across the wilderness and struck the four corners of the house, and it fell on the young people, and they are dead; and I alone have escaped to tell you!"

JOB 1:18-19

Along with everything else, Job must have been blessed with a strong heart. Can you imagine taking in such news? He was devoted to his children, constantly bringing them before God. Despite all his intercession, they have died in one fell blow. He faces ten fresh graves and an aching silence from heaven. *Why, God?*

The book of Job has always been the go-to book to help people cope with the existence and effects of evil. At the outset, the book shows us three major sources of evil. First, there are evil individuals, such as the Sabeans and the Chaldeans who killed Job's servants and stole his oxen and donkeys. Then it shows the destructive evil of natural disasters in the fire that destroyed Job's livestock and herders and the windstorm that killed Job's children. And behind it all, we see evil on a cosmic level in the hand of Satan who, with God's permission, orchestrated the entire disaster.

Since scholars consider Job to be the oldest book in the Bible, we know that the problem of natural disasters has been with us for as long as human beings have walked the earth. The Bible doesn't gloss over the tougher questions of life; it doesn't try to make us avert our gaze. We're invited to stand with Job in the cemetery, looking down at the ashes of his dreams, and ask God *why?* The first question evoked by this story in particular and natural calamities in general is this: What do these recurring disasters say about God?

## NATURAL DISASTERS AND THE REALITY OF GOD

### *God Cannot Be Divorced from Disasters*

Some say that God should not even be included in the discussion of disasters since He would have nothing to do with such evil. The explanation goes something like this: God created the world, but He is not involved in the operation of it. This philosophy is called deism. It accepts the existence and goodness of God but distances Him from anything that happens in the world He created.

I think many Christians often adopt a sort of deism in an attempt to get God off the hook. It allows us to affirm the goodness of God in the face of terrible evils simply by saying it's not His fault. He created a good world, and He should not be blamed if it goes wrong. But Scripture is clear that God is actively at work in the universe (Job 37).

Another way we extricate God from responsibility for disasters is to blame them all on Satan. But we know from our study of Job that Satan cannot do anything without God's permission (Job 1:8-12). If Satan has to get permission from God to do what he does, then God is still in control and reigns in human affairs. People sense His control over everything when they call natural disasters "acts of God."

So for us to say that God is not involved in these cataclysmic events is too simplistic to explain all the facts. Whether it's comfortable or not, we must discuss this issue with theological integrity. The Bible teaches us that God is sovereign—He reigns in the nice moments and in those that aren't so nice. Let's look at some of the reasons disaster exists in a world that God controls.

#### GOD EMPLOYS THE ELEMENTS OF NATURE IN THE OPERATION OF THE WORLD

The Bible contains many passages refuting the idea that God set nature in motion and now lets it run as it will. These Scriptures present a hands-on God who is intimately involved in controlling and sustaining all events in the natural world. Here is a small sampling:

> Whatever the LORD pleases He does,
> In heaven and in earth,
> In the seas and in all deep places.
> He causes the vapors to ascend from
> the ends of the earth;
> He makes lightning for the rain;
> He brings the wind out of His treasuries.
>
> PSALM 135:6-7

> He makes His sun rise on the evil and on the good, and
> sends rain on the just and on the unjust.
>
> MATTHEW 5:45

> He says to the snow, "Fall on the earth";
> Likewise to the gentle rain and the heavy
>       rain of His strength. . . .
> By the breath of God ice is given,
> And the broad waters are frozen.
> Also with moisture He saturates the
>       thick clouds;
> He scatters His bright clouds.
> And they swirl about, being turned by
>       His guidance,
> That they may do whatever He commands
>       them
> On the face of the whole earth.
>
> JOB 37:6, 10-12

## GOD EMPLOYS THE ELEMENTS OF NATURE IN HIS OPPOSITION TO EVIL

Not only does God use the elements of nature to keep the world running, He also uses them as punishment or to drive His people toward righteousness.

Early in the Bible, we find God sending a flood to destroy a sin-blackened world, sparing only righteous Noah and his family (Genesis 6–8). Later, when the Israelites were wandering in the desert, God sent judgment upon Dathan, Abiram, and Korah, who had rejected Him. The "earth opened its mouth and swallowed them up . . . with all their goods" (Numbers 16:32).

God sent fire to destroy Sodom and Gomorrah because of their wickedness (Genesis 19:24); He sent plagues to punish Egypt (Exodus 7–12); He crafted a plague that killed seventy thousand men because of David's sin in numbering the people (2 Samuel 24:15); He sent a fierce storm to get Jonah's attention and bring him to repentance (Jonah 1:4-17).

In Amos 4, there is an extended passage describing God's dealings with the disobedience of His people. If we're ever tempted to separate God from natural disaster, this passage should stop us in our tracks. Here is Eugene Peterson's vivid paraphrase:

> "You know, don't you, that I'm the One
> who emptied your pantries and cleaned out your
> cupboards,
> Who left you hungry and standing in bread lines?
> But you never got hungry for me. You continued to
> ignore me."
> GOD's Decree.
>
> "Yes, and I'm the One who stopped the rains
> three months short of harvest.

I'd make it rain on one village
    but not on another.
I'd make it rain on one field
    but not on another—and that one would dry up.
People would stagger from village to village
    crazed for water and never quenching their thirst.
But you never got thirsty for me.
    You ignored me."
    GOD's Decree.

"I hit your crops with disease
    and withered your orchards and gardens.
Locusts devoured your olive and fig trees,
    but you continued to ignore me."
    GOD's Decree.

"I revisited you with the old Egyptian plagues,
    killed your choice young men and prize horses.
The stink of rot in your camps was so strong
    that you held your noses—
But you didn't notice me.
    You continued to ignore me."
    GOD's Decree.

"I hit you with earthquake and fire,
    left you devastated like Sodom and Gomorrah.
You were like a burning stick
    snatched from the flames.
But you never looked my way.
    You continued to ignore me."
    GOD's Decree.

AMOS 4:6-11, *THE MESSAGE*

When we distance God from responsibility for the calamities of the world, we are claiming more than we know. For if God is not in control of the world's disasters, then how can we depend on Him to be in control of our lives and the future? Either He is involved in all the world's operations, or He's involved in none of them.

Before we move on, it is critical that I make a distinction between God's general judgment on the sin of humankind and His supposed judgment on the sin of particular men and women. It is true to say that all God's judgment is because of sin and that He uses disasters in administering judgment. But it is not true to say that every particular disaster is His judgment of some particular sin committed by some particular person or nation.

After 9/11, some people were quick to point out that the disaster was God's judgment on our nation for our rebellion against Him. While that may have been true, how would anyone on earth know for sure?

Almost all the disasters and tragedies that have befallen our nation in the last several years have incited some pundit to declare the tragedy a particular judgment for a particular sin that had been committed in the immediate context of the disaster. The truth is, we don't know the mysteries of God's heart and will. In Luke's Gospel, Jesus warns against playing the armchair prophet. Pilate had murdered some Galileans, and others had been killed when a tower collapsed at Siloam. When asked about it, Jesus said,

> Do you suppose that these Galileans were worse sinners
> than all other Galileans, because they suffered such
> things? I tell you, no; but unless you repent you will all
> likewise perish. Or those eighteen on whom the tower
> in Siloam fell and killed them, do you think that they

were worse sinners than all other men who dwelt in Jerusalem? I tell you, no; but unless you repent you will all likewise perish.

LUKE 13:2-5

Jesus was reminding us that in our fallen world, disasters happen, and they happen to both evil and righteous people without distinction or explanation. It's not up to us to label this one as misfortune or that one as God's judgment but simply, as Jesus pointed out, to ponder the sin in our own hearts.

## God Cannot Be Discredited by Disasters

Some people, of course, remove God from the equation entirely; He simply doesn't exist, they argue, and disasters are all the proof we need. Apologist Dinesh D'Souza summarizes this line of reasoning in his book *What's So Great about Christianity*:

> If God exists, He is all-powerful. If He is all-powerful, He is in a position to stop evil and suffering. But we know from experience that evil and suffering go on, scandalously, mercilessly, without even a hint of proportion or justice. Thus there cannot be an omnipotent being capable of preventing all this from happening because if there were, He surely would. Therefore God does not exist.[1]

Atheist George Smith speaks for those who would attempt to make this case with tidy logic: "The problem of evil is this. . . . If God knows there is evil but cannot prevent it, he is not omnipotent. If God knows there is evil and can prevent it but desires not to, he is not omnibenevolent."[2]

Sometimes it is sheer emotion rather than cut-and-dried reasoning that provokes such a conclusion. After the 2010 tsunami, a commentator in Scotland's newspaper *The Herald* wrote,

God, if there is a God, should be ashamed of Himself. The sheer enormity of the Asian tsunami disaster, the death, destruction, and havoc it has wreaked, the scale of misery it has caused, must surely test the faith of even the firmest believer. . . . I hope I am right . . . that there is no God. For if there were, then He'd have to shoulder the blame. In my book, He would be as guilty as sin and I'd want nothing to do with Him.[3]

But wait a minute—not so fast. C. S. Lewis, once an atheist himself, saw disasters not as a proof against the existence of God but, reasoning as he did when he came to faith in Christ, as actual proof of God's existence:

My argument against God was that the universe seemed so cruel and unjust. But how had I got this idea of *just* and *unjust*? A man does not call a line crooked unless he has some idea of a straight line. What was I comparing this universe with when I called it unjust? If the whole show was bad and senseless from A to Z, so to speak, why did I, who was supposed to be part of the show, find myself in violent reaction against it? . . . Thus in the very act of trying to prove that God did not exist—in other words, that the whole of reality was senseless—I found I was forced to assume that one part of reality—namely my idea of justice—was full of sense. Consequently atheism turns out to be too simple. If the whole of the universe has no meaning, we should never have found out that it has no meaning: just as, if there were no light in the universe and therefore no creatures with eyes, we should never know it was dark. *Dark* would be without meaning.[4]

The fact that we have a strong idea of justice and perfection in a world contaminated with injustice and imperfection gives compelling evidence that a good God does exist.

One truth we often overlook is that massive deaths caused by disaster cannot discredit God any more than a single death can. We know who brought death into the world, and it wasn't God. We must remember that every one of the people who died in the Haiti earthquake would eventually have died anyway. The fact that they died simultaneously is really no more tragic than if their deaths had been spread out over the next several decades. It's just that the sudden and unexpected simultaneous deaths shock us more.

## God Cannot Be Defined by Disasters

In the aftermath of every disaster, we often hear something like this: "I could never believe in a God who would allow such awful things to happen to His creatures."

The God these people want to believe in is the "helicopter parent" God who hovers just above us at all times, insulating us from all unpleasantness like an overprotective father. They want a God who guarantees safety, security, and happiness and spares us from all tragedy and pain, even disciplinary pain. God is better than that. He does not indulge our every desire but rather administers discipline to help us become the kind of creatures who can inhabit a blissful eternity.

Those who define God solely by the evil He allows overlook the flip side of their complaint. Yes, there is evil in the world, but there is also an enormous amount of good. If God is not good, as they claim, how do they account for all the good we experience? Is it fair to judge Him for the evil and not credit Him with the good?

In his book *Where Was God?* Erwin Lutzer writes,

Often the same people who ask where God was following a disaster thanklessly refuse to worship and honor Him for years of peace and calmness. They disregard God in good times, yet think He is obligated to provide help when bad times come. They believe the God they dishonor when they are well should heal them when they are sick; the God they ignore when they are wealthy should rescue them from impending poverty; and the God they refuse to worship when the earth is still should rescue them when it begins to shake.

We must admit that God owes us nothing. Before we charge God with not caring, we must thank Him for those times when His care is very evident. We are ever surrounded by undeserved blessings. Even in His silence, He blesses us.[5]

In a world that contains tragedies, we must realize that they're vastly outnumbered by blessings. A little clear thinking underlines the point that we can't allow others to define God for us. The Bible and good common sense erase a lot of confusion.

There's no denying that we live in a world where many bad things happen, and much of it seems undeserved. "Why do bad things happen to good people?" Dinesh D'Souza asks. "The

Christian answer is that there are no good people. None of us deserves the life that we have, which is a gratuitous gift from God."[6]

God is loving, and His gifts abound in our world. So does His discipline. That is why we must refuse to let only one side of the equation define God for us.

### God Cannot Be Defeated by Disasters

When disasters happen, we are sometimes tempted to think that God's purposes have been thwarted. Let's allow God to speak for Himself on this subject:

> I am God, and there is no other;
> I am God, and there is none like Me,
> Declaring the end from the beginning,
> And from ancient times things that are not yet done,
> Saying, "My counsel shall stand,
> And I will do all My pleasure." . . .
> Indeed I have spoken it;
> I will also bring it to pass.
> I have purposed it;
> I will also do it.
> ISAIAH 46:9-11

One reason we fear disasters is that their occurrence makes it seem that God is not in control, that somehow things have slipped out of His grasp. At such times we must remember that a single thread in the grand tapestry cannot comprehend the pattern of the whole. Our view is too limited to perceive any ultimate meaning in a calamity—how our present suffering fits into God's ultimate purpose. Yet, as Paul tells us, "We know that all things work together for good to those who love God, to those who are the called according to His purpose" (Romans 8:28).

Like every other piece of this entangled subject, this verse is easy to confuse in its meaning. As James Montgomery Boice tells us, Paul is not saying that evil things are good:

> The text does not teach that sickness, suffering, persecution, grief, or any other such thing is itself good. On the contrary, these things are evils. Hatred is not love. Death is not life. Grief is not joy. The world is filled with evil. But what the text teaches . . . is that God uses these things to effect his own good ends for people. God brings good out of evil.[7]

God brought good out of the work by which Satan meant to destroy Job's faith. And He used the awful reality of the crucifixion of a perfect Christ for wonderful purposes. In God's wise and powerful hands, evil events are used as tools to work toward good ends.

The clue is in the ordering of the words in the original language: "We know that for those who love God," the Greek text reads, "He is working." In other words, God is ceaselessly, energetically, and purposefully active on their behalf. He is involved; He is busy creating a glorious destiny for those who love Him.

The phrase Paul uses to describe how God works on our behalf is interesting. He says that "all things work together." This expression is translated from the Greek word *sunergeo*, from which we get our word *synergism*. Synergism is the working together of various elements to produce an effect greater than, and often completely different from, the sum of each element acting separately.

So things do not just work out somehow if we let nature take its course. God causes this synergism to happen. He is the One who stirs the mix! This is why disaster cannot defeat God or derail His plans and purposes. All nature is under His control: *all things* work together. The One who controls nature holds us in His hands.

Donald Grey Barnhouse explains that the "we know" part of Romans 8:28 is a superb antidote to the fear of disaster:

> It is possible here and now for us to know that all things
> work together for our good. To lay hold of that fact is
> to calm the turbulence of life and to bring quiet and
> confidence into the whole of life. Nothing can touch me
> unless it passes through the will of God. God has a plan
> for my life. God is working according to a fixed, eternal
> purpose.[8]

In the following poem, Annie Johnson Flint uses the intricate workings of factory machinery to give us a creative picture of God's complete control of "all things":

> *In a factory building, there are wheels and gearings,*
> *There are cranks, pulleys, belts either tight or slack—*
> *Some are whirling swiftly, some are turning slowly,*
> *Some are thrusting forward, some are pulling back;*
> *Some are smooth and silent, some are rough and noisy,*
> *Pounding, rattling, clanking, moving with a jerk;*
> *In a wild confusion in a seeming chaos,*
> *Lifting, pushing, driving—but they do their work.*
> *From the mightiest lever to the smallest cog or gear,*
> *All things move together for the purpose planned;*

*And behind the working is a mind controlling,*
*And a force directing, and a guiding hand.*
*So all things are working for the Lord's beloved;*
*Some things might be hurtful if alone they stood;*
*Some might seem to hinder; some might draw*
       *us backward;*
*But they work together, and they work for good,*
*All the thwarted longings, all the stern denials,*
*All the contradictions, hard to understand.*
*And the force that holds them, speeds them and*
       *retards them,*
*Stops and starts and guides them—is our*
       *Father's hand.*[9]

Several years ago my wife and I were reminded of an inspiring example of one couple who trusted God's control over all things. While we were visiting Jerusalem, some friends took us to lunch at the American Colony Hotel. As we sat down to eat, we were handed a small brochure that told the story of the hotel and its restaurant.

I was shocked to discover that the hotel belonged to the family of Horatio Spafford, the man who wrote the words to my favorite Gospel hymn, "It Is Well with My Soul." I have often recounted the tragic circumstances that surrounded the writing of that song, but the brochure included facts I hadn't known. Here is that story:

In 1871, Horatio Spafford lived in the Lake View suburb of Chicago. He was a young lawyer with a wife, Anna, and four little girls. In October of that year, the whole center of the city was devastated by fire. No one is certain how the fire started, but it killed hundreds of people and destroyed whole sections of the city.

All across town, people were wandering homeless and hungry. The Spaffords were deeply involved in doing what they could to help families in distress. But it was no short-term ministry. Two years later, exhausted from their work, they planned a trip to Europe for rest. But at the last minute, business kept Horatio in town. Anna and the four girls boarded a ship and left the harbor.

Late one night during the voyage, another ship rammed the steamer, which sank within twenty minutes. One of only forty-seven who were rescued, Anna was pulled from the water, unconscious and floating on a piece of debris. But the four Spafford girls perished. Anna sent a telegram from Paris to her husband: "Saved alone. What shall I do?" She remarked to another passenger that God had given her four daughters and taken them away and that perhaps someday she would understand why.

Horatio boarded a ship to find his wife and bring her home. When the ship's path crossed the very point where his daughters had been lost, the captain called him to his cabin and told him so. Horatio, deeply moved, found a piece of paper from the hotel in which he had stayed before the voyage. He jotted down the words to "It Is Well with My Soul," now one of the world's favorite hymns.

Back in Chicago, the couple tried to start over again. A son was born to them, and then another daughter. Maybe the worst was over. But then, another tragedy: the boy died of scarlet fever at four years old.

Inexplicably, the family's church took the view that these tragedies were surely the punishment of a wrathful God for some unspecified sin on the part of the Spaffords. An elder in a church he had helped build, Horatio was asked to leave rather than being taken in and comforted by a healing community.

In 1881, the little family left the United States to begin a new life in Jerusalem. They rented a house in the Old City section, with the goal of imitating the lives of the first-century Christians as closely as possible. Soon the family was widely known for their love and service to the needy, as well as for their devotion to the Scriptures. Even today, the Spafford Children's Center serves Jerusalem and the West Bank by providing health care and educational support to as many as thirty thousand children annually under the leadership of the Spaffords' descendants.[10]

Anna and Horatio Spafford suffered severe testings of their faith, but they did not blame God for their suffering. They knew He was in control of all things, and because He could not be defeated, neither could they. Their faith allowed them to learn through their testings and to use their pain to bless others and further the Gospel.

I hope this section has helped lift the fog that obscures our understanding of God's connection with disaster. When our pain leads us to see Him as uninvolved in calamity, powerless to control it, or defeated by it, we saw off the limb that supports us, and we plunge into fear. This leaves us without hope, for an all-powerful God is our only solace in tragic times.

Now we will look at ways in which the experience of disaster can actually bless us.

## NATURAL DISASTERS
## AND THE RESPONSIBILITIES OF MAN

In the midst of pain and grief, it's hard to realize that disasters can bring vital benefits. Just as destructive forest fires clean out the underbrush that would eventually stifle the trees, disasters in our lives can cause us to see our blind spots and address them with clearer vision.

## Disasters Teach Us to Repent of Our Sin

Earlier in this chapter we discussed an occasion from Luke 13 in which Jesus refers to two contemporary tragedies. Did the victims die because they were more sinful than the survivors? No, He replies; we all perish unless we repent. In other words, the greatest natural disaster of all happened in the Garden of Eden; the rest is collateral damage. The Fall makes us all victims unless we allow Jesus Christ to handle the problem of our sin.

When you read about people losing their lives in fires, floods, hurricanes, tornadoes, and tsunamis, do you ever wonder how many of them were prepared to meet their God? Does the question cause you to examine your own readiness (2 Corinthians 13:5)? Our readiness to meet God greatly reduces our fear of disaster.

Many factors are at work in the scope of a disaster, but one of them is surely the work of God drawing our attention to Himself. In truth, we are surrounded by unrecognized tragedies and disasters: a dark, sex-obsessed, violent culture; the rapid decline of morality; the deterioration of Christian influence in our world. How many more are victims to these man-made poisons than to the forces of wind and weather? Sometimes it requires the dramatic power of a hurricane or some other force in nature to capture our attention and turn our minds to matters of eternity.

God uses disasters and tragedies to accomplish His perfect will in us and through us—and sometimes to bring us to Himself in the first place. In the church I pastor, almost all who give testimony to their faith at their baptism have one thing in common: they are brought to Christ through some difficult experience. Often it is the loss of a loved one or a divorce or the loss of employment. God uses difficulty and disaster to get the attention of those He is pursuing.

How does this work? Erwin Lutzer tells us,

Disasters might drive some people away from God, but
for others it has the opposite effect, driving them into the
arms of Jesus. The destruction of nature has helped them
distinguish the temporary from the permanent. Disasters
remind the living that tomorrow is uncertain, so we must
prepare for eternity today. Today is the accepted time;
today is the day of salvation.

When disasters come, God is not on trial, *we are.*[11]

### Disasters Teach Us to Reflect on God's Goodness

When I watch reports of natural disasters as they are instanta-
neously delivered to us through the media, my first thoughts are
for the lives lost and the families torn apart. I also experience a
sense of gratitude that my family and people I know were not
touched by these events.

I used to feel guilty about this in the same way I felt guilty
about people who got cancer at the same time I did but did not
survive. But I have since come to understand that it is proper to
be grateful that I have been saved even while I mourn for those
who have been lost.

Mark Mittelberg writes,

It's common in the middle of a drought . . . to forget that
rain is the norm. Or in the middle of a flood to forget
that floods rarely happen. Or when bad news comes from
the doctor to forget that, for most of us, this comes after
many years of relatively good health.[12]

God's blessings abound; they are the norm, and it's proper to be grateful for them at all times, regardless of surrounding circumstances.

### Disasters Teach Us to Respond to the Hurting

The Southern California wildfires of 2003 and 2007 destroyed the homes of several of our church families and decimated a community in the mountains above our place of worship. I had never experienced anything that touched our church so directly.

To this day, people still talk about the ways they were changed for the better from an event that couldn't have seemed any worse. When the devil sends a wildfire, God sends the holy fire of Spirit-filled followers of Christ. When the devil sends a flood, God sends the refreshment of living water.

During those tragic events, many of our people did exactly what Job's friends did at first: they sat with hurting people. Sometimes silent presence is the most powerful ministry. When folks are grieving, for example, spiritual rationalizations and the wholesale quoting of Scripture verses can fall flat. People don't need our answers—they simply need our shoulders to cry on, our company in the darkness. These are the moments when the church of Jesus Christ is at its very best. And when someone finally turns to us and asks why, we can say, "I'd love to sit down with you over coffee and work on those questions together soon. But right now, I'm here to serve you. What can I do?"

In 1940, C. S. Lewis published his first popular book on Christian doctrine, *The Problem of Pain*. It was an intellectual attack on the view that suffering and evil rule out the existence of God. It was a book for the mind—and a good one. But it didn't really touch the heart; that came twenty-one years later, when Lewis found himself writing a very different kind of book.

In *A Grief Observed*, Lewis's aching sadness and even anger radiated from every page. He had lost his beloved wife to bone cancer, and he was overwhelmed with sorrow. He was no longer interested in debating points; now his heart was broken. This new book held more questions than answers. It read as a journey of mourning that somehow arrived at a safe harbor for faith.

When he finished writing, Lewis understood that the world had never seen him this raw and emotional. He decided to publish *A Grief Observed* under the pen name N. W. Clerk. Yet soon an army of loving friends were bringing him "Clerk's" book, saying, "Here, perhaps this little volume will help you." Lewis had to come out from behind his pseudonym and admit that he was the book's author and the owner of the pain it displayed. It was the book born out of pain, even more than the book with the intellectual answers, that ministered to others who were suffering.[13]

Disasters perform a painful surgery in our inmost parts, but the Physician's hand is tender and sure. He wants to make us better, stronger, more capable of ministry in a world of broken hearts. As we minister to our own pain and the pain of others, we take on a growing resemblance to the Savior who healed pain everywhere He encountered it.

### Disasters Teach Us to Remember God's Promise

God has given us a spectacular, all-encompassing promise that provides the ultimate cure for our fear of disaster. Revelation 21:3-4 says, "I heard a loud voice from heaven saying, 'Behold, the tabernacle of God is with men, and He will dwell with them, and they shall be His people. God Himself will be with them and be their God. And God will wipe away every tear from their eyes; there shall be no more death, nor sorrow, nor crying. There shall be no more pain, for the former things have passed away.'"

Disasters remind us that God doesn't intend for this fallen earth, with its death, disaster, and corruption, to be our permanent home. As the old spiritual says, "This world is not my home; I'm just a passin' through." The calamities we experience here are only temporary phenomena. Each disaster reminds us that a disaster-free eternity awaits us and inspires our hearts to long for it.

Paul affirms this longing: "The earnest expectation of the creation eagerly waits for the revealing of the sons of God. . . . For we know that the whole creation groans and labors with birth pangs together until now" (Romans 8:19, 22).

Dinesh D'Souza sums up how this promise of God assures our ultimate victory over disaster:

> The only way for us to really triumph over evil and suffering is to live forever in a place where those things do not exist. It is the claim of Christianity that there is such a place and that it is available to all who seek it. No one can deny that, if this claim is true, then evil and suffering are exposed as temporary hardships and injustices. They are as transient as our brief, mortal lives. In that case God has shown us a way to prevail over evil and suffering, which are finally overcome in the life to come.[14]

### Disasters Teach Us to Rely on God's Presence and His Power

We began this chapter by looking into the terrible experience of a man named Job. It's fitting that we return to his life again to discover how the tragic events of his life fully played themselves out.

Job experiences severe depression as he struggles to deal with his losses. But soon he finds within himself a powerful, trusting commitment to God. "Though He slay me," Job resolves, "yet will I trust Him" (Job 13:15).

By the grace of God, Job manages to maintain his strong faith and reliance on God, certain that something better is in store for him:

I know that my Redeemer lives,
And He shall stand at last on the earth;
And after my skin is destroyed, this I know,
That in my flesh I shall see God,
Whom I shall see for myself,
And my eyes shall behold, and not another.
How my heart yearns within me!

JOB 19:25-27

Finally God speaks to Job and his friends. But instead of explaining His ways, He proclaims His almighty power and puts to shame their bumbling attempts to explain suffering. On hearing the voice of God, Job humbles himself and repents of his questioning of God:

I have heard of You by the hearing of the ear,
But now my eye sees You.
Therefore I abhor myself,
And repent in dust and ashes.

JOB 42:5-6

But that wasn't the end of Job's story. In the last chapter of his book we are told that "the LORD blessed the latter days of Job more than his beginning," giving him a superabundance of livestock and ten more children (Job 42:12-15). Thus Job was amply rewarded for his patience, his faith, and his complete trust in God's power.

We should not take this to mean that all who suffer disaster will have everything restored in this life. The promise is that no matter what those who love God suffer here, a time is coming when God's blessings will cause us to forget every pain we ever endured.

Famed devotional author Hannah Whitall Smith was plagued with terrible pain and unanswered questions. It seemed to her, just as it seems to you and me, that no one could possibly understand what she was experiencing. She didn't know where to turn for help until she was told of a deeply spiritual Christian woman living nearby:

> I summoned up my courage, therefore, one afternoon, and went to see her, and poured out my troubles; expecting that of course she would take a deep interest in me, and would be at great pains to do all she could to help me. . . . When I had finished my story, and had paused, expecting sympathy and consideration, she simply said, "Yes, all you say may be very true, but then in spite of it all, there is God."
>
> I waited a few minutes for something more, but nothing came, and my friend and teacher had the air of having said all that was necessary. "But," I continued, "surely you did not understand how very serious and perplexing my difficulties are."
>
> "Oh, yes, I did," replied my friend, "but then, as I tell you, there is God." And I could not induce her to make any other answer. It seemed to me most disappointing and unsatisfactory. I felt that my peculiar and really harrowing experiences could not be met by anything so simple as merely the statement, "Yes, but there is God." . . .

At last . . . I came gradually to believing, that, being my Creator and Redeemer, He must be enough; and at last a conviction burst upon me that He really was enough, and my eyes were opened to the fact of the absolute and utter all-sufficiency of God.[15]

*God is enough.* Do these words of guidance seem to you as they did at first to Hannah—a trite oversimplification? They could be viewed that way until, like Hannah, we think a little more deeply. The fact is, God *must* be enough, for if He isn't, where do we go for plan B? If the God of heaven and earth—who is mightier than all the world's armies, who can cause the earth to melt into the sea—is not Lord of your crisis, you're in deep trouble. And so am I.

God *is* sufficient. He is in control. He holds the destiny of the galaxies in His hands, all the while knowing the precise number of hairs on your head. Above all else, He loves you and chose to pour that love out, not in words, but in blood.

So let the winds blow. Let the earth itself open beneath us. We find our fortress in God alone . . . and He is enough:

God is our refuge and strength,
A very present help in trouble.
Therefore we will not fear,
Even though the earth be removed,
And though the mountains be carried into the midst of
    the sea;
Though its waters roar and be troubled,
Though the mountains shake with its swelling.
PSALM 46:1-3

# CHAPTER 2

# DISEASE:
## The Fear of Serious Illness

*I, the* Lord *your God, will hold your right hand, saying to you,*
*"Fear not, I will help you."*
Isaiah 41:13

As I write this chapter, I have just completed my semiannual CT scan. For nearly twenty years, I've been making this round-trip journey to the Scripps Clinic in La Jolla, California. It all began in 1994 when I was diagnosed with non-Hodgkin's lymphoma at the Mayo Clinic in Rochester, Minnesota. I arranged to receive chemotherapy at Scripps, nearer to my home. With each passing year, the staff there has risen higher on my list of heroes.

It was on my first day at Scripps that I met Dr. Alan Saven, the oncologist. After two decades, he still examines me twice yearly. He and Dr. Charles Mason, who presided over my stem cell transplant, saved my life.

Make no mistake, to *God* be the glory—He and only He holds my life in His hands. But I also know that He raises up caring and gifted people to apply their skills as God's agents in delivering His gift of health. I'm so grateful for these talented specialists, and I let them know it in every way I can.

I won't recount all the details of my bout with cancer. You can find them in my book *When Your World Falls Apart*. But here in this book about fear, I can't help but revisit those memories. People know I'm a pastor, and they know my thoughts on spiritual issues. Therefore they want to know whether I was afraid as I struggled with cancer. I'm more than happy to answer that question, but I must warn you that it may be difficult for you to truly understand what I'm saying.

Cancer is one of those subjects that can't be comprehended secondhand. It's larger than life; it carries such powerful implications that it changes a person forever. Whenever I open the door at Scripps, the feelings come flooding back, even though I've had consistently good reports for two decades. The good news never quite washes out the memory and emotions of those uncertain times.

So was I afraid? Is it fear that comes creeping back even now? Here's what I wrote in that previous book:

Absolutely! I was *desperately* afraid. There's no disputing that. Was I afraid to die? No. I'm not afraid to leave this life, although I'm not eager to do so either. A good bit of my fear focused on losing precious years with the people I love. Some of it was simply about pain. Some of it was about the unknown. How would you respond to the news that you were suffering from a possibly fatal disease? Imagine the thoughts and feelings that might flood your heart at such a time, and you'll know the same things I experienced.[1]

Missionary Isobel Kuhn wrote a book entitled *In the Arena*, in which she explains a wonderful truth: a life filled with problems and setbacks can become a life filled with unique tools for sharing the Gospel. Every issue she faced brought one more opportunity to glorify God through the wisdom she learned.

In her final chapter, Isobel told of how she coped with breast cancer. Health became her great concern, and knowing how cancer could spread, her natural impulse was to panic—to anticipate the worst. If she coughed, it must be lung cancer. A toothache meant mouth cancer. Every minor ache or twinge was a harbinger of dire health consequences. She learned that disease is the host of fear.[2]

Eventually, however, Isobel learned that Christ overcomes every fear. That message can change the world, and it can change your life.

## THE PREVALENCE OF DISEASE

It's hard for us to imagine anyone living in perfect health, but Adam and Eve did. Their bodies were absolutely flawless. The very concept of disease would have been foreign to them. Their sin, of course, shattered that reality. It cost them God's gift of perfection and corrupted the whole created order. As Paul tells us, God's creation, now afflicted with disease and corruption, groans in agony (Romans 8:20-22). Because of Adam and Eve's rebellion, disease is now a prevalent factor of our existence. Each of us will spend a certain portion of our lives sick, wounded, or dying.

We view sickness with revulsion and dread, and somewhere in our spirits we sense that things weren't meant to be this way. God has placed eternity in our hearts, and thus threats to life come as odious intrusions. We long for the day when the curse of sin will be lifted—"eagerly waiting for the adoption, the redemption of our body" (Romans 8:23). Until then, we must cope with the inevitability of bodily corruption.

As we lose the naive sense of invulnerability of youth, we fret over aches and pains and what they may foretell. We feel anxious over the doctor's call with a test result or the look on his face as he walks into the room. We panic over a strange feeling in the chest or a lump where none should be. These are basic, primal fears. Death does its work in increments: the erosion of teeth, the growing inflexibility of limbs, the dulling of the senses. There are only so many ways to do maintenance work on the human body. We jog, we work out, we eat right, and then, as comedian Redd Foxx put it, someday we lie down in a hospital, "dying of nothing."

The diversity of the human body allows many points of entry for the grim reaper. According to the Federal Centers for Disease Control, the leading causes of death by disease in the United States are (in descending order) heart disease, cancer, respiratory diseases, stroke, Alzheimer's disease, diabetes, kidney disease, and pneumonia.[3]

Not only do diseases take a physical and an emotional toll, they take a financial one as well. The United States is the most expensive nation when it comes to treating illness.[4] In 2010, the total cost for health care was more than $2.5 trillion.[5] Because of these astronomical costs, a major medical incident can wipe out a family living on the financial edge. When our bodily health declines, so does the health of our wallets.

Disease (dis-ease) literally means "not easy" or "not at ease." Our experiences confirm the accuracy of that definition. Disease disrupts the patterns of life, robbing us of control and forming barriers with other people. It sends us to expensive medical facilities where we place our fate in the hands of strangers. It builds our dependence on mystifying medications. Commercials for these medicines show happy, healthy people who don't seem to have a care in the world. But at the end of the ad, the announcer lists ominous side effects in a hushed voice and with the speed of an auctioneer on steroids.

Hospitals are not fun places. They're a conglomeration of needles, tubes, monitors, pills, thermometers, call buttons, and bedpans—not to mention the total absence of modesty and privacy. During one of my hospital stays, a friend sent me the perfect poem that describes it all:

*I was sitting here minding my business,*
*Kind of letting my mind go slack,*
*When in comes a nurse with a bright sunny smile*
*And a gown with a split down the back.*
*"Take a shower," she said,*
*"And get ready. And then jump into this sack."*
*What she's really talking about*
*Was the gown with the split down the back.*
*"They're coming to do some tests," she said.*
*They're going to stretch me out on a rack*
*With nothing twixt me and the cold, cruel world*
*But a gown that's split down the back!*
*It comes only to the knees in front.*
*In the sides there is no lack.*
*But by far the greatest shortcoming*
*Is that blooming split down the back.*
*Whoever designed this garment*
*For humor had a great knack,*
*But I fail to see anything funny*
*About a gown that is split down the back.*

*I hear them coming to get me,*
*The wheels going clickety clack.*
*I'll ride through the halls on a table*
*In a gown with a split down the back.*
*When I get to heaven, I'll make me no odds*
*If my robe is white, red, or black,*
*The only thing I ask is please!*
*Give me one with no split down the back.*

We all fear disease, yet one or more will eventually catch up with each of us. Maybe you're battling an illness right now. Maybe it's just around the next corner, or perhaps someone dear to you is fighting desperately for his or her health. Disease is prevalent and inevitable, but how we understand it makes a great difference. It's no surprise that the Bible has a great deal to say about disease and how people coped with it.

## PROMINENT BIBLICAL EXAMPLES OF DISEASE

I've never preached a sermon series on "Diseased Characters from the Bible," nor has any pastor I know. But there would be a wealth of material to mine. For example:

- Paul and his "thorn in the flesh," which may have been a physical illness (2 Corinthians 12:7)
- Job sitting in his ash heap, covered with boils (Job 2:7-8)
- Lazarus, a young man with a terminal illness (John 11:1-4)
- The woman with the issue of blood (Mark 5:25-29)
- Naaman and his leprosy (2 Kings 5:1)
- King David and the "evil disease" that clung to him (Psalm 41:8)

- King Asa and his foot disease (1 Kings 15:23)
- King Jehoram and his diseased intestines (2 Chronicles 21:15)
- Christ's Galilean friends with "all kinds of sickness and all kinds of disease" (Matthew 4:23)
- Epaphroditus, who was "sick almost unto death" (Philippians 2:26-27)
- Dorcas, who fell sick, died, and was raised from death by Peter (Acts 9:36-41)

As we read of people in Scripture who suffered with various diseases, we recognize the same emotions we feel today. One compelling example is Hezekiah, a king of Judah. Let's look first at his life, and then we'll explore his approach to illness. His battle with disease is recounted three times: in 2 Kings 20, 2 Chronicles 32, and Isaiah 38.

Hezekiah was one of Judah's greatest kings. "He trusted in the LORD God of Israel, so that after him was none like him among all the kings of Judah, nor who were before him" (2 Kings 18:5).

Hezekiah ascended the throne at the age of twenty-five and inspired a period of religious revival in which he was encouraged by Isaiah, perhaps the noblest and the most eloquent of the Hebrew prophets. Hezekiah opened the long-closed doors of the Temple in Jerusalem and began its renovation, issuing this charge to the priests and Levites: "Hear me, Levites! Now sanctify yourselves, sanctify the house of the LORD God of your fathers, and carry out the rubbish from the holy place" (2 Chronicles 29:5).

The final verses of this great chapter describe the lavish Temple consecration services and the joy of the king and his people, who felt that God was doing a great thing among them. (Reading this account makes us long for a similar revival today.) In chapter 30, we learn that God's hand was on this nation, bringing its people together in unity and obedience under God. We find a glowing summary of Hezekiah's reign in 2 Chronicles 31:20-21:

> Hezekiah did . . . what was good and right and true
> before the LORD his God. And in every work that he
> began in the service of the house of God, in the law and
> in the commandment, to seek his God, he did it with all
> his heart. So he prospered.

It was a golden age of faith and prosperity in Judah, and all things went well for ten to fifteen years. Then, when Hezekiah turned thirty-nine, he became ill. The prophet Isaiah came to him and said, "Thus says the LORD: 'Set your house in order, for you shall die and not live'" (Isaiah 38:1).

## PAINFUL EMOTIONS OF DISEASE

How would you react if you learned that your death was imminent? If a godly man like Hezekiah "wept bitterly" (Isaiah 38:3), then we can understand it's no sin to express grief when we're hit with terrible medical news. Hezekiah was not just a godly king; he was a godly *human* king. And humans naturally grieve in the face of bad news. As we follow the progress of Hezekiah's illness, we'll gather helpful insights into the art of managing poor health.

### The Prayer

Hezekiah turned his face toward the wall, and prayed to the LORD, and said, "Remember now, O LORD, I pray, how I have walked before You in truth and with a loyal

heart, and have done what is good in Your sight." And
Hezekiah wept bitterly.

ISAIAH 38:2-3

Hezekiah, horrified and in earnest grief, soaked his sickbed with
sweat and tears. Later he wrote a memoir of his illness, which we
find in Isaiah 38:10-15. The first few verses of that passage offer
a vivid and wrenching picture of Hezekiah's troubled heart. Here,
in Eugene Peterson's memorable paraphrase, are the reflections
of this king upon the news of his impending death:

In the very prime of life
   I have to leave.
Whatever time I have left
   is spent in death's waiting room.
No more glimpses of GOD
   in the land of the living,
No more meetings with my neighbors,
   no more rubbing shoulders with friends.
This body I inhabit is taken down
   and packed away like a camper's tent.
Like a weaver, I've rolled up the carpet of my life
   as God cuts me free of the loom
And at day's end sweeps up the scraps and pieces.
   I cry for help until morning.
Like a lion, God pummels and pounds me,
   relentlessly finishing me off.
I squawk like a doomed hen,
   moan like a dove.
My eyes ache from looking up for help:
   "Master, I'm in trouble! Get me out of this!"

But what's the use? God Himself gave me the word.

He's done it to me.

I can't sleep—

I'm that upset, that troubled.

ISAIAH 38:10-15, *The Message*

In my own memoir of illness, I shared that it took me three days simply to be capable of telling my wife the doctor's news. On the day after my diagnosis, she was scheduled to leave town to visit her mother, and I decided not to burden her. I knew she'd immediately cancel her trip, and for what? There was no point in disturbing her until further tests were done.

So I kept my silence. I drove her to the airport the next day, watched her plane vanish into the clouds, and suddenly felt the pangs of loneliness; it was time to confront the dark jungle of my thoughts. I longed for her comfort, but it would only be a three-day wait. We met in another city where I was scheduled to speak, and that's where I quietly told her what the doctors had said.

We wept, but not bitterly. Even at such a low moment, we knew we had our faith and we had each other. We held each other for hours as the gray dusk of a new morning gathered outside.

During my previous three days of solitary meditation, I walked in Hezekiah's sandals. *Master, I'm in trouble—get me out of this!* I prayed, just as Jesus prayed for the cup to be taken from Him. But just as He set His own desires within the will of the Father (Luke 22:42), I knew what all serious Christians know: my prayers would cycle through a process that would end at the same destination: *Your will, not mine, O Lord.*

I'm not comparing my plight to that of the Son of God, of course. I just followed His example to the resolution I knew was inevitable. His will, I knew, is infinitely wiser than my feeble comprehension. The cycle of every anguished prayer must move from our frantic human desires to loving, trusting obedience.

Tears and prayer are understandable responses to disease, whether we're the one afflicted or we're grieving for a loved one. Though we can't predict how the Lord will answer, we know the tears and prayers of His suffering people always move Him (Psalm 56:8).

### The Promise

The word of the LORD came to Isaiah, saying, "Go and tell Hezekiah, 'Thus says the LORD, the God of David your father: "I have heard your prayer, I have seen your tears; surely I will add to your days fifteen years."'"

ISAIAH 38:4-5

Here Hezekiah received the joyful news he was longing to hear: God would heal him. Why did God do this? Why did he heal the king and give him fifteen more years of life? In part, it was because He saw Hezekiah's tears and was moved by compassion.

Recall the basis of Hezekiah's prayer for healing: "Remember now, O LORD, I pray, how I have walked before You in truth and with a loyal heart, and have done what is good in Your sight" (Isaiah 38:3). Hezekiah laid out his case before God: "I've been faithful to You. I've cleansed the land of idols and restored the Temple worship. So in return, please be gracious and heal me."

We must remember, however, that no matter how great a king Hezekiah was, God had no obligation to heal him. We cannot earn His favor with our works. God's healing is about His faithfulness, not ours. Healing comes the same way salvation does— by grace: "By [the Messiah's] stripes we are healed" (Isaiah 53:5).

Healing is part of the very nature of God, and in His grace, He offers it to those who fear Him: "To you who fear My name the Sun of Righteousness shall arise with healing in His wings" (Malachi 4:2).

We find another reason for Hezekiah's healing in Isaiah 38:5: God said to the king: "Thus says the LORD, the God of David your father." God had made a covenant with David that the throne of Judah would always go to one of David's descendants. The reference to David in this passage is God's reminder that He is faithful to His promises. That faithfulness was demonstrated when, three years after Hezekiah's healing, his son Manasseh, who would be the next king, was born (2 Chronicles 33:1).

After Hezekiah was healed, God reminded him again of His faithfulness to His promise to David. He said He would defend Jerusalem against the invading Assyrians "for My own sake and for My servant David's sake" (2 Kings 19:34).

God's dealings with Hezekiah and his nation were part of a much bigger story than Hezekiah could see. It was also about the glory of God—as it always is—and about a promise made long ago to David. God is always good, gracious, and compassionate.

Why does God heal us? Essentially for the same reasons He healed Hezekiah: first, because of His grace and compassion, and second, for the sake of Jesus Christ—a son of David. Like Hezekiah's story, ours also is part of a much greater one that we cannot yet see.

### The Prescription

Isaiah had said, "Let them take a lump of figs, and apply it as a poultice on the boil, and he shall recover."

ISAIAH 38:21

Hezekiah's fatal disease stemmed from a boil somewhere on his body. We can probably assume it had become infected and was leaching poison into his system. God gave Isaiah directions for healing, which were to be passed on to the court physicians attending the king.

The prescription was a poultice (or paste) made of crushed figs to be applied to the boil. It's not likely that today's physicians would think of using pharmaceutical figs, which might be seen as alternative or herbal medicine. It's more likely they would lance and drain the boil, then administer an antibiotic.

You might wonder why God bothered to use the court physicians at all. Why not heal Hezekiah through a simple miracle? But God has a habit of using people, their gifts, and their resources to carry out His plans. In fact, we were created to be God's deputies, doing His work on earth (Genesis 1:28). As C. S. Lewis said, God "seems to do nothing of Himself which He can possibly delegate to His creatures."[6] Clearly, God used doctors and prescriptions in Hezekiah's time just as He does now.

In 1994, doctors treated my lymphoma with chemotherapy. When the lymphoma returned in 1998, I received a stem cell transplant. That's the scientific part of the story. But behind the scenes, a great many people were praying for my recovery. That's the faith part of the story.

This raises a question. How much of my healing should be credited to medicine, and how much to prayer? We can't know, but it really makes little difference: either way, healing comes from above. We are the ones who draw distinctions between the natural and the supernatural. All of it is God's realm. I simply feel blessed to have both available to me—friends on praying knees as well as doctors with skilled hands.

One positive aspect of medical solutions is that they get

us involved. Becoming active agents of God in our own healing process builds our faith by giving us hope. Following the
recommendations of my caring and committed doctors was a
powerful encouragement to me. I have complete faith that God
led me to those specific doctors, and I thank God for them
every day.

When we face a serious disease, the first thing we should do
is talk to God. Ask Him for guidance, and then take advantage of
the best medical assistance available, as Hezekiah did. Ultimately,
our God is *Jehovah-Rophe*—"the LORD who heals you" (Exodus
15:26)—whether He heals us with a miracle, with medicines, or
in the world to come.

### The Praise

Hezekiah's memoir of his experience with disease continues in
Isaiah 38:17-20, where he records a testimony of praise to the
God who healed him:

> It was for my own peace
> That I had great bitterness;
> But You have lovingly delivered my soul from the pit of
>     corruption,
> For you have cast all my sins behind Your back. . . .
> The LORD was ready to save me;
> Therefore we will sing my songs with stringed instruments
> All the days of our life, in the house of the LORD.
> ISAIAH 38:17, 20

Hezekiah gave all the credit to God for the miracle of healing.
I can't read his memoir without being reminded of this psalm:

Bless the LORD, O my soul;

And all that is within me, bless His holy name!

Bless the LORD, O my soul,

And forget not all His benefits:

Who forgives all your iniquities,

Who heals all your diseases.

PSALM 103:1-3

These passages remind us that upon recovering from illness, our first order of business should be to praise God. Some people never think of such a thing; they pray in the time of peril and quickly forget God when they are healed. Do you see a lack of consistency here—or worse, a lack of gratitude? If we pray for healing, why wouldn't we thank God when healing comes?

Are some illnesses so small and insignificant that we shouldn't bother God with them? Absolutely not! It's common for people to thank God when they've experienced a close brush with death, as in a barely missed traffic collision, but far too few of us praise Him after getting over the flu or a migraine headache. If we can pray over serious illnesses, why shouldn't we pray over *all* illnesses? Nothing that hurts us is too small for His concern.

In fact, Scripture teaches us to pray not just about our health, but about *everything* (1 Thessalonians 5:17; Philippians 4:6-7). If we pray about everything, shouldn't we also praise God in everything (1 Thessalonians 5:18)? It's fairly simple. When can we pray? All the time. When should we praise God? Whenever we pray.

### The Problem

Hezekiah did not repay according to the favor shown him, for his heart was lifted up; therefore wrath was looming over him and over Judah and Jerusalem.

2 CHRONICLES 32:25

Unfortunately, Hezekiah's medical adventure has a tragic epilogue. After all God had done for him, after the gift of fifteen precious years added to his life span, Hezekiah lost favor with God. How did this happen? His miraculous recovery caused him to lose his near-death humility.

As the heat died down on his problems, so did his passion for God. Rather than living humbly before his Lord, his heart began to swell with pride. And he became obsessed with wealth, looking not to God but to goods.

Hezekiah's pride in his wealth led him to make the political mistake of showing off his treasury and armory to envoys from Babylon, the empire that would later defeat his nation (Isaiah 39). The king of Babylon had sent his representatives to Hezekiah, supposedly to pay their respects during his convalescence. Their true motive, however, was to curry Hezekiah's favor toward a mutual alliance against a common enemy: Assyria. This wasn't on God's agenda.

In Hezekiah's prideful strength and overconfidence, he failed to consult the Lord on these developments, and he confided state secrets to his visitors: "There was nothing in his house or in all his dominion that Hezekiah did not show them" (Isaiah 39:2). His new "allies" took careful note.

Isaiah's heart was grieved when he heard of the king's foolhardy actions. The prophet foretold God's judgment on the nation (Isaiah 39:3-7), which later came to pass when the Babylonians destroyed Jerusalem and escorted the people of Judah into seventy years of captivity. They easily looted the treasury and the Temple because they knew where all the wealth was stored. Hezekiah, who had blessed his people by turning their hearts toward God, ultimately failed them just as deeply.

When Hezekiah died, his son, Manasseh, became king at age twelve and completely reversed all the good his father had done. For half a century, Manasseh left a trail of blood, violence, idolatry, and even sorcery through his reign. His father had lovingly cleansed the Temple; the son desecrated it with a carved image of a false god. The result of his evil leadership was military invasion and the blood of children sacrificed at pagan altars. The kingdom of Judah was on the slippery slope from which it would not recover.

God had His reasons for healing Hezekiah, even though He knew the future. Yet we can't help but observe that sometimes everyone is better off when God says no. The nation paid an exorbitant price for those fifteen extra years of Hezekiah's life. As the psalmist reminds us, be careful what you pray for; you might just get it:

> He gave them their request,
> But sent leanness into their soul.
> PSALM 106:15

Our problem is that our perspective doesn't extend much further than our noses, while God's perspective is infinite. We only know that we hurt, and we want it to stop. But if we could see how our suffering fits into God's perspective, we would realize there are things worse than our present darkness. Illness may be a necessary cog in the divine plan to bring about some good.

Sometimes it is only through pain that we become who God wants us to be.

Charles H. Spurgeon, in his wry way, once declared, "I daresay the greatest earthly blessing that God can give to any of us is health, *with the exception of sickness.*"[7]

Instead of quickly pleading for deliverance, we might more wisely ask God about the purpose of our sufferings. *How can I grow through this, Lord?* We please Him deeply when we pray as Jesus did: "Nevertheless not My will, but Yours, be done" (Luke 22:42).

## PRACTICAL ENCOURAGEMENTS WHEN FACING DISEASE

If a sadder but wiser Hezekiah could join us for questions and answers today, what advice might he give that would help us deal with disease? Let me suggest five possibilities.

### Center Your Mind

God has not given us a spirit of fear, but of power and of love and of a sound mind.

2 TIMOTHY 1:7

The human imagination is a powerful force that can create beautiful visions of a desirable future or conjure up every worst-case scenario. These dark products of the imagination can put us in the grip of fear—a place God would never have us go. As this Scripture verse shows, the power that banishes fear is a sound mind.

We maintain a sound mind by "bringing every thought into captivity to the obedience of Christ" (2 Corinthians 10:5). Paul wrote those words when false apostles in Corinth were spreading lies about his ministry. When a thought that is not from God enters our heads ("I'm sick; I'm going to die!"), we examine it in light of "the knowledge of God" (verse 5). Does this thought have any basis in reality? If not, we take it captive. No longer can it run free and lead our imaginations away from God's goodness and into unhealthy fear.

When Isobel Kuhn was fighting cancer, she realized that the real enemy was something too deep for the surgeon's scalpel. It lay in the invisible world of her imagination. She wrote,

> I had to refuse to allow my imagination to play with my future. That future, I believe, is ordered of God, and no man can guess it. For me to let myself imagine how or when the end would come was not only unprofitable, it was definitely harmful, so I had to bring my thoughts into captivity that they might not dishonor Christ.[8]

How different would your life be if you could simply take your thoughts captive for Christ? How much better would you sleep at night? How much happier and less anxious would you be? How much more joyful would friends find you?

Gaining a sound and centered mind is not as difficult as you think. If we simply read the Scriptures deeply, thoughtfully, and openly every day, we will invite the Holy Spirit to whisper new strength into our thoughts. He and He alone can tame the reckless power of the human mind. A mind centered on the truth of God is the key to being sustained and not losing heart.

### Count Your Blessings

In everything give thanks; for this is the will of God in Christ Jesus for you.

1 THESSALONIANS 5:18

What would you think if you opened your Bible to Ephesians 1 and read, "Blessed be the God and Father of our Lord Jesus Christ, who, *when we are well and healthy*, has blessed us with every spiritual blessing in the heavenly places in Christ" (verse 3)?

You probably know that the italicized words I inserted in that verse are nowhere to be found in Ephesians or anywhere else in the Bible. God has blessed us with every spiritual blessing in the heavenly places in Christ—period! Whether we are strong or weak, sound of body or wracked with pain, we are blessed. "From the fullness of his grace we have all received one blessing after another" (John 1:16, NIV).

You may wonder how in the midst of debilitating illness we can possibly feel blessed. It's not a matter just of feeling blessed, as if it is something we must conjure up from our imaginations; it is a matter of seeing the enormous blessings that are truly there. In her book *Gold by Moonlight*, Amy Carmichael compares living with pain and disease to a hike through a rugged terrain. Even a bleak landscape, she observes, has cheering surprises, like "bright flowers of the edelweiss waiting to be gathered among the rough rocks of difficult circumstances."[9]

In times of sickness, our blessings become clearer, richer, and more meaningful. Something therapeutic happens deep in our hearts when we count those blessings. We can rejoice in the prayers of our friends, in a note from a loved one, in the compassionate care of a conscientious nurse, in the smile of a doctor, in the verse of a hymn that comes to mind, in a neighbor who mows the lawn, in a Bible verse that shows up at just the right time, in a prescription that lessens our pain, in a column of sunlight that cuts through the window of the room, in the intricate design of a flower in a nearby vase, or in the innocence and cheer of a grandchild who visits us. In sickness, our focus sharpens, and our perception of what's truly important narrows to exclude the peripheral values that clutter our lives when good health keeps us too busy to appreciate the simple blessings, which are often the best ones.

Training ourselves to spot these "wildflowers in the wilderness" is the secret to learning to "count it all joy" (James 1:2). This may not be easy, but it is essential to maintaining our spiritual and attitudinal health. It frees us from the tyranny of being limited to a deteriorating physical frame. It's liberating to realize that disease does not define who we are—that we are more than our aches and pains.

Illness also leads us to shift our focus in another way—from the earthly to the heavenly. This is a vital shift that can play an important part in our eventual healing.

Dr. Ed Dobson was senior pastor of Calvary Church in Grand Rapids, Michigan, when he was diagnosed with ALS (Lou Gehrig's disease)—a degenerative and terminal illness. For several years he tried to maintain his pastoral ministry with the earnest support of his church. When it became obvious that he couldn't continue, he stepped out of his pastoral role with great reluctance.

But nothing could stop Ed from continuing to bless the Lord in all things and to develop the disciplines of praise and personal worship. Ed and his oldest son had once taken a course in Judaism at a local synagogue, where they'd learned the traditional Jewish blessing that begins, "Blessed are you God our God, King of the universe. . . ." Dobson wrote,

In the midst of my disease, I began blessing God for all the gifts of life. I use this official formula (I learned to do it in Hebrew), and I bless God for each day. I bless God for the ability to shower and clothe myself. I bless God for the ability to button buttons. I bless God for the ability to lift food to my mouth even though I can no longer do it with my right hand. I bless God for everything I can do and for every gift that comes from Him.[10]

As I write, Ed Dobson continues to show Christians how to count their blessings, naming them one by one. It is always good spiritual arithmetic. If we ask God for a calm, thankful heart that sees all the blessings His grace imparts, He can teach us many lessons in illness that can never be learned in health. As the old Puritan preacher Thomas Watson put it, "A sick-bed often teaches more than a sermon."[11]

The Bible doesn't say we have to be thankful *for* all things, like the pain and discomfort of illness. But it does say we should give thanks *in* all things—including illness: "In every thing give thanks: for this is the will of God in Christ Jesus concerning you" (1 Thessalonians 5:18, KJV). Be thankful that even your sickness gives you an opportunity to glorify God.

### Continue Your Work

We are His workmanship, created in Christ Jesus for good works, which God prepared beforehand that we should walk in them.

Ephesians 2:10

Many Christians know how God saved them—by grace through faith—but not all know *why* God saved them: "for good works, which God prepared beforehand that we should walk in them" (Ephesians 2:10). And as the great NBA star and Hall of Famer Jerry West once said, "You can't get much done in life if you only work on the days when you feel good."

As long as we're on this earth, there is work we can do. Even when we can't walk in the body, we can walk in the Spirit. On his deathbed, the prophet Elisha continued to counsel Joash, the king of Israel (2 Kings 13:14). History is filled with examples of saints who served God as long as body and breath would allow.

As Isobel Kuhn battled cancer, she discovered that staying busy was good medicine for her. Though largely confined to bed, she drew up a daily schedule that fit within the limits of her strength. She worked on her book, engaged in a ministry of prayer, read, studied, and rejoiced in letters and cards that came from all over the world.

When she lacked the strength even for these activities, she wrote, "Sound health and a normal life I cannot have while on this platform. Therefore I accept the fact and do not fret about it."[12]

Isobel Kuhn passed away on March 20, 1957, full of faith and joy. "Facing the end of one's earthly pilgrimage is not a melancholy thing for a Christian," she wrote. "It is like preparation for the most exciting journey of all. . . . And so the platform of a dreaded disease becomes but a springboard for heaven."[13]

The Englishman John Pounds (1766–1839) is another example of someone who faced illness faithfully. He was a tall, muscular, teenage laborer at the docks of Portsmouth who fell from the top of a ship's mast.

> When workers reached him, he was nothing but a mass of broken bones. For two years he lay in bed as his bones healed crookedly. His pain never ceased. Out of boredom, he began to read the Bible.
>
> Eventually, John crawled from bed, hoping to find something he could do with his life. A shoemaker hired him, and day after day, John sat at his cobbler's bench,

a Bible open on his lap. Soon he was born again through faith in Christ. John gathered enough money to purchase his own little shoe shop, where he developed a pair of orthopedic boots for his crippled nephew. Soon he was making corrective shoes for other children, and his cobbler's shop became a miniature children's hospital.

As John's burden for children grew, he began feeding homeless children, teaching them to read and telling them about the Lord. His shop became known as "the Ragged School." John often limped around the waterfront with food in his pocket, looking for more children to tend. John Pounds rescued five hundred children from despair and led every one of them to Christ. His work became so famous that a Ragged School movement swept England. In John's honor, Parliament passed a series of laws to establish schools for poor children—boys' homes, girls' homes, day schools, and evening schools. All had Bible classes in which thousands heard the Gospel.

John collapsed and died on New Year's Day in 1839 while tending a boy's ulcerated foot. He was buried in a churchyard on High Street. All of England mourned, and in the church was hung a tablet that reads, "Thou shalt be blessed, for they could not recompense thee."[14]

What might John Pounds have become had he not been severely injured? We don't know. But we do know what he became in spite of his injury—or perhaps because of it. It's an inspiring reminder that our afflictions and limitations don't mean God is finished with us. The weaker we become, the more God's grace is multiplied (2 Corinthians 12:9). Going through a rough patch often equips us for further service. It also allows us to empathize with and minister to people who otherwise would never have crossed our paths.

We would discard suffering as a vile thing, but God wastes nothing. In His hands, suffering becomes the means for miracles. He will open new doors of witness, and His strength will shine through our weaknesses.

### Claim Your Promises

[Jesus said,] "This sickness is not unto death, but for the glory of God, that the Son of God may be glorified through it."

JOHN 11:4

I said earlier that healing has a dual purpose—our good and God's glory. Jesus went a step further when He said that even death can glorify God.

Perhaps the greatest truth in the entire Bible as it relates to sickness among Christians comes from the words of Jesus in John 11:4. His friend Lazarus was ill and went on to die, and when Jesus arrived, his friend had been in the tomb four days. But Jesus didn't say that Lazarus's sickness wouldn't *include* death. He said that it wouldn't *end* in death. It would provide instead an occasion for God to be glorified.

Because of the resurrection of Jesus Christ, we must claim the promise that, although our illnesses may include death, they will not end in death; we, too, will be resurrected. Armed with this truth, we can see how God can glorify Himself even through disease. And when we are faced with life-threatening sickness, our fear can be replaced by a determination to glorify the One who "works all things according to the counsel of His will" (Ephesians 1:11).

### Consider Your Future

> I consider that the sufferings of this present time are not worthy to be compared with the glory which shall be revealed in us.
>
> ROMANS 8:18

Suppose you won a free trip around the world for you and a loved one. It included first-class accommodations at five-star hotels, private planes, lavish gifts, and personal tours. (See how powerful the imagination is?) But suppose as you opened the envelope containing the tickets, you suffered a paper cut on the end of your finger. You might say to your companion, "Oh, I cut my finger!" You'd grimace for about half a second before grinning from ear to ear and saying, "Who cares? We're about to take the trip of a lifetime!"

I would say nothing to trivialize disease; I know the misery of it firsthand. But according to Paul, and from the perspective of our eternal God, the sufferings of this present world are less than a paper cut in relation to the glory yet to be revealed to us.

Although Christ has conquered sin and death, the effects of both linger. But only temporarily. Disease must be accepted, but only for now—and always with the knowledge that its master, death itself, no longer has power over us. If this life were all we had, then cancer and every other life-threatening illness would truly be tragic. But because death's prison doors have been destroyed, death can no longer hold us captive. This is why Paul says, "To live is Christ, and to die is gain" (Philippians 1:21). We look forward to our new resurrection bodies, perfect and free from all defects. As Paul explains, Christ will "transform our lowly body that it may be conformed to His glorious body, according to the working by which He is able even to subdue all things to Himself" (Philippians 3:21).

It would be nice to be healed here and now, as Lazarus and Hezekiah were. But if not, we'll simply be healed later. Every one of us who belongs to Jesus Christ holds a Lazarus coupon. What Jesus did for him, God will do for us. The big difference is that our restored lives will be eternally free from further disease. "God will wipe away every tear from [our] eyes; there shall be no more death, nor sorrow, nor crying. There shall be no more pain, for the former things have passed away" (Revelation 21:4).

Dr. Jonathan Thigpen, former president of the Evangelical Training Association, was forty-five years old when he began having some muscular disorders. The diagnosis was the same as that of Ed Dobson—ALS, or Lou Gehrig's disease. This disease is debilitating and terminal: it has no known cause or cure.

Thigpen describes the chilling fear he felt after learning of his diagnosis: "I remember walking out of the doctor's office in Carol Stream, Illinois, and deep in the pit of my stomach there was a feeling of overwhelming fear. . . . It felt like I was being hugged by something so dark and so horrible that I can't describe it."[15]

Then an old, familiar voice echoed through his memory—the voice of his father, Dr. Charles Thigpen, reading the words of Psalm 46:

God is our refuge and strength, a very present help in trouble.
Therefore we will not fear,
Even though the earth be removed,
And though the mountains be carried into the midst of
    the sea;
Though its waters roar and be troubled,
Though the mountains shake with its swelling.
PSALM 46:1-3

Many times Jonathan had tagged along as his dad visited hospital patients and read those soothing and powerful words. Now it was his own soul that was soothed. As he reached his car, the dark clouds overshadowing his spirit began to dissipate. God was still in control—he knew it for a certainty. Jonathan didn't have any answers, but he knew that "fear cannot stand in the face of a faith and a God who does not change. My fear had left."[16]

Jonathan took hold of Psalm 46 as so many of us often do with particular Scripture passages that hold remarkable power just when we need it. In the months that followed, Jonathan's spirit was willing but his flesh was increasingly weak as he traveled the country sharing those words about his refuge and his strength, the help he had found to be very present in his time of trouble. Once again, Christ claimed victory in the face of what had seemed a meaningless misfortune.

A Puritan preacher once wrote, "Sickness, when sanctified, teaches us four things: the vanity of the world, the vileness of sin, the helplessness of man and the preciousness of Christ."[17] The last of those, I submit, overpowers the emptiness of the others. If heaven is what lies ahead for us, what can we possibly complain about?

Instead, think of the best: we have a Great Physician who raised His own Son from the dead, leaving behind an empty tomb. We have a heavenly home with welcoming doors opened wide. We have a sympathetic Savior who never imparts a spirit of fear but a spirit of power, love, and a sound mind. To understand that is to enjoy a spiritual health that overcomes the darkest days that disease can inflict.

# CHAPTER 3

# DEBT:
## *The Fear of Financial Collapse*

*Oh, fear the L*ORD*, you His saints!*
*There is no want to those who fear Him.*

PSALM 34:9

Ethelda Lopez was ready to let go and enjoy the golden days of her time on earth. She'd been a hard worker her whole adult life, and she had planned well for retirement. Now, when that pension check arrived each month, she felt a nice sense of security.

Then one month, the check didn't come.

It had to be a mistake. After Ethelda made a few phone calls, her discomfort increased. A Sacramento accounting firm had managed her investments, but the company was no longer to be found. Every time she phoned she got a repeated recording: "This number is no longer in service."

Ethelda had worked for AT&T for three decades. Her benefits should have been rock solid. She'd paid into her investment plan all those years, and now she was cut off and cast adrift like a boat from its moorings. Her ultimate worst-case scenario was looming: she couldn't make the mortgage payment.

Ethelda fired off more phone calls—to mortgage companies, to her political representatives, to bank managers—to anyone at all who might be able to shed light on this craziness. But it was all to no avail. Her money was all gone—lost, embezzled, stolen. What difference did it make how it had happened? She was suddenly, unexpectedly destitute. Every night she cried herself to sleep.

Her worst fears were realized the day she stood on the lawn of the county courthouse and watched as her dream home was auctioned off to strangers. Someone wanted to know why she was crying; did she need some kind of assistance? Oh, yes. But when she tried to explain that it was her home on the auction block, nothing but unintelligible whimpers came out.

Ethelda's story is tragic, but it's hardly unique. In 2006 such auctions were occurring across the nation as banks repossessed homes at an alarming rate. Everywhere, families were boxing up their possessions in shock.

In Ethelda's county, one of every seven homes was subject to foreclosure. And the nightmare continues. Today, roughly 1.5 million homes in America are in foreclosure, and another 10.9 million are "under water."[1] Many homeowners, trying desperately to stave off this disaster, are rapidly depleting their cash reserves.

Our homes are our sanctuaries, the places where we retreat, relax, and regroup. If even this space is up for grabs, what certainties are left in the world? The idea of losing a home hits us—well, as they say—right where we live.

Loss is an inevitable part of life. Nothing that's visible is lasting, and one of the first harsh realities we face is the moment we first learn that truth. We lose a friend or we lose a job or we lose our fortune, yet life goes on.

The larger the loss, the deeper the pain. Financial collapse is a major loss that has inflicted immeasurable sadness and suffering on countless heartbroken families in the last few years. Even if the current economic collapse spared you, you know it could happen. You know that this world contains no permanent dwellings.

In a very real sense, we're all nomads—pilgrims bound for an eternal world who are just passing through this physical one. This world is not our home, and when we leave it, any possessions that outlast us will be owned by someone else. The impermanence of this world and all that is in it is actually good news for those of us who have faith in God. It means we'll be moving on to better things.

But other people live only for the here and now, as typified in Jesus' story of the prosperous but ignorant homeowner. This man placed his faith in his holdings, and then one night he heard the voice of God: "Fool! This night your soul will be required of you; then whose will those things be which you have provided?" (Luke 12:20).

The error is in thinking of home, property, and possessions as everything we have. In reality, they're the least important and most superficial of what we have. Material things dazzle us because of their one advantage: they're tangible. They can be seen, touched, and held. On the other hand, faith, hope, and the fruit of the Spirit can't be picked up and examined, bought or sold, photographed or filmed. When we allow the tangible but transient to block our perception of the invisible but imperishable, we've lost our perspective on true value.

Henry David Thoreau, the Enlightenment philosopher,

understood that principle. In *Walden*, he observed that people in his village spent their lives accumulating objects that needed constant dusting. They doted on these things, even built their lives around them. Then when they died, men gathered up all their stuff, carted it to the town square, and auctioned it off to other people who would spend their lives dusting it.[2]

I am not denying the value of tangible things. Everything God created is good, including the material world (Genesis 1:31). My wife and I have a houseful of possessions, which we value at varying levels. Family pictures and heirlooms, for example, mean more to us than furnishings or automobiles. We enjoy our stuff, but we never forget that it is *stuff*. Even so, I have no desire to see it all carted to the town square. I, too, would be terribly upset to lose my home. But I know that such things can and do happen.

So the question arises: When we've lost our homes, our possessions, our bank accounts, and our investments, and the very concept of financial security has been swept away—where do we turn? Does God have anything to say that will give us comfort?

Questions don't come any more rhetorical than that, do they? *Of course* the Bible has words of comfort. The book of Psalms, our go-to book for comfort, provides a one-stop destination for all the significant emotional issues of life.

One of my favorites, Psalm 37, speaks to our hearts when the fear of calamity is stalking us. David wrote this psalm when he was an older man reflecting on the great questions of his life. Here he divides humanity into two general groups: the righteous and the wicked. Like many of us who saw so many good people lose their possessions in recent economic recessions, David, too, has often seen bad things happen to good people and good things happen to bad people. He wants to know why. Isn't God at work, rewarding good people and striking down the bad? David thinks, considers all the evidence, and draws this conclusion:

> I have been young, and now am old;
> Yet I have not seen the righteous forsaken,
> Nor his descendants begging bread.
>
> PSALM 37:25

As David wrote this, he was well aware that wicked people were doing record business and oppressing good, God-fearing people. Earlier in the psalm he addresses this abuse, using the word *wicked* thirteen times. Here is a typical example:

> The wicked have drawn the sword
> And have bent their bow,
> To cast down the poor and needy,
> To slay those who are of upright conduct.
>
> PSALM 37:14

The term *wicked* refers to the negative moral conditions of guilt, ungodliness, and evil. It's one of those words we've more or less retired. We allow its use only for witches in fairy tales, even though we know that real wickedness abounds all around us.

How should we respond when righteous people lose their possessions to those who are prospering through evil means? We need answers, and the Bible tells us that ultimately it's an issue of trust. Do we trust God to sort out these glaring injustices? Do we trust Him more than our own finances and possessions?

Let's explore Psalm 37 and discover seven solid principles that will increase our reliance on God and anchor us in these days of instability.

## DECIDE TO TRUST IN THE LORD

Trust in the LORD.

PSALM 37:3

One of the themes of this psalm is the principle of trusting. David uses the word *trust* three times—in verse 3, cited above, and in the two following references:

Commit your way to the LORD,
Trust also in Him,
And He shall bring it to pass.

PSALM 37:5

The LORD shall help them and deliver them;
He shall deliver them from the wicked,
And save them,
Because they trust in Him.

PSALM 37:40

We find true stability in this unstable world only when we trust in God. To trust is to be confident—to possess a strong sense of security. When we trust, we place confidence in someone or something. Trust is not an emotion that just springs up in our hearts as does anger, jealousy, or sadness. It is always a choice based on reason. We use evidence and discernment to conclude that this man or that bank or this investment is "trustworthy." Yes, God gives us the faith to act, but He first gives us a choice to make.

To illustrate the process, let's take a look at the stock market, which is based on high-level choices of trust. If you don't trust in a company, you don't buy its stock. The stock price represents an index of the overall trust people have in a company. Wise people investigate to determine if there are grounds for trust, then they depend on God to guide their decisions. Having placed their trust in God, they need not live in fear of loss. Even if material loss occurs, God promises to meet the needs of His children, and the Bible is filled with repetitions of that promise.

For example, Psalm 23 tells us that the Lord is our Shepherd, so we shall not lack. Jesus pointed to the birds and the flowers and noted that if God feeds and clothes them, won't He do the same for His very own children (Matthew 6:25-33)? And here in Psalm 37, David tells us that in his long life, he has never seen God fail to meet needs (verse 25). His experience has proved God to be worthy of our trust. He will work things out.

Paul says the same: "My God shall supply all your need according to His riches in glory by Christ Jesus" (Philippians 4:19). Then, in 2 Corinthians 9:8, the Lord promises that He "is able to make all grace abound toward you, that you, always having all sufficiency in all things, may have an abundance for every good work."

It's easy to say we believe in these promises, but when financial anxiety looms like an approaching storm, we're forced to confront our faith level. Do we really believe God is in control? Easy living does nothing for faith; when the weather is fine, we drift into the illusion of adequacy. We think we have it all figured out and under control.

The recent financial collapse destroyed that illusion for many. People found themselves falling on their knees and saying, "Lord God, I have nowhere else to turn—can You help me?"

Can God help? It's another obviously rhetorical question, isn't it? He helps by offering the only stability possible in our lives.

Christian leaders attending a YMCA convention in Carlisle, Pennsylvania, in 1873 witnessed firsthand how God can provide stability when our financial world is collapsing. Presiding over the convention was John Wanamaker, the famous retailer known today as the father of modern advertising. On the second day of the conference, a telegram arrived with shocking news. The banking house of Jay Cooke & Company had failed, resulting in terrible losses for Wanamaker and others at the convention.

When reports of other failing firms flowed into the hall, it became apparent that this was a nationwide financial crash. A tidal wave of panic swept the convention, making it hard to continue.

One of the delegates, Erastus Johnson, came across a comforting Bible verse:

> From the end of the earth I will cry to You,
> When my heart is overwhelmed;
> Lead me to the rock that is higher than I.
> PSALM 61:2

Based on that verse, Johnson wrote a song that was instantly put to music at the convention and sung over and over. It became a favorite hymn of its day, and the words are still applicable today:

> *Oh! Sometimes the shadows are deep,*
> *And rough seems the path to the goal,*
> *And sorrows, sometimes how they sweep*
> *Like tempests down over my soul.*
>
> *Oh, then to the Rock let me fly*
> *To the Rock that is higher than I.*

We've lived for too long in a world in which nothing is "higher than I." We've placed ourselves above everything else, and where has it taken us? Into a world as broken as Humpty-Dumpty—and just as impossible to put back together. The one great loss we need is the loss of the illusion that we're in any way self-sufficient. We need the Rock that is higher than we are, higher than this world. We need the Rock upon which we can make our stand, even with empty pockets, even without property or claim, even without a shred of worldly hope, because at the end of our vain hope lies the beginning of the knowledge of God and His grace.

Another great hymn says, "On Christ the solid rock I stand/ All other ground is sinking sand." When the sinking sand of nest eggs and 401(k) plans destroys our sand castle, nothing but trust in God provides stability.

Trust in God will not make the pain go away; it means we know He will provide what we truly need. In Christ our hope stands tall, solid, and untouchable. In Him we have a home that outshines the sun, an inheritance that can never perish, and treasures that can never be taken from us. The deed to our heavenly home is signed and sealed with the blood of Christ; the contract is ratified by the Resurrection. And no one will ever foreclose on that.

## DO THINGS THAT HONOR THE LORD

Trust in the LORD, and do good.
PSALM 37:3

Here David tells us that we respond to God first by trusting and then by doing good—trust and obey. Trust is an act of the mind, while obedience is an act of the hands and feet. Once we've set our minds on the wisdom of God, we get busy doing the things He would have us do. It's simple but empowering: "Trust in the LORD and do good."

Let's look first at the trust step—the "think right" step. Paul's advice to his protégé, Timothy, captures it well: "Godliness with contentment is great gain. For we brought nothing into this world, and it is certain we can carry nothing out. And having food and clothing, with these we shall be content" (1 Timothy 6:6-8).

Godliness with contentment is the mind-set for right thinking—the pinnacle of wisdom in the Christian life. Don't crave more than you need; demonstrate your trust in God by being content with what you have. It's why Paul could be stripped of all he owned and thrown into prison, yet still manifest incredible joy.

The world is filled with wealthy, miserable people who have everything but contentment. Their money is an empty god that can never fill the vacuum in their souls with peace. Here Paul points those with money toward right thinking: "Command those who are rich in this present age not to be haughty, nor to trust in uncertain riches but in the living God, who gives us richly all things to enjoy. Let them do good, that they be rich in good works, ready to give, willing to share, storing up for themselves a good foundation for the time to come" (1 Timothy 6:17-19).

Paul stresses the idea of both thinking rightly (trust) and then acting rightly (obedience). Right thinking means trusting in an unshakable God instead of riches that we can't take with us. Right acting means doing good, which builds a heavenly nest egg of riches waiting just for us.

These insights echo throughout the Scriptures, and they are summed up in Paul's restatement of Job's famous observation: "We brought nothing into this world, and it is certain we can carry nothing out" (1 Timothy 6:7). Someone has observed that life is ultimately like a board game of Monopoly: you go around a few times; you collect paper money and houses; and then, sooner or later, it all goes back in the box.

What we often hear of wealth is true: you can't take it with you. But you can send it on ahead. Jesus said we can lay up treasures in heaven. That means we can live now in a way that earns a kind of interest for the next life. Whenever we serve a fellow human being, we're earning that kind of spiritual capital. Jesus said that even giving a cup of cold water to someone in need is rewarded in heaven (Matthew 10:42). He also said that when we amass "treasures in heaven," no moth can eat them away, and no robber can steal them (Matthew 6:19-20).

The great Christian leader John Wesley lived in a time of financial disruption, and he took those words of Jesus very seriously. The Industrial Revolution was causing a massive move to the cities. Farms were lost, small-town economies collapsed, and epidemics of crime and disease plagued the cities. The rich grew richer, and the poor grew in number.

Wesley saw the crowds of hurting people as Jesus would see them, and he designed ministries to care for them. His ministry became a financial success, and his annual salary grew to be the modern-day equivalent of $160,000. Wesley calculated the small sum that he really needed and gave the rest away. He saw it as investing in the things of God, which never perish. Wesley said, "If I leave behind me ten pounds, . . . you and all mankind [can] bear witness against me, that I have lived and died a thief and a robber."[3]

By no means was John Wesley against the idea of wealth; his problem was with "storing up treasures on earth" when wealth could be such a marvelous tool for ministry. He once preached a sermon in which he proposed the best attitude we can have toward wealth: "Gain all you can, save all you can, give all you can."[4]

When we do things that honor the Lord, we invest in eternity.

## DWELL ON THE FAITHFULNESS OF THE LORD

Feed on His faithfulness.

PSALM 37:3

Your mercy, O LORD, is in the heavens;
Your faithfulness reaches to the clouds.

PSALM 36:5

These verses draw our attention to the faithfulness of the Lord. But let's take a peek at the final verse of Psalm 37 to learn the outcome of God's faithfulness:

The LORD shall help them and deliver them;
He shall deliver them from the wicked,
And save them,
Because they trust in Him.

PSALM 37:40

To trust in Him is to respond in faith to His faithfulness. David knew from experience that God rewards faith with blessings. As a young man, David had been anointed as the next king of Israel. Then he spent years living in forests and caves as the reigning king hunted him down. He had to do more than merely assent to the idea of God's faithfulness—he had to stake his life on it. Life was hard during those long, perilous years. But in time, Saul died, David became king, and he could attest to the fact that God keeps His promises.

Timothy George, the dean of Beeson Divinity School, recalls a story from one of his professors, Dr. Gardner Taylor, who had once preached in Louisiana. He had been assigned to a poor, rural church with a sanctuary lit by a single lightbulb hanging from the ceiling. One evening he was preaching the Gospel with gusto when suddenly the power went out. Dr. Taylor had no idea what the protocol might be, so he stumbled around in the dark until an elderly deacon cried out, "Preach on, brother! We can still see Jesus in the dark!"

Sometimes, George concludes, we see Him *best* in the dark. "And the good news of the gospel is that whether or not we can see him in the dark, he can see us in the dark."[5]

## DELIGHT YOURSELF IN THE LORD

Delight yourself also in the LORD,
And He shall give you the desires of your heart.

PSALM 37:4

Even when our circumstances hold nothing delightful for us, we find delight in the Lord. We could be facing loss and oppression, but these things don't define us. Because we trust in God, we find an inner joy in Him.

What gives you delight? The word refers to extreme satisfaction or gratification. I find delight in a good football game or in Frank Sinatra singing a terrific old song. I find deeper delight in having my family all around and hearing about what's new in the world of my grandchildren. One of my deepest delights is time alone with my wife, my soul mate of all these years. No one on earth knows me as she does, and we create our own little world when we're together.

But my deepest delight is found in the Lord. I can go to Him no matter what is happening in my world, and the amazing truth is that He finds delight in me. I can't even begin to imagine why, but He does. My children and grandchildren realize that there's never a time when I'm not overjoyed to see them. God has this kind of delight in His children, and we should delight in Him—not because we "ought to" but because there is no deeper joy in life.

David squeezed every drop out of life the way some do an orange. He had many delights, many gifts. He could sing, he could dance, he could write poetry, he could devise battle plans, and he had an aching desire to design a temple for God. He was a passionate man who found the best in life, and he wanted us to know that one's greatest delight is found in the knowledge of God. And as usual, there's a breathtaking promise attached to that delight.

The promise is that if we delight ourselves in the Lord, He will give us the desires of our hearts. Can anything so wonderful be true? Absolutely! But it's important to understand this promise. It isn't a shortcut to prosperity, as some ill-informed preachers claim. We don't delight in the Lord *so that* He will give us what we want. That approach confuses faith with greed.

No, when we find true and genuine pleasure in God, with no thought of gain other than gaining intimacy with Him, we find our own desires coming into conformance with His desires. We begin to live in His will, and we pray accordingly. We find the joy of the Lord by following the Lord of joy into His joy. The following promises capture this idea:

> He said to them, "Go your way, eat the fat, drink the
> sweet, and send portions to those for whom nothing is
> prepared; for this day is holy to our Lord. Do not sorrow,
> for the joy of the LORD is your strength."
> NEHEMIAH 8:10

You will show me the path of life;
In Your presence is fullness of joy;
At Your right hand are pleasures forevermore.
PSALM 16:11

When things go wrong and loss overtakes us, misery often follows. And the more we struggle against the pit of discouragement, the deeper it becomes. But if we've placed our trust in God no matter what, His joy becomes our strength. We delight in Him and find new energy, new insights, and new resources to keep on going.

How can we delight in God or anything else when our world is crashing down on us? We can begin by turning to Psalm 119, which uses the word *delight* six times and shows us the first step in finding it.

I will delight myself in Your statutes;
I will not forget Your word.
PSALM 119:16

Make me walk in the path of Your commandments,
For I delight in it.
PSALM 119:35

The proud have forged a lie against me,
But I will keep Your precepts with my whole heart.
Their heart is as fat as grease,
But I delight in Your law.
PSALM 119:69-70

Let Your tender mercies come to me, that I may live;
For Your law is my delight.

PSALM 119:77

Unless Your law had been my delight,
I would then have perished in my affliction.

PSALM 119:92

I long for Your salvation, O LORD,
And Your law is my delight.

PSALM 119:174

Did you pick up on the common theme these six verses express? The first step in delighting in God is to delight in His Word. Immersing ourselves in the Word of God reveals a God we can delight in. The psalmist takes such a delight in God's Word that he uses every possible term to express the range of its meaning: statutes, commandments, precepts, law. In the same way, other writers of Scripture delight in God by using His various names. Isn't that just what people do when they're in love? They come up with pet names for their beloved, and each name has a special meaning that conveys a particular facet of the delight they find.

Delighting in God's Word leads us to delight in God, and delight in God drives away fear.

## DEDICATE YOUR LIFE TO THE LORD

Commit your way to the LORD,
Trust also in Him,
And He shall bring it to pass.

PSALM 37:5

Having found our deepest delight in God, we realize that we must give *all* of our lives to Him. This isn't a temporary commitment, a halfway intention, or the feeling of a moment. It's a choice and a contract of the heart. As in marriage, we commit ourselves to that partnership for the rest of our lives.

How does committing to the Lord help us in times of material loss? In committing to Him, we cast all our burdens upon Him. He becomes our life—the place where we bring our problems, our joys, our marriages, our families, our careers. Life and happiness are no longer dependent on financial success or material possessions. It's now all about Him.

The verse above ends with the phrase "And He shall bring it to pass." When we trust Him, depend on Him, and respond to Him in faith, He will make our greatest dreams come true by elevating them from the material to the eternal.

God is also the answer when our losses leave us unable to help ourselves:

The helpless commits himself to You;
You are the helper of the fatherless.
PSALM 10:14

When we dedicate ourselves to God, *helpless* becomes a word without meaning. When we've lost our jobs, our houses, or our savings, and debt or bankruptcy stares us in the face, it's as if we're crushed under the weight of an enormous sack filled with every problem facing us. It's a burden too heavy to bear. We can't take another step. We can't lift it—but God can. He gently says, "May I take that upon Myself? My shoulders are stronger." As we say yes, life brightens and becomes joyful.

Cast your burden on the LORD,
And He shall sustain you;
He shall never permit the righteous to be moved.
PSALM 55:22


[Cast] all your care upon Him, for He cares for you.
1 PETER 5:7


Why keep struggling with your losses on your own? Why not give the burden to Him? Nothing could be more liberating.

William Carey, the "father of modern missions," established a large print shop in Serampore, India, where he worked for years translating the Bible into many Indian languages.

On March 11, 1812, Carey had to travel to another town. His associate, William Ward, was working late when suddenly he smelled smoke. He leaped up to discover black clouds belching from the printing room. He screamed for help, and workers carried water from the nearby river until 2 a.m. But it was to no avail; nearly everything was destroyed.

The next day, missionary Joshua Marshman entered a Calcutta classroom where Carey was teaching. He placed a gentle hand on his friend's shoulder and said, "I can think of no easy way to break the news. The print shop burned to the ground last night."

Gone was Carey's massive translation work of nearly twenty years: a dictionary, two grammar books, and whole versions of the Bible. Gone were sets of type for fourteen Eastern languages, twelve hundred reams of paper, fifty-five thousand printed sheets, and thirty pages of his Bengal dictionary. Gone was his complete library. "The work of years—gone in a moment," he whispered.

In that moment he understood the pain of loss. "The loss is heavy," he wrote, "but as traveling a road the second time is usually done with greater ease and certainty than the first time, so I trust the work will lose nothing of real value. We are not discouraged; indeed the work is already begun again in every language. We are cast down but not in despair."

William Carey had dedicated his life to God, and he trusted Him to bring blessings in the ashes of his dreams. "There are grave difficulties on every hand," he once wrote, "and more are looming ahead. Therefore we must go forward." As Carey moved forward, so did God. News of the fire caused all England to start talking about William Carey. Money for support flowed in. Volunteers enlisted to help. The print shop was rebuilt and enlarged. By 1832, complete Bibles, New Testaments, or separate books of Scripture had issued from the press in forty-four languages and dialects.[6]

Because Carey had dedicated his life to God, he understood what it meant to cast all his burdens on the Lord, even when all seemed lost.

## DOWNLOAD YOUR WORRY TO THE LORD

Do not fret because of him who prospers in his way,
Because of the man who brings wicked schemes to pass.
PSALM 37:7

The year 2008 changed the landscape of American expectations. We were a prosperous nation, and many of us believed our economy was "too big to fail." Recovery continues to move at a snail's pace, and many senior citizens are no longer certain they can retire. If they do retire, they wonder whether they will be able to keep the pantry stocked.

Economic chaos also affects younger people who are having trouble finding jobs. Many have simply given up searching and have been dropped off the unemployment rolls, making the employment picture much worse than reported. These conditions are producing a new level of anxiety, and for believers, these times can become a real challenge to faith.

Remember, there are two strategies for facing the future: with fear or with faith. If you've decided to follow Christ, that means walking by faith (2 Corinthians 5:7). That does not mean Satan will forget about you. He will try to chip away at your faith by pointing you to the fear of the moment. At this time in our nation, that fear focuses heavily on finances. But fear about money—or about anything, for that matter—is never part of God's plan for us. As Paul writes, "God has not given us a spirit of fear, but of power and of love and of a sound mind" (2 Timothy 1:7). Embed this verse in your mind, and bring it to the forefront whenever you feel that first pang of fear.

Many other Bible promises will strengthen your faith and help you overcome the fear of the moment:

- Romans 8:35-39 assures us that nothing is able to separate us from the love of God.
- First John 4:18 reminds us that God's perfect love casts out our fear.
- Philippians 4:6-7 invites us to lay our anxieties before God by faith with thanksgiving, allowing the peace of God to guard our hearts and minds in Christ Jesus.

We need to understand that faith in God does not immunize us from financial failure. As long as we live in this fallen world, there will be no such thing as complete financial security. There is no ultimate security in anything but the grace of God. To be human means that loss, including heartbreaking loss, is always possible. As tough as times are, they can and may become much worse. But faith in God assures us that He holds our lives in His powerful, loving hands, which means no collapses, no losses, and no fears can truly harm us. As the Lord of this universe, He is, indeed, too big to fail.

Because God loves and cares for us, David urges us not to worry, or as he puts it, "Do not fret." This phrase *do not fret* essentially means "relax; don't react." It occurs only four times in the entire Bible—three times in Psalm 37 and once in Proverbs.

- Psalm 37:1: "Do not fret because of evildoers."
- Psalm 37:7: "Do not fret because of him who prospers in his way."
- Psalm 37:8: "Do not fret—it only causes harm."
- Proverbs 24:19: "Do not fret because of evildoers, nor be envious of the wicked."

The English word *fret* comes from the Old English *fretan*, meaning "to devour, to eat, to gnaw into something." The Hebrew word David used is *charah*, which has at its root the idea of "growing warm" and "blazing up."

Here we have a mix of two metaphors illustrating the same idea—a word picture of gnawing and a word picture of fire. In the first metaphor, fretting is seen as a rat inside your soul, gnawing away at your joy and peace. (I didn't say it was a pretty picture. But it's a true one.)

The fire metaphor pictures Satan as the arsonist of hellfire, setting blazes of distress inside your heart. Both pictures illustrate the destructiveness of fretting. In Psalm 37 David tells us not to put up with fretting: kill the rats and douse the fires, because fretting will kill you from the inside out.

Someone has observed that the prosperous people of the previous generation known as the "jet set" have now become the "fret set." Once they were flying high, and now they're flying off the handle.

One of the most frustrating things about massive losses is that we look around and see evil people prospering—sometimes even because of their evil. It violates our sense of justice. But in Psalm 37 David assures us that justice will be done. God is not yet finished with these people. Five times in this psalm, David gives us reason not to envy the prosperous wicked:

They shall soon be cut down like the grass,
And wither as the green herb.
PSALM 37:2

For yet a little while and the wicked shall be no more;
Indeed, you will look carefully for his place,
But it shall be no more.
PSALM 37:10

The wicked shall perish;
And the enemies of the LORD,
Like the splendor of the meadows, shall vanish.
Into smoke they shall vanish away.
PSALM 37:20

When the wicked are cut off, you shall see it.
PSALM 37:34

I have seen the wicked in great power,
And spreading himself like a native green tree.
Yet he passed away, and behold, he was no more;
Indeed I sought him, but he could not be found.
PSALM 37:35-36

As a creative exercise, pastor and author Leonard Griffith transplanted Rip Van Winkle, the beloved Washington Irving character, into 1930s Germany. You remember the story: Rip falls asleep for twenty years, then walks through town to find that everything has changed and no one remembers him.

In Griffith's version, Van Winkle is horrified as he watches Hitler rise to power and begin conquering Europe. He retreats into the Alps to get away from the terrifying events. There he falls asleep. When he wakes up, the 1950s are under way and the world is vastly different. The Nazis are gone—no more swastikas, no more eager Hitler youth, no more arrogant attitudes of world domination. The masterminds of the Third Reich are all dead or imprisoned or being hunted down.

Rip Van Winkle then understands the words of the psalmist: "I have seen the wicked in great power, and spreading himself like a native green tree. Yet he passed away, and behold, he was no more."[7]

Many in the 1930s wondered why God allowed the Nazis to prosper. He didn't. He dealt with them by His own timetable, and He dealt with them thoroughly.

There's another point to be considered here. What if the wrong people do come out on top in this life? Would we really want to trade our kind of security for theirs? Spurgeon wrote, "What if wicked devices succeed and your own plans are defeated! There is more of the love of God in your defeats than in the successes of the wicked."[8]

## DISCIPLINE YOURSELF TO WAIT ON THE LORD

Rest in the LORD, and wait patiently for Him.

PSALM 37:7

Waiting doesn't come easily for us. In this age of instant gratification, we're conditioned not to wait for anything. If the fast-food line is too long, we rush to the restaurant across the street. If the TV show doesn't quickly become interesting, we surf impatiently through hundreds of channels. If the car ahead doesn't move the instant the traffic light changes, we hit the horn.

When we face loss, we know we must trust God's timetable for dealing with it. But what we'd like better is for Him to accede to ours. The fact that we cannot see into the future can convince us that the future is up for grabs. But rest assured, God is completely in control. Though His timing may seem slow to us, from the viewpoint of eternity, it is perfect. God is never early and never late.

When we truly believe this, we acquire the mind of Christ, which enables us to wait on Him with patience and trust. Waiting means . . .

- Not lagging behind His leading and direction
- Not walking ahead of His leading and direction
- Not ignoring His leading and direction
- Not fretting about what He is doing or planning for you

The word *wait* is found two additional times in this psalm:

Evildoers shall be cut off;
But those who wait on the LORD,
They shall inherit the earth.

PSALM 37:9

Wait on the LORD,
And keep His way,
And He shall exalt you to inherit the land.

PSALM 37:34

Waiting is difficult in the face of loss, but it's a discipline with a huge payoff. Those who wait on the Lord will "inherit the earth" because those pushers and shovers in life's express line have all burned out, victims of their own impatience. Patient people are happier and healthier, and God will exalt them.

One writer explained that there are two kinds of faith: one based on *if* and the other on *though*. The first says, "*If* everything goes the way I want, then I'll agree that God is good." The other says, "*Though* evil may prosper, *though* I may sweat in Gethsemane, *though* my road leads to Calvary—even so, I trust in God." The first wants instant results; the second has learned the wisdom of waiting, as Job did when he cried out, "Though He slay me, yet will I trust Him" (Job 13:15).[9]

Almost two hundred years ago, our nation went through another economic upheaval: the Panic of 1837. Anna and Susan Warner and their father, Henry Warner, lived in a mansion filled with art treasures, high-class furnishings, and an army of servants. Then came the deluge.

The market crashed and took Henry Warner's investments

down with it. The family lost everything and, deeply in debt, moved to a decrepit old house up the river from New York City. Henry's financial collapse devastated him emotionally, and he was never the same. The daughters, accustomed to expensive parties and the social whirl, now realized they had to pitch in to work down the family's staggering debt.

All they could think to do was write. Though they struggled to find a publisher, eventually Putnam accepted Susan Warner's novel *The Wide, Wide World*. Success followed. The sisters wrote more than one hundred books, all built on the foundation of the Gospel that warmed their lives. One of the books, *Say and Seal*, contained a little poem Anna had woven into the story. It began with the words "Jesus loves me, this I know." Songwriter William Bradbury added music, and now "Jesus Loves Me" is loved throughout the world. Untold millions of children have first encountered Christ through its simple yet powerful words. In 1943, when John F. Kennedy's PT-109 was sunk in the Solomon Islands, local islanders and American marines sang the song as they rescued the survivors. You may have sung it as a child. I did.

If you had been part of this disconsolate family, standing in the ashes of financial failure and watching as your lifetime possessions were hauled away, you might have thought that life was unfair. But if you knew the ways of God, you might have known even then that He had special things in mind. From the cold rubble and debris of today's misfortune, God raises the bricks and beams of tomorrow's miracle.

Yes, we know that "all things work together for good to those who love God" (Romans 8:28), but this long-term promise does not provide a quick fix for the heartbreak of loss. There's no bypass to avoid it. Yet the promise remains true, and it gives us something to cling to and focus on through the blur of our tears.

The devil may win today, but the God who owns tomorrow "works out everything in conformity with the purpose of his will, in order that we, who were the first to put our hope in Christ, might be for the praise of his glory" (Ephesians 1:11-12, NIV).

Philip Yancey points out that two of the primary days we've named on the church calendar are Good Friday and Easter Sunday. One held the worst event imaginable, and the other the greatest. Yet we live most of life on the day between—Saturday—a day we've given no special name. Like the disciples, we sit in the wake of life's heartbreak with no clue that what the morning will bring is brighter than our most brilliant dreams.

Life is about deciding how to live in that interim between cross and crown. Just how much do we trust God? Do we really believe He can take a world that includes genocide in Bosnia and Rwanda, inner-city ghettos, capacity prisons, and wipe out losses, then fashion something beautiful out of it? We know what Friday feels like. Is there going to be a Sunday?

Yancey observes that the day of Christ's beatings, crucifixion, and death is called *Good* Friday. It only earns that adjective in light of Sunday's developments. The empty tomb refashions the shame of the Cross into a victory. Easter, says Yancey, offers a clue into the greater workings of God. Our souls rise above the loss of Friday, knowing that blessing will come on Sunday. In the meantime, Saturday becomes a day of waiting.[10]

Waiting is not always a bad thing; it can bring its own joy—the thrill of anticipation. Do you remember waiting for Christmas as a child? Waiting for your wedding day? Waiting for something good makes the heart sing. It fills us with hope. It changes us internally so that the ups and downs of this fickle, undependable life can exert no real power over us. The world may take away our homes and every cent we have. We may cry out, but our hope is intact because our losses are only a reminder of the grand gift that, once received, can never be lost. And it's worth waiting for.

# CHAPTER 4

# DEFEAT:
## *The Fear of Failure*

*The LORD, He is the One who goes before you. He will be*

*with you, He will not leave you nor forsake you;*

*do not fear nor be dismayed.*

DEUTERONOMY 31:8

Lyndon Baines Johnson was ambitious from the start. He moved smoothly through the House of Representatives, was elected to the Senate, and then became the Senate's majority leader. Still, his eyes never left one address: 1600 Pennsylvania Avenue—the White House.

He was a tall Texan—six foot four—not to mention wealthy and influential. He had a reputation for getting things done, even if he had to cut a few corners along the way. By the end of a typical day, he had outworked and outmaneuvered everyone in the room. He wouldn't take no for an answer on anything, including his drive to be president of the United States.

In the two years leading up to the 1960 campaign, it seemed like his greatest dream lay within his grip. He was the highest-ranking

Democrat in the nation and one of the most respected men in America. His opponent was considered a lightweight in politics— a skinny, sickly young man who, in Johnson's view, was little more than a playboy living on his father's money: John F. Kennedy.

Summoning advisers to his Texas ranch in 1958, Johnson told them plainly that it was his destiny to be president and that he was going to run for the office.

So the men around him began to lay the foundation for a campaign to put their man in the White House. Since the Republicans had held the presidency for two terms, the Democrats poured all they had into their leading light. The planners waited for Johnson's announcement that he would throw his ten-gallon hat in the ring.

Then they waited some more.

Johnson, who had spoken of this dream for as long as anyone had known him, had cold feet. He was, according to the White House press secretary at the time, "a man badly torn."[1] Meanwhile, Kennedy was racing across the nation sewing up delegates to win the nomination for himself. By the time Johnson got around to announcing his candidacy, it was too late. Kennedy had beaten him to the punch.

Historians have speculated why such a driven and powerful man stalled at the most important moment of his career. Biographer Robert A. Caro has a theory. He believes that for all his drive and bravado, Johnson was paralyzed by a fear of failure—the fear that he would end up like his father.

When Lyndon was a child, his family was among the most respected in town, living in a large house on a sprawling Texas ranch. His father, Samuel, was a successful man—a member of the state House and the most prosperous businessman in the area.

Sam bought the first car anyone had ever seen in those parts, and he had a chauffeur to drive it. The Johnson family was riding high.

But just as young Lyndon came into his teenage years, disaster struck: the business failed. The family lost its ranch and moved into a little shanty house, the next step up from homelessness. From being the highest in society, the Johnsons plummeted to the lowest. Townspeople brought food to keep them from starving. Lyndon was humiliated beyond words. One classmate recalls that when Lyndon was taunted at school, he responded that one day he would be president of the United States. His classmates laughed and said they wouldn't vote for him. He retorted that he wouldn't need their votes.

From that moment, LBJ dreamed of being president. But when the prize was finally within his grasp, he was traumatized by a fear of failing in a way that would bring public humiliation, as had happened to his father. He was so afraid of defeat that it became a self-fulfilling prophecy.

Caro writes,

His father's fall had shown him that failure could mean not merely failure but terror, the terror of living in a house that, month by month, you were afraid would be taken from you by the bank; that failure could mean not merely terror but ruin, permanent ruin; that failure— defeat—might be something from which you would never recover. And failure in public—failing in a way that was visible: having to move off your ranch; having your credit cut off at stores you had to walk past every day; no longer holding your public office—could mean a different, but also terrible, kind of pain: embarrassment, disgrace, humiliation.[2]

According to Caro, that's why Johnson anguished and languished over his run for office. And that's why Kennedy beat him for the 1960 nomination and history took the strange and twisted course that followed. He did eventually make it to 1600 Pennsylvania Avenue, but it wasn't by a course he ever would have scripted out for himself.

It has a name: *atychiphobia*—the paralyzing, recurring fear of failure. It's a harsh taskmaster, leading its victims to a life of restraint and retreat. The worst of its side effects is that it results in a persistent refusal to try anything new.

Those who fear failure are paralyzed by the "*r* word": *risk*. They may undermine their own efforts without even realizing it in an attempt to escape the anxiety of looming failure. Have you known people like that? I have—gifted people who might have done great things in life but wouldn't, and couldn't, because they were protecting themselves from disappointment.

Perhaps only a few of us are atychiphobes, but nearly all of us have felt the fear of failure to some degree. In fact, many of the most-admired people in the Bible experienced it. As I mentioned in the introduction to this book, the Bible identifies more than two hundred people who were afraid at one time or another. Some of them were afraid of failure!

We see this consistently in the "call narratives" of the Bible— those accounts in which God summons a person to a particular task. The more prominent examples are Moses, Gideon, Isaiah, Jeremiah, and Ezekiel.

In the Old Testament, these call narratives have a similar form and progression. First there is an encounter with God, either directly or through one of His angels. This encounter occurs not in some sacred place but within the normal routines of life. Moses is tending sheep, and Gideon is threshing wheat. A divine encounter ensues, bringing a call and challenge: *Your moment has arrived—I am sending you on the mission of your life!*

The calling is usually followed by objections from the person called—many of them born out of a fear of failure. Moses responded to his call by saying: "Who am I that I should go to Pharaoh, and that I should bring the children of Israel out of Egypt?" (Exodus 3:11). Even after God's assurances of success, Moses continued to object: "O my Lord, I am not eloquent . . . but I am slow of speech and slow of tongue" (Exodus 4:10).

When God called Gideon to fight against the Midianites, his initial response was similar: "O my Lord, how can I save Israel? Indeed my clan is the weakest in Manasseh, and I am the least in my father's house" (Judges 6:15). When God called Jeremiah to speak words of prophecy to God's people, Jeremiah's objection follows the same pattern: "Then said I: 'Ah, Lord GOD! Behold, I cannot speak, for I am a youth'" (Jeremiah 1:6).

Obviously, the fear of failure is not a modern phenomenon; it is a timeless human fear. Some of God's choicest servants through the ages displayed this fear in spite of God's promises of success. Their stories provide insight into how God responds to human fears. In every case, He draws alongside His servant with assurance and affirmation.

Nowhere is God's concern for a fearful servant more evident than in Joshua 1, where He prepares Joshua to lead Israel after the death of Moses. In this chapter, I will focus mainly on this call and its accompanying assurance, because here all the principles scattered throughout the other call narratives come together in an organized, step-by-step strategy for dealing with the fear of failure.

The theme of Joshua's call is transition—the transition of Israel's leadership from Moses to Joshua. To fully appreciate the magnitude of this transition, we must remember the greatness of Moses.

He is certainly the most revered figure in Judaism, and he ranks among the greatest men in history. An entire generation of Israelites followed Moses out of slavery and into the wilderness. Deuteronomy 34 tells how he died at the ripe age of 120, still a sharp and vigorous man. Israel had seen no other prophet of Moses' caliber—a man so close to God, so endowed with God's miraculous power. They had seen him raise his staff as God parted the waters of the Red Sea. They had seen him stand up to Pharaoh and call down bread from heaven. They had waited at the base of the mountain as God dictated His Ten Commandments to him.

The book of Exodus makes a statement about Moses that is not said of any other person in Scripture: "The LORD spoke to Moses face to face, as a man speaks to his friend" (Exodus 33:11). On more than one occasion, Moses even spent forty days on a mountain in fellowship with Him. God grants this kind of intimacy only to those who desire it. Moses belonged to an inner circle of people who enjoyed holy intimacy with God.

The people would grumble against Moses, but in the end they would always follow him, for they knew he was God's man. His leadership filled them with frustration at first, then deeper devotion. And when the great man finally died, they wept in the plains of Moab for thirty days (Deuteronomy 34:8).

There's no question—Moses would have been a hard act to follow. That was the call to greatness that thrust itself upon Joshua.

Moses' death came at a perilous time in Israel's history. The previous generation had been too fearful to believe God's promise of victory and refused to enter the Promised Land at its very border (Numbers 13–14). That entire generation had died off during thirty-eight years of wandering in the wilderness. Now an all-new generation was gathered on the east bank of the Jordan River, ready to cross over and take possession of the Promised Land. They were ready to step out in faith and claim their home. But it wasn't going to be easy—it never is.

For one thing, after four decades of peace, the children of Israel indeed felt like children. They hadn't fought a serious battle for forty years, and the Canaanites they would soon face were said to be tall, sturdy, battle-hardened warriors who made the Israelite spies feel "like grasshoppers" in comparison (Numbers 13:33). The enemy waited behind strong, fortified walls. They even had horses and chariots (Joshua 17:16).

Then there was the problem of food. The people had grown accustomed to receiving manna from the hand of God at their doorstep each morning. Now, as we read in Exodus 16:35 and Joshua 5:12, the manna would cease, and the Israelites would be responsible for cultivating food from the land.

How would you like to have been Joshua, taking the reins of leadership from someone like Moses at such a critical time? If you had been called in as a consultant to help Joshua prepare for his new role, what would your counsel have been? Actually, Joshua did have a consultant—God Himself. God delivered to Joshua one of the greatest motivational speeches I've ever read. His words have often encouraged me at times of great personal challenge.

If you are afraid about your future, if you are being called to a new assignment that seems beyond your abilities, or if you just need encouragement to continue on in whatever God has called you to do, you, too, will find courage as you study God's charge to Joshua in the face of his greatest challenge. We'll explore six powerful principles from Joshua to send you forth as a conqueror rather than a hostage to your own fear of failure.

## THE PRINCIPLE OF DIVINE PERSPECTIVE

As I was with Moses, so I will be with you. I will not leave
you nor forsake you.

JOSHUA 1:5

God looked upon an anxious new leader and gave him the words
of a lifetime. He began by reminding Joshua of the adventures
he had enjoyed as Moses' protégé through the years. Joshua had
been witness to a rich history of miracles and magnificence, of
God proving His faithfulness in a trek through a hostile empire
and then into the wilderness.

God encouraged Joshua to remember what he had experienced as Moses' partner in ministry—how He had led Moses
and how He had performed mighty acts to help Moses lead the
people. God assured Joshua, "As I was with Moses, so I will be
with you." Joshua was to view his daunting task through the
perspective of God's previous demonstrations of power and
faithfulness.

I love to read biographies of Christian leaders because they
remind me of the principle of divine perspective. As God has
been faithful to His followers in the past, He will be faithful to
us in the present. He has put no limits on what He is willing to
do for you and me. His actions might even exceed what He has
done in the past. He is able "to do exceedingly abundantly above
all that we ask or think" (Ephesians 3:20).

Fear of failure is nothing new—nor is overcoming it. Think
of the seventeenth-century Pilgrims who left their homes to
find freedom of worship in the New World. They must have
been daunted by the prospect of crossing the Atlantic in their
tiny ships and surviving in an uncharted wilderness. But they

overcame their fear because they had faith in God's power and provision. That is the benefit of perspective—it allows us to see beyond the trials that frighten us in the here and now.

God has never called anyone to a task and then abandoned him or her by the side of the road. So if we fear what God wants us to do, our perspective needs adjusting so that we focus not on the size of the job but on the size of God.

## THE PRINCIPLE OF DIVINE PURPOSE

> Arise, go over this Jordan, you and all this people, to the land which I am giving to them—the children of Israel. Every place that the sole of your foot will tread upon I have given you, as I said to Moses.
>
> JOSHUA 1:2-3

God gave Joshua a specific thing to do! He told Joshua to walk on every piece of ground in the land of Canaan and promised him that every piece of ground he walked on would be given to him and to his people forever. God was giving Joshua *focus*.

The 1993 movie *The Fugitive*, starring Harrison Ford, was nominated for seven Academy Awards, winning one. It grossed nearly $369 million worldwide. But the movie almost didn't get made. The script was in development for five and a half years. Nine different writers produced at least twenty-five different screenplays. Producer Arnold Kopelson said,

> There were times that everyone would say, "You're wasting your time. Why are you doing this? You're wasting money." Warner Brothers put the property into turn-around. . . . We had spent about two million dollars in writing costs and they were concerned that this would

never bear out. And I said, "Listen, I have an instinct about this. My gut tells me that this is going to be a success."[3]

Granted, sometimes instincts and gut feelings don't work out. But in this case, they did. Kopelson's determination illustrates an important point: maintaining purpose and focus in the face of obstacles can be the difference between failure and success.

Seeing *The Fugitive* through to opening day meant the producer had to stay focused for more than five years. But Joshua had to maintain his own focus for fourteen years, the time required to win the Promised Land. It helped that Joshua didn't have to trust his gut feeling; he had the promises of God.

J. Oswald Sanders helps us understand this promise to Joshua:

The land belonged to Israel by direct gift from God, Possessor of heaven and earth. The land became theirs experientially only when they walked around it and actually took possession. This fundamental spiritual principle carries over into the experience of the New Testament Christian. "According to your faith let it be to you" (Matthew 9:29).[4]

But having a promise from God is no guarantee of success if we lose our focus. God's responsibility is to make the promise; ours is to stay focused on it in the face of fear. To achieve success, Joshua and the new generation of Israelites had to focus their minds and hearts on the purpose God had given them.

There's a special, liberating power in knowing exactly what it is we must do. That's why people derive great satisfaction by making and checking off to-do lists. To boil down all the complexities of the day into bullet points of activity is to see our way to productivity. On the other hand, whole organizations fail because people are confused about their job descriptions.

Set a clear focus in your life, and fear will be crowded out. The more you fix your eyes on God's purpose for you, the more you will overcome your fear.

## THE PRINCIPLE OF DIVINE PERSUASION

Have I not commanded you? Be strong and of good courage.

JOSHUA 1:9

While Reverend William Sykes was the chaplain of University College, Oxford, he described a group of undergraduates with physical disabilities he had known. Their limitations were many, but what linked them together was a quiet courage within them. This experience caused him to ponder the meaning of that word. Looking to the writings of Cardinal Manning, he found this entry:

The Italians call it *Coraggio*, or greatness of heart; the Spaniards, *Corage*; the French, *Courage*, from whom we have borrowed it. And we understand it to mean manliness, bravery, boldness, fearlessness, springing not from a sense of physical power, or from insensibility to danger or pain, but from the moral habit of self-command, with deliberation, fully weighing present dangers, and clearly foreseeing future consequences, and yet in the path of duty advancing unmoved to its execution.[5]

Somehow, the students had found a strength inside that transcended their physical limitations. Faith is an inestimable power, and often it grows by the convincing words of someone who persuades us that we, too, can live courageously.

Who among us does not have some kind of disability—in skill, desire, motivation, strength, experience, courage, or the countless other traits required to make good progress in life? It's called being human—and it's why every person needs the same exhortation Joshua needed when he stood on the banks of the Jordan River and looked across to a hostile land.

He must have remembered what happened when the Israelites stood at the borders of the Promised Land almost forty years earlier. They had God's promise, yet the challenge paralyzed them. It wasn't the giants in the land that disabled them; it was their giant fear. To prevent this new generation from making the same mistake, Joshua needed to display strength and courage. This meant he needed to be persuaded that God would enable them to meet the challenge. God had just the right words for Israel's new leader:

> Be strong and of good courage. . . . Only be strong and
> very courageous. . . . Have I not commanded you? Be
> strong and of good courage.
> JOSHUA 1:6-7, 9

This is the heart of God's motivational speech to Joshua. Three times He tells him to be strong and courageous. The word *strong* means to be resolute, firm, and not easily swayed. *Courageous* conveys a sense of daring, an openness to risk.

Joshua had proved that he had that inner strength within him. We witness it on the day the spies returned, ten of them giving a fearful report of unconquerable giants. Only two men, Joshua and

Caleb, wanted to take hold of God's promises and push forward despite the obstacles. The ten insisted, "We are not able to go up against the people, for they are stronger than we" (Numbers 13:31). The tales of terror drowned out the counsel of courage.

When we face such a situation, we'll either focus on the problem or on the solution. Ten men turned into grasshoppers in their own eyes simply by giving rein to their fear; two men focused on God and His power. Ten spoke of the size of the enemy; two spoke of the size of their God.

Sometimes the majority gets it wrong. The wisdom of God is often found on the narrow path that few travel rather than in the easy and popular choice. Leadership is a great deal more than gauging which way the wind is blowing. It often requires standing firm as the current tries to bend you in another direction.

Paul Laurence Dunbar's little poem makes this point:

*Minorities, since time began,*
*Have shown the better side of man;*
*And often in the lists of Time*
*One man has made a cause sublime!*[6]

When I've faced challenges in my life, I've drawn inspiration from envisioning Joshua at the banks of his river, learning to be strong and courageous, or from holding on to the words of Paul: "If God is for us, who can be against us?" (Romans 8:31). These inspiring passages persuade me to be firm and willing to take risks for God. I believe this practice will work for you as well.

## THE PRINCIPLE OF DIVINE PRIORITY

Do not turn from it to the right hand or to the left, that you may prosper wherever you go. This Book of the Law shall not depart from your mouth, but you shall meditate in it day and night, that you may observe to do according to all that is written in it.

JOSHUA 1:7-8

Now we come to the heart of the matter: God's Word is the only path to success.

God didn't tell Joshua that his priority needed to be military strategy, financial backing, or bilateral relations with neighboring countries. These things have a place, but they are not the priority. Here was Joshua's priority: meditate day and night on the principles of the Word of God.

This requires dedication somewhat like that of a long-distance runner who is training to compete in an Olympic marathon. The runners I've read about are incredibly focused. They live with a Spartan's commitment to a single priority—winning that marathon and standing on an Olympic podium. Running informs every aspect of their lives. They eat specific foods, weighing the grams and counting the calories. They monitor their weight, body fat, water weight, and bone density. They run in only a certain kind of shoe. They have limited social lives because running, training, eating, and sleeping dominate their days. Their training schedule is the paradigm into which all of life's activities fit. Their conversations and their daily decisions reflect their mission. When planning and executing their lives, everything flows through the grid of training.

When asked what he would be doing if he weren't a runner, one marathoner from Kenya laughed and said, "I don't know. For me, running is everything." I urge you to read the following five points about Scripture with that perspective so you can say, "For me, the Word of God is everything. It informs all my decisions and values. I arrange my life around its principles. I study it consistently to reinforce my life goals. I consult it before I make plans or decisions. What the Bible says takes precedence over whatever anyone else says. It is, after all, *God's* Word."

Scripture is my weapon of choice in the fight against the fear of defeat. As we seek courage to conquer the giants in our lives, we need to make our top priority the Word of God.

### Talk about the Word Constantly

This Book of the Law shall not depart from your mouth.
JOSHUA 1:8

Let's clarify what Joshua would have understood to be the "Book of the Law." For him it was the first five books of our Bible—the Pentateuch, as that collection of books is called. Nothing more of Scripture had yet been written. God told Joshua that this book was to be his plan of action. He was to take this book in his hands and commit it to his heart. It was the key to his ability to accomplish the assignment God was giving him.

The Book of the Law was also to be the topic of his conversation with others—not talking about it as we would a novel or a biography, but allowing the law of God to inform, guide, and temper all conversations and deliberations. Later in the book, we see Joshua doing that very thing:

Afterward he read all the words of the law, the blessings and the cursings, according to all that is written in the Book of the Law. There was not a word of all that Moses had commanded which Joshua did not read before all the assembly of Israel.
JOSHUA 8:34-35

Part of what Joshua would have read to the people was the passage in Deuteronomy 6:6-9, Moses' instructions to parents about how to weave the Word of God into their children's lives: "You . . . shall talk of [God's words] when you sit in your house, when you walk by the way, when you lie down, and when you rise up" (verse 7).

Notice the word *talk*. God's words, commands, and statutes—His perspective on everything—were to be embedded in every family conversation. Children would grow up with God's law deeply entrenched in their very thinking.

The Deuteronomy passage also uses a figure of speech that involves making a point by giving opposites: when you're in the house, when you're outside; when you're lying down, when you're up and about; when you're sitting, when you're standing. The idea is that we teach the law all the time—now, then, and every moment in between.

God's law should live on the tongue. There is no inappropriate time for sharing it, and we should be as driven to discuss it as a bird is to sing. The Lord provides all the various venues of life—relaxed family time, outdoor chores, coming-of-age milestones—for discussing the law in every context. Think what would happen today if Christians, instead of discussing politics, TV shows, movies, sports, and traffic, started talking more about the Word of God!

"What did you learn from the Word today?"

"Before we discuss our plans, let's see what counsel we can find in the Bible."

Wouldn't that be a refreshing way to live? Wouldn't it be a powerful step in conquering our fears and failings?

### *Meditate on the Word Continually*
You shall meditate in it day and night.

JOSHUA 1:8

The very idea of meditation is out of step with the times. We don't like anything slow or deliberate, and we particularly hate the idea of quiet. We like things to be fast paced. We like more action and less reflection. We like 140-character tweets instead of in-depth information.

But meditation—biblical meditation, not the emptying of the mind featured in Eastern religions—is central to the life to which God calls us. It requires that we give up our hurry and listen quietly and deeply to what God has to say. J. I. Packer describes the right way to do it:

> Meditation is the activity of calling to mind, and thinking over, and dwelling on, and applying to oneself, the various things that one knows about the works and ways and purposes and promises of God.
>
> Its purpose is to . . . let his truth make its full and proper impact on one's mind and heart. . . . It is, indeed, often a matter of arguing with oneself, reasoning oneself out of moods of doubt and unbelief into a clear apprehension of God's power and grace.[7]

Like a cow that chews the same grass over and over to digest it and benefit from it, we meditate on the Word of God by going over and over it in a way that allows God to speak to our hearts and quiet our fears.

Meditation is preventive maintenance for the mind. We fill every corner of our thinking with rich, eternal truth before the errors of the world can take root there and infect us. We live in this world, and we'll be exposed to all that is wrong about it. But we can make ourselves resistant to the virus of false ideas. Meditating on God's Word is inoculation against "every wind of doctrine" (Ephesians 4:14).

David understood the power of meditation. He wrote,

Oh, how I love Your law!
It is my meditation all the day.
You, through Your commandments, make me wiser than my
    enemies;
For they are ever with me.
I have more understanding than all my teachers,
For Your testimonies are my meditation.
I understand more than the ancients,
Because I keep Your precepts.
PSALM 119:97-100

Try meditating each day on Philippians 4:13, which reads, "I can do all things through Christ who strengthens me." Think about how much more resistant you'd be to the insidious whispers that say, *Give up—you can't do this; God isn't going to help you.* The implanted Word is a bulwark against the lies of the evil one.

Whichever of those two messages touches your soul most frequently—the voice of courage or the voice of defeat—that's the one that wins the battle for your mind.

### Read the Word Obediently

. . . that you may observe to do according to all that is written in [the Book of the Law]."
JOSHUA 1:8

Notice the phrase *observe to do* in this passage. It's easy to pass over these three words as negligible, but in reality they present one of the great concepts of the Old Testament. We are not to read the Bible for information only or just to increase our knowledge. We are to study the Bible to discover God's will for our lives. We *observe* in order to *do*. We observe the Bible in order to obey the Bible.

One of the most subtle and dangerous errors we can fall into is to view the Bible simply as interesting reading. Yes, it's timeless literature—fascinating, entertaining, and moving. But at all times the Word of God is no mere book. It's meant to change who we are and how we live. The Bible's message can't simply stop with the mind; it must go on to the heart and the will. We are to be "doers of the word, and not hearers only" (James 1:22).

When we fear living counterculturally as God's light in the world, obedience is the single key to banishing the fear. Disobey, and fear remains. Obey, and fear departs. The role of the Word of God is to tell us what to do. But courage is only realized when we obey.

### Follow the Word Exclusively

Do not turn from [the Book of the Law] to the right hand or to the left.

JOSHUA 1:7

In recent years a new buzz phrase has entered our common language: *zero tolerance*. We began to hear it more frequently after 1994 legislation outlawed bringing firearms to school. There would be no tolerance for a violation of that decree. Expulsion for one year would follow, and if the school failed to comply, it could lose its federal funding. Zero tolerance meant a strict, clear-cut policy banning guns in schools. The phrase caught on, and soon we were discussing other areas that deserved zero tolerance: bullying, cheating, dealing drugs.

The term didn't exist in Joshua's day, but as the passage above shows, its application did. God gave Joshua a zero-tolerance policy concerning spiritual infidelity, telling him that when Israel entered Canaan, he was to follow the Word of God without turning "to the right hand or to the left."

He wasn't to compromise morality or principles to conform to the practices of the land's inhabitants. He wasn't to massage the meaning of God's law to make it politically correct. He wasn't to use it as a proof text for his own point of view. He was to obey God's law and nothing else.

At the heart of the law was the covenant, the agreement between God and His people. It would not change; a new generation must hold to old revelation. In a time of uncertainty, facing a new world, this would be their assurance: *Nothing important has changed. I, the Lord, do not change. Keep following Me.*

We know the history that followed. The people of Israel took many steps to the left and to the right. God was patient and forgiving, but finally the nation had to suffer for its lack of faithfulness to God and His law. The nation split in two. Its people were exiled first to Assyria, then to Babylon. The Israelites paid the price, living in constant fear of enemies and invasions. They turned to the right hand and the left to serve other gods, and eventually their fears were realized when God removed His umbrella of protection.

We have a choice: we can follow the gods of this world and live with the fear that we'll be caught in the outcomes that inevitably fall on all disobedience, or we can follow God and His Word exclusively and live without fear.

## *Accept the Word Totally*

... all that is written in it.

JOSHUA 1:8

Sometimes people ask me why I preach from the Old Testament. Nearly everyone likes the Gospels of Jesus and the letters of the apostles. But why worry about all those wars and kings and prophets?

There is good reason. I include the Old Testament in my teaching because God's message is incomplete without it. Theology recognizes two kinds of inspiration of Scripture: verbal inspiration means that the words were inspired by God; plenary or full inspiration means that *all* of the Bible comes directly from God. We believe, then, that every word of the Scriptures has God as its source. This is reflected in Joshua 1:8, where the word *all* takes center stage. We aren't to pick and choose from God's law any more than we are to pick and choose what federal laws we obey.

Did Joshua listen? Many years later, when he was nearing death, he gave his final address to the people of Israel, now established in the Promised Land. He echoed the words that were given to him many years earlier by God: "Be very courageous to keep and to do all that is written in the Book of the Law of Moses, lest you turn aside from it to the right hand or to the left" (Joshua 23:6).

In Deuteronomy 17:18-19, God made deep immersion in His law the first priority for Israel's future kings. No doubt this is why David, nearing the end of his life, prepared his son Solomon for accession to kingship with words that echoed God's charge to Joshua:

I go the way of all the earth; be strong, therefore, and prove yourself a man. And keep the charge of the LORD your God: to walk in His ways, to keep His statutes, His commandments, His judgments, and His testimonies, as it is written in the Law of Moses, that you may prosper in all that you do and wherever you turn.

1 KINGS 2:2-3

It is no small thing that God called Joshua to the Word as he stood on the banks of the Jordan. Those who desire to do anything for God and experience the richness He desires for them must be people of the Word.

The "spiritual greats" of our times have made the Word a first priority. Some pastors, leaders, teachers, and laymen have read through the Bible more than a hundred times. It is said that George Müller read it two hundred times. Missionary David Livingston read it four times in succession while he was detained in a jungle town. Charles Spurgeon said, "A Bible that is falling apart usually belongs to someone who is not."

The Bible is the greatest source of encouragement available today. When we read it, we are changed because it is a living book. Whenever we are afraid of failure or feel as if we are failures, the Word of God should be our highest priority. The words we find there will infuse our hearts and minds with strength and courage. The more we focus on God and His Word, the less room there will be for fear.

## THE PRINCIPLE OF DIVINE PRESENCE

I will be with you. I will not leave you nor forsake you. . . . The LORD your God is with you wherever you go.

JOSHUA 1:5, 9

Earlier in this chapter, we discussed the similarities in the call narratives of the Old Testament—the challenge from heaven, the fear from earth, the reaffirmation and assurance from God. There's one other key element: God's consistent promise to accompany us on the journey. He never says, "You go, and I'll wait here for you." He says, "Let's go."

- God said to Moses: "I will certainly be with you. . . . Now therefore, go, and I will be with your mouth and teach you what you shall say" (Exodus 3:12; 4:12).
- To Gideon: "Surely I will be with you, and you shall defeat the Midianites as one man" (Judges 6:16).
- To Jeremiah: "'Do not be afraid of their faces, for I am with you to deliver you,' says the LORD. . . . 'For I am with you,' says the LORD, 'to deliver you'" (Jeremiah 1:8, 19).
- And to Joshua: "As I was with Moses, so I will be with you. I will not leave you nor forsake you" (Joshua 1:5).

For forty years, Joshua had witnessed God's faithful presence with his mentor, Moses. Now God promised Joshua that he, too, would be blessed by the presence of God in his life and leadership.

Nothing is more important, or more confidence boosting, in the call of God than the promise that God will be with us. God's promise of His active presence and power always accompanies every person He calls. This renders meaningless any excuse or objection to the call. Whether the person called feels inadequate or incapable becomes irrelevant, because he carries with him God's power to accomplish what God calls him to do.

In the New Testament, God makes the same promise to us that He made to His Old Testament saints:

"I will never leave you nor forsake you." So we may boldly say:

"The LORD is my helper;
I will not fear.
What can man do to me?"
HEBREWS 13:5-6

## THE PRINCIPLE OF DIVINE PROSPERITY

You will make your way prosperous, and then you will have good success.
JOSHUA 1:8

This is undoubtedly one of the boldest promises in the entire Bible. To most people today, success means the accomplishment of goals and financial achievement. In the Hebrew language, however, it means to be prudent or to act circumspectly. In a spiritual sense, this means letting one's life be guided by God. Joshua had this kind of success and prosperity. He ran into his share of bumps in the road, and he had his failures. But the great scope of his life indicated prudence and wisdom, and he was a successful man.

Now picture this with me: Joshua learns that his new job assignment is to lead these nomadic people against the Canaanites. It's a great promotion, but he fears it's too much for him. Filled with anxiety, he goes into the Divine Consultant's office, where he is given these six principles to overcome his fear of failure and guarantee his success. He walks out standing straight and tall, with a confident spring in his step. He has received a transfusion of courage.

As Joshua came to the end of his life, he gave testimony to the power of these principles to bring prosperity and success to his nation:

> Behold, this day I am going the way of all the earth. And
> you know in all your hearts and in all your souls that
> not one thing has failed of all the good things which the
> LORD your God spoke concerning you. All have come to
> pass for you; not one word of them has failed.
> JOSHUA 23:14

I know these principles work, because I have made them the core principles for my own walk with God. On many occasions when I've faced the challenges of ministry, these powerful words have given me the shot of courage I needed to push on and find the success God promises.

As I write this chapter, I am reminded of the times when I was most afraid of failure. The first was my last year in seminary. I had spent four years in college and four years in graduate seminary training, and within weeks I would have to step out of that comfort zone into the real world. I remember thinking, *I wonder if I'll be able to do this. What if I'm just not cut out for the ministry?*

My first assignment after graduating was to serve as a youth pastor and Christian education director at a large church in New Jersey. Those were great days for Donna and me. We hung out with the high school kids day and night, and God gave us the privilege of mentoring some of the greatest young people we had ever met. We still hear from some of them to this day.

During the last months of our second year in New Jersey, I began to feel a growing desire to preach. My few preaching opportunities made me eager to do more. We didn't have to wait long for that desire to be met. A longtime pastor friend was building a network of churches in Fort Wayne, Indiana. Out of the blue, he called me to ask if I would have any interest in becoming the pastor of their newest church plant.

With many reservations, Donna and I agreed to visit the church. I would preach in the mother church and then meet with the seven families who had agreed to help start this new work. I was pretty certain that God did not want me to do this, but I felt obligated to listen to their proposal.

As we traveled home afterward, we were both overwhelmed with the faith and excitement of this core group of people. And we were shocked that they wanted us to come to lead them in this venture of faith. They gave us a couple of weeks to make our decision, and we ended up taking every single day! As the deadline drew near, I was conflicted. Looking back, I now realize that a big part of my indecision was the fear that I would not be able to accomplish what they wanted me to do. What if we went to Indiana and failed to make the new church a success?

Other issues also clouded my mind. During our visit, I had driven around the area where this church was to be planted, and I counted at least five well-established churches. And I was to be the pastor of seven families meeting in a mobile home! That's right—a mobile home. One of the core members of the new church sold mobile homes, and he had agreed to assemble four of them into an L-shaped arrangement that resulted in an "auditorium" that would seat one hundred people, with the other section housing a nursery, a few classrooms, and a small office.

If you were driving around Fort Wayne, Indiana, looking for a new church home, would you have chosen the mobile home church over one of the five beautiful churches in our part of town? Neither would I! The fear of failure was palpable, and I knew how to get rid of it—stay right where we were in an established, comfortable church.

With only a few days left before the deadline, I drove to the New Jersey shore to spend the day thinking and praying. It was colder than I'd anticipated, so I popped into a coffee shop on the boardwalk to get warm. I took my coffee and a copy of the *Philadelphia Inquirer* to a booth and settled in—and began reading a story that changed our lives.

It was an article about Vince Lombardi, the fabled coach of the Green Bay Packers. He had just left Wisconsin to become head coach of the struggling Washington Redskins. It was the talk of the sports world: Why would Lombardi leave his spectacularly successful franchise in Green Bay and move to what was then the worst franchise in the NFL? What caught my attention was a line in the middle of the article—a pullout quote from the coach set in bold type: "I have discovered in my life that it is more challenging to build than to maintain."

I finished my coffee, drove the hour back to Haddon Heights, and told Donna that we were moving to Fort Wayne. God had vanquished my fear of failure—for the moment.

The fear returned as we spent the next few weeks preparing our transition to Indiana. I believed God had spoken to me that day at the Jersey Shore, but I was still nervous and afraid—until we arrived. When we walked into the little house where we would live, we saw a sign taped on a kitchen cabinet door:

God's commandments are God's enablements.

To this day, I don't know who put the sign there, but I believe God moved them to do it. It suddenly dawned on me: God wouldn't tell me to do something that He wouldn't enable me to accomplish! Why should I be afraid if God had committed Himself to my success? What God did for Moses, Gideon, Jeremiah, Joshua, and others, He would do for me. And He did. For twelve years, God patiently helped me learn to be a pastor and caused the church to grow. When we left Fort Wayne, God had proved to Donna and me that the only way we learn to trust Him is to step out of our comfort zones into the "fear zone" and say yes to Him.

If you are in a similar place today, may I encourage you to replace your fear of the unknown with confidence in God and His Word? If there is something God wants you to do, let your actions put your fear to flight.

**CHAPTER 5**

# DISCONNECTION:
## *The Fear of Being Alone*

*Do not be afraid, nor be dismayed, for the* LORD *your God is*
*with you wherever you go.*
JOSHUA 1:9

During the summer of 2008, *New York Times* writer Hal Niedzviecki decided to explore the brave new world of social media, particularly Facebook. So he set up an account and dived in. He added friends quickly—people he'd known over the years, relatives, friends of friends, and even a few tangential acquaintances here and there. He was soon astonished to discover he had seven hundred online friends. He had to admit: it was a rush! He had a new, enhanced view of his place in the world.

But he wondered how Facebook friends translated into traditional friendships. He was a bit of an introvert who focused on his career. Still, this was the age of Facebook—maybe he had underestimated his social abilities.

So he put it all to a test. He planned a Facebook party designed to help him convert digital acquaintances into real, in-the-flesh friends. Niedzviecki invited all seven hundred of his connections to a local bar for a party. People could respond that they were "attending," "maybe attending," or "not attending."

He watched the early returns as if it were election night. Fifteen said they'd be there. Another sixty gave him a solid maybe, some said no, while others failed to respond. He crunched the numbers and decided he could reasonably expect twenty friends to show.

Niedzviecki was excited about the get-together. He showered and shaved, splashed on a little cologne, and dressed nicely, ready to put his best foot forward and meet his Facebook public. It felt like a first date. He walked into the neighborhood bar, found a seat, and waited.

Then he waited some more.

After some time, he greeted his first attendee—a nice lady who was the friend of a friend. They made a little awkward small talk, and she finally left. Niedzviecki sat by himself until midnight, nursing his drink and wondering where the seven hundred were.

"Seven hundred friends," he wrote, "and I was drinking alone."[1]

Hal Niedzviecki's experience summarizes something many of us are beginning to feel. We've invented so many new ways to connect with others, yet we feel more disconnected than ever. Paradoxically, our world is filled with bustling crowds of isolated people.

Today's average American may meet as many people in one year as his great-grandfather met in a lifetime. So why is he lonelier than his great-grandfather ever was? We all recognize that there's *alone* and then there's *lonely*, and they're not the same thing. Hardly anyone today is alone. We move among crowds almost continually. But being near people isn't the same as connecting with them.

This sense of disconnection is generating a new brand of fear: autophobia. No, it's not a fear of cars. An autophobe is someone who is afraid of loneliness. The term comes from two Greek words meaning "self" and "fear." This fear of disconnection is an abnormal and persistent fear of being alone. Sufferers of this fear experience abnormal anxiety even though they may realize that being alone does not threaten their well-being.

The autophobe may not be physically alone, but he or she has the persistent feeling of being ignored, unloved, or disconnected. Those who have endured the trauma of being deserted—by a parent or a spouse, for example—are candidates for autophobia. Since love is our greatest need, rejection by a loved one is enormously devastating.

Sometimes the least likely people are the loneliest—or among those most frightened by the prospect of loneliness. You wouldn't expect famous or wealthy people to be lonely. They have the advantages of wealth, friends, contacts, engagements, appointments, and adulation. Yet appearances often hide unexpected fears:

- Oscar-winning actress Anne Hathaway confessed, "Loneliness is my least favourite thing about life. The thing that I'm most worried about is just being alone without anybody to care for or someone who will care for me."[2]
- Joss Whedon, director of *The Avengers*, said, "Loneliness is about the scariest thing out there."[3]
- Comedic actress Lily Tomlin said, "We're all in this alone."[4]
- Speaking of former president Richard M. Nixon, Henry Kissinger wrote, "The essence of this man is loneliness."[5]
- Albert Einstein wrote, "It is strange to be known so universally and yet to be so lonely."[6]

- Author Ernest Hemingway wrote, "I live in a vacuum that is as lonely as a radio tube when the batteries are dead and there is no current to plug into."[7]
- Marilyn Monroe said, "Sometimes I think the only people who stay with me and really listen are people I hire, people I pay."[8]

Disconnectedness has spread like a disease in our world, where most people live without the support of a community, where the Internet replaces face-to-face conversation, where the average job lasts only two years, where people often move from state to state and from marriage to marriage. In this age of technology, the possibilities of being alone have increased exponentially. Actor Emilio Estevez put it this way: "We have all these devices that keep us connected, and yet we're more disconnected than ever before. Why is that?"[9]

In 1998, researchers from Carnegie Mellon University studied the effects of addiction to the Internet, a new phenomenon then. They found that the more time people spent online, the more depressed and lonely they became. Robert Kraut, the lead author of the study, said that people saw the Internet as a social medium, yet they derived from it only negative symptoms such as depression and loneliness.[10]

Similar studies abounded, but few people listened. A 2008 survey found that adults were spending 30 percent of their leisure time online. By 2009, the average jumped to twelve hours a week—double the average in 2005.[11] Today most Americans spend between eight and nine hours per day staring at some kind of glowing screen, be it a TV, a computer, or a phone. Are we screening out healthier relationships?

I am not labeling electronic connections as evil. There are

occasions when texts and social media provide beneficial links between people who need to share a real-time prayer request or find quick help for a flat tire. Now, however, these forms of quick communication have become the primary basis for our social interactions. We need less Facebook and more "face time"—and I'm not talking about the iPhone app by that name; I mean old-school, face-to-face, eyeball-to-eyeball connection. We need closeness, and there's no app for that.

Many younger people will identify with another brand-new phobia: nomophobia—the fear of being phoneless. Can you imagine? For thousands of years before Alexander Graham Bell, no one even imagined that such a thing as a phone could exist. And now the thought of being without one every minute of the day can strike terror in people's hearts. We must have access to instant communication with all our connections. One woman texted several instant messages to her husband but received no reply. Impatient for a response, she texted, "What's wrong? Has the cat got your thumb?"

SecurEnvoy, a digital password specialist, found that 66 percent of those surveyed in the United Kingdom genuinely fear the possibility of finding themselves with no cell phone.[12]

Watch the advertising, and you'll see that new communication gadgets are marketed toward the human craving for connection. It's ironic, because the device-centric life further isolates us. Tech is not touch. The glow of the colorful screen won't replace the glow of a colorful friendship.

Lisa, a seventeen-year-old high school junior, writes, "I come home from school and go online, and I'm feeling okay, and I talk for two hours on the Web. But then I still have no friends. I'll never know the people I spoke to."[13]

Hannah, sixteen, has known "Ian" for five years without ever meeting him in person. Yet, in her judgment, he is the one who knows her best.[14] But neither Hannah nor Ian really knows the other, because when we're online, we need not be real; we can be carefully created symbols of ourselves. We can hide our shortcomings and defects, real or imagined, behind the facade of a carefully crafted fantasy self. The *New Yorker* magazine ran a cartoon in 1993, the dawn of the Internet age, that was an instant sensation. A dog sits in a desk chair with a paw on the computer keyboard. He turns and says to another dog, "On the Internet, nobody knows you're a dog."[15]

Internet companions may not know each other at all. Bytes and pixels can't capture the heart and soul of a human being. Authentic connection requires much more than quick words and emoticons. It must have the intricate vocabulary of body language: facial expressions, verbal nuances, and tones of voice. It's when we sit together and look into one another's eyes that we truly connect. A phone call narrows the "bandwidth" of connection; a text or post narrows it still more. Digital communication is twenty-five thousand miles wide and a half-inch deep. In digital connections, we lose out on the opportunity to know and be known. Technology promises the comfort of connection, but it lowers the threshold of intimacy.

In short, electronic communication has moved us away from authentic community. We seem to have little idea how dangerous this can be to our emotional and spiritual health.

## THE DANGERS OF ISOLATION

Most of us don't realize just how insidious true isolation can be. Going without food or water will kill the body, but the lack of relationship will kill the mind and spirit.

An article in *Psychology Today* called isolation "a potent killer." It continued, "There is no more destructive influence on physical and mental health than the isolation of you from me and of us from them. [Isolation] has been shown to be a central agent in the etiology of depression, paranoia, schizophrenia, rape, suicide, mass murder, and a wide variety of disease states."[16]

There is something in us that doesn't like too much solitude. Erle Stanley Gardner, the creator of Perry Mason, also wrote a few early sci-fi and Western novels. In one of his Westerns, a crusty old gold prospector says,

There are lots of people you could put down in the middle of the desert, go away and leave 'em for a week, and come back and find 'em completely crazy. I've seen it happen.

A man sprained his ankle and couldn't travel. The party he was with had to go right on, but they left him with lots of food. All he had to do was keep quiet for three or four days. He showed up in civilization just about half-crazy. His ankle was all inflamed. He said he'd rather have lost the whole leg than to have stayed in that desert another ten minutes. People can't bear it, because out there they are alone with their Maker.[17]

Is it such a fearful thing to be alone with one's Maker? Could that be one of the reasons many people can't stand utter quiet—because they can't shut out the quiet voice of God, calling them to a new life?

That's a part of it, but there's certainly more. Isolation and disconnection hurt us so severely because we were created with a built-in desire for social interaction. To put it simply, we need each other. The song from *Funny Girl* claims, "People who need people are the luckiest people in the world." But I submit to you that they're the *only* people in the world. None of us can live sanely without interaction with other people.

In two related parables, Jesus tells of a man finding a lost sheep and a woman finding a lost coin. After recovering their losses, both invite friends to rejoice with them (Luke 15:4-10). Though human connection is not the primary point of the parables, these stories show an ingrained aspect of human nature. We have a powerful need to share our experiences with others—to rejoice in our good times and find comfort in the bad ones. After watching a movie, reading a book, seeing a ball game, or attending a concert, we want someone with whom we can share our thoughts about it. After getting a new hairdo, a wife craves her husband's admiring comments. After taking a vacation, we want someone to look at our photos and hear about our adventures. We are made that way. We cannot be happy or healthy without relationships.

Modern technology, in seeking to bring us together, has succeeded only in driving us apart. If we are to remain spiritually and emotionally healthy, we cannot succumb to the temptation of depending on electronic interaction as the basis for our social connections.

## ANCIENT EXAMPLES OF DISCONNECTION

Though isolation is more pervasive in today's world of electronic communication, it isn't anything new. We see many examples of disconnection and loneliness among our biblical heroes:

- Noah was spiritually lonely. He preached to a wicked generation for 120 years without a single convert. All connections but his immediate family were wiped out in a world-destroying flood (Genesis 6–7).

- Hagar, Sarah's handmaid, was consigned to the desert through no fault of her own. She was so alone she despaired for her life (Genesis 16).
- Abraham waited many years for a son, only to make a lonely walk to Mount Moriah believing he would have to sacrifice the boy to the Lord (Genesis 22).
- Joseph's brothers sold him into Egyptian slavery, where he spent seventeen lonely years as a prisoner and a slave (Genesis 37, 39).
- For forty years Moses was banished to the rustic outback of Midian, far from the luxury of his former royal home (Exodus 2–3).
- David, perhaps more than any other person in the Old Testament, experienced disconnection—especially when King Saul, jealous of David's growing popularity, stalked him like an animal with intent to kill. David sometimes expressed his loneliness in his psalms:

Turn Yourself to me, and have mercy on me,
For I am desolate and afflicted.
PSALM 25:16

Look on my right hand and see,
For there is no one who acknowledges me;
Refuge has failed me;
No one cares for my soul.
PSALM 142:4

These are just a few of the Bible characters who experienced isolation and disconnection. But the man whose life I have chosen to explore on this topic may surprise you—the apostle Paul.

Your first thought may be, *How could this man possibly be a model for dealing with isolation?* The Bible makes it abundantly clear that this energetic, charge-ahead, type-A, goal-oriented man was a thoroughgoing people person. For example, he wrote his letter to the Roman church before he had ever been there. Yet in that letter he greets no fewer than twenty-six people by name and several others indirectly. He also mentions eight others who are with him as he writes his letter. Many people today would be hard pressed to greet personally or reference as friends nearly three dozen people (Facebook friends aside).

But near the end of Paul's life, this man who knew so many people by name was utterly alone, confined to the infamous Mamertine Prison in the bowels of Rome. From that depressing location, Paul wrote to Timothy the final letter of his apostolic ministry—the letter we know as 2 Timothy. In 2 Timothy 4:9-21, we find Paul mentioning another seventeen people (in addition to two others in chapter 1). These were friends and associates he remembered in what he knew were his final days on earth.

How does a person whose life and ministry have been so people oriented handle the isolation of death row? Not only was Paul alone physically, he was likely alone spiritually and emotionally as well, vulnerable to the crushing reality of isolation. If anyone would be prey to loneliness, it would be a gregarious people person like Paul. And if anyone had a spiritual answer for it, it would be this man.

## THE DISCONNECTION OF ISOLATION

What effect can forced aloneness have on an outgoing, highly connected person like Paul? News correspondent Terry Anderson knows firsthand. He was an American living in Beirut, Lebanon, in 1985. On March 16, he was kidnapped by three men; he was held as a hostage, along with several other Americans, for nearly six years. For much of that time, he was kept in isolation. An article for the *New Yorker* describes the effects of Anderson's isolation:

> He missed people terribly, especially his fiancée and his family. He was despondent and depressed. Then, with time, he began to feel something more. He felt himself disintegrating. It was as if his brain were grinding down. A month into his confinement, he recalled in his memoir, "The mind is blank. . . . I always thought I was smart. Where are all the things I learned, the books I read, the poems I memorized? There's nothing there, just a formless gray-black misery. My mind's gone dead. God, help me." . . .
>
> One day, three years into his ordeal, [Anderson] snapped. He walked over to a wall and began beating his forehead against it, dozens of times. His head was smashed and bleeding before the guards were able to stop him.[18]

Reflecting later on the horrors of his isolation, Anderson said, "I would rather have had the worst companion than no companion at all."

Paul's time in prison could have produced effects similar to those Terry Anderson experienced. We don't know the details, but we have a pretty good picture of how Paul responded to isolation. Facing trial before Nero, he knew his days were winding down. He writes to Timothy, "I am already being poured out as a drink offering, and the time of my departure is at hand" (2 Timothy 4:6).

In this verse we can see Paul's picture of death. The Greek word for "departure" is *analysis*, from which we get our English word. It literally means to "unloose" or "untie" or "separate." When we analyze something, we "untie" it and separate it into its various parts. In Paul's time, the word often referred to loosing a ship from its mooring or breaking up (untying) an army's camp in preparation for moving.

So Paul sees his departure as loosing (untying and separating) himself from this world and beginning his journey to join the Lord Jesus Christ. He uses the same word in Philippians 1:23: "I am hard-pressed between the two, having a desire to *depart* and be with Christ, which is far better" (emphasis added). As a lover of people, Paul deeply felt his strong ties to his friends, yet he also felt the knot loosening. Of course, he wasn't the one loosening the knot; it was Rome's doing. Nevertheless, soon he would sail over the horizon to his eternal destination.

No matter how mature Paul was in his spiritual understanding, he was still disconnected and alone, facing his final departure and enduring miserable surroundings. John Phillips imagines his misery:

Paul . . . was in the Mamertine Prison. . . . He was
stripped of his outer garments and left naked, except
for his tunic. . . . Paul was then taken over to a trapdoor
in the floor. The door was lifted, ropes were passed

under his armpits, and he was lowered into the terrible Tullianum dungeon. Paul's feet touched the floor, the ropes were drawn up, and the trapdoor was slammed into place. He was now in the dark.

In Paul's day, the name of that dungeon was spoken in whispers. It was a black pit, a hole in the ground. It was damp and chilly. The bed was a clump of stale, damp straw, and the floor was heaped with filth. There was a spring, at least, but the air was foul. Food was lowered to prisoners from time to time—rough fare to keep body and soul together—and perhaps a kidskin of thin, sour wine. Prisoners had been known to be eaten by rats in that dreadful hole.[19]

Fortunately, most of us will never experience this kind of forced isolation. But we don't have to be in a cold, wet place to feel all alone. There are lonely office cubicles, church pews loaded with friendless individuals, and sky-high condominiums dense with individuals residing in close proximity without knowing one another's names.

Divorce is a grinding factory for loneliness. Not only do victims of divorce lose a mate, they lose friends as well. Some friends choose a side; others back away from both parties. One woman told me that she had never felt so alone as in the days that followed the end of her marriage.

Military families know about isolation; it occurs on both sides of a military marriage. When one spouse is deployed, the other can suddenly feel isolated, especially if left in a new community or on a military base where social relationships haven't been established. The deployed spouse can also experience waves of isolation, especially if stationed halfway around the world.

The church I pastor is in San Diego, California—home to a giant US Navy base. Our members see this pain of disconnection on a routine basis. When the ships leave harbor for months-long deployments, a kind of collective depression settles over our congregation. And when the ships come home, Christmas comes even if the calendar says July. I love the moments when I see those joyful reunions.

Today a growing number of people live alone. In 1950, fewer than 10 percent of American households were home to just one person.[20] By 2010 that figure escalated to almost 28 percent.[21]

I believe we can explain something of our growing disconnection by comparing it to a primary principle of physics. The second law of thermodynamics is known as the law of entropy. To state it simply, life, energy, and matter move toward disorder and disorganization. Things break down; centers don't hold. Entropy happens in all systems. Social systems exhibit the same tendency, but with one difference: it is preventable. And if our society is to survive, we must resist relational entropy. When we come together, we enrich each other simply by virtue of our different gifts and personalities. Together, we're greater than the sum of our parts.

People in relationships have a better chance of resisting entropy—thus keeping culture ordered and organized—than those who are isolated. Broken marriages send shock waves through society and hurt us all by adding to the tendency toward disintegration. Schismatic churches hurt God's Kingdom, as well as their communities, by breaking relational bonds and destroying unity. Revolving-door workplaces are bad for our society because they break down permanence and foster chaos. Long-lasting relationships are the unifying force that creates accountable, healthy social stability.

## THE DISCONNECTION OF INFIDELITY

The last verses of 2 Timothy 4 are a litany of desertion and departure. Of the seventeen friends Paul names, six are fellow workers who are in other places for legitimate reasons: Crescens is in Galatia, Titus is in Dalmatia, Tychicus is in Ephesus, Carpus is in Troas, Erastus is in Corinth, and Trophimus is in Miletus.

But Paul mentions one who was a deserter: "Demas has forsaken me, having loved this present world, and has departed for Thessalonica" (2 Timothy 4:10). Two others, Phygellus and Hermogenes, had deserted Paul earlier (2 Timothy 1:15).

Demas is mentioned two other times in the New Testament—both in the context of ministry, and both in letters written during Paul's first Roman imprisonment (Colossians 4:14; Philemon 24). At that time, Demas was faithful to Paul. But here, toward the end of Paul's life, Demas has walked away. Apparently he was in Rome during Paul's second imprisonment there, but for some reason forsook him and left for Thessalonica.

Demas's departure was obviously not a positive exit; he "loved this present world" more than he loved Paul. It appears that he demonstrated infidelity—he was disloyal and unfaithful toward both Paul and his fellow Christians. Some scholars speculate that the Romans had turned up the heat on the Christian community, resulting in Paul's imprisonment, and Demas didn't want to end up in confinement like his friend. Kent Hughes suggests,

> Perhaps Demas never truly counted the cost. It may be he did not understand that when we come to Christ, we will face troubles because we will always collide with the world. . . . There is not a single soul that is not swayed by the lure of comfort. And the older we get, the more

alluring the siren songs are. This is the short-sighted temptation to love the present world instead of Christ's appearing.[22]

For whatever reason, Demas turned his back on Paul and left Rome. But he wasn't the only one to demonstrate this kind of infidelity. When Paul first stood before Caesar, he stood alone (2 Timothy 4:16). No one but faithful Luke stayed behind to keep him company and endure the long days of waiting while the Roman bureaucratic processes took their ponderous course (2 Timothy 4:11, 16).

Imagine what a devastating feeling it must have been for Paul to be left in Rome nearly alone at such a time of great need. We cannot doubt that he must have remembered that Christ Himself endured similar abandonment. On the night Jesus was arrested, all the disciples "forsook Him and fled" (Mark 14:50). Paul's friends left him in the hands of the Romans just as Jesus' disciples had left Him in the hands of the Jewish mob.

Nothing, it is said, hurts as much as betrayal, in whatever form. We most often use the term *infidelity* in the context of marriage, but no matter the situation, abandonment, disloyalty, and betrayal leave us with a sick feeling in the pits of our stomachs. Even if there isn't a betrayal, desertion hurts, especially when we're facing danger or trauma or when others leave us to shoulder a load alone.

## THE DISCONNECTION OF INTERFERENCE

Demas's desertion hurt Paul—but Alexander's interference hurt him even more. Paul writes, "Alexander the coppersmith did me much harm. May the Lord repay him according to his works. You

also must beware of him, for he has greatly resisted our words"
(2 Timothy 4:14-15).

In Paul's final letter from prison, he also pinpointed
Alexander as someone who caused disunity. We know little about
Alexander—not even whether he is the same Alexander mentioned in 1 Timothy 1:20 and Acts 19:33. The phrase *did me much
harm* literally means "informed many evil things against me."
Some speculate that Alexander was a Judas figure who betrayed
Paul to Roman authorities, resulting in his imprisonment. That
makes sense in light of Paul's warning to Timothy: "You also must
beware of him."

Regardless of the details, Alexander was a man who resisted
Paul's ministry—a man who interfered. Such people are not
strangers to leaders. There are always some who, for their own
reasons, will resist us and attempt to disrupt what we are trying
to accomplish.

The greater our commitment to Christ, the more we will be
disconnected from the values of the crowd. Disconnection from
the culture's pervasive values often breeds resentment, and resentment breeds opposition. Those who lack our commitment will
often desert us or disappoint us as they retreat into society's less
demanding values, finding comfort in numbers. Sometimes they
will be people we have poured our lives into, and we will be devastated. That's what happened to Paul. But it is part of the calling to
discipleship. We cannot worry about what others do; we can only
stay focused on not becoming deserters or interferers ourselves.

The great preacher and missions leader A. B. Simpson offers
this reflection on the perils of leadership: "Often the crowd does
not recognize a leader until he is gone, and then they build a
monument for him with the same stones they threw at him
in life."[23]

## WHAT WE NEED IN TIMES OF DISCONNECTION

What can help us when we are overcome with a fear of being disconnected and alone? How can we help others who experience isolation? I have discovered at least four needs we experience when the fear of disconnection begins to set in, and based on Paul's experience in prison, we have clues and suggestions as to how these needs can be met.

### We Need Companionship

Remember Paul's location: sitting, probably alone, in the dank Mamertine Prison in Rome, the last stop on the road to death for the empire's most-feared prisoners.

Where was the church of Rome when Paul needed it? Its members were still in the city, but they were probably lying low to avoid suffering Paul's fate. We don't know the visitation policies at the Mamertine, but I suspect they were limited. So Paul's final words to Timothy come as no surprise: "Be diligent to come to me quickly. . . . Get Mark and bring him with you. . . . Do your utmost to come before winter" (2 Timothy 4:9, 11, 21).

If the apostle Paul—perhaps the strongest and most mature Christian in history—longed and pleaded for companionship in his final days, how much more should we acknowledge our own need for companions? And I mean friends in the flesh, not just friends in pixels and digital sound bites. I mean friends who can wipe our tears and hug our necks and squeeze our hands as they pray earnestly with us.

John Stott reminds us that friendship is a gift from God:

One sometimes meets super-spiritual people who claim that they never feel lonely and have no need of human friends, for the companionship of Christ satisfies all their needs. But human friendship is the loving provision of God for mankind. It was God himself who said in the beginning: "It is not good that the man should be alone" (Gn. 2:18). Wonderful as are both the presence of the Lord Jesus every day and the prospect of his coming on the last day, they are not intended to be a substitute for human friendships.[24]

Perhaps the most poignant longing Paul expresses is to see John Mark, for it shows us a healed disconnection. Years earlier, John Mark abandoned Paul and Barnabas on their second missionary journey (Acts 15:36-41), and Paul counted it against him then. But over time they have reconciled to the point that, in Paul's time of need, it is John Mark for whom Paul calls— someone "useful to [him] for ministry" (2 Timothy 4:11).

One of the greatest omissions in the life of the average American Christian is the failure to cultivate close companions in the faith. In nations where Christianity is outlawed, restricted, or persecuted, Christians survive by means of hidden, underground relationships with other believers. They must remain connected to one another in order to remain strong and courageous to Christ in spite of opposition: "Though one may be overpowered by another, two can withstand him. And a threefold cord is not quickly broken" (Ecclesiastes 4:12).

Simply attending Sunday morning worship is not enough to create those connections. Many churches have implemented small-group programs to foster the kinds of relationships needed to "stir up love and good works" (Hebrews 10:24). Every Christian needs to have close companions in the faith, whether through small groups or other means. Finding ourselves alone in the middle of a crisis is not the time to realize we have no one to send for.

Small groups are not just a sociological fad or a clever gimmick to pump up church attendance. Small groups are a ministry format with a solid biblical foundation. The first and foremost small group in human history is the family, which tells us that God intends for people to be intimately connected with one another. Such connections are the first line of defense against the fear of disconnection.

### We Need Compassion

Among Paul's physical needs was a good, sturdy blanket to stave off the chill of the underground cells. Alas, socks and gloves as we know them had yet to be invented. But at least he could have used a nice lamp and oil to keep it burning, along with writing supplies, food, water, and the Scriptures. More than anything, of course, he simply desired human company.

My point is this: one reason we fear disconnection is that when our deepest needs rise to the surface, we worry we'll have no one to meet those needs. There's no doubt Paul's few remaining companions became even more precious to him during his imprisonment; he knew he could call on them to meet those needs. When we need something desperately, we shouldn't hesitate to ask our loyal friends for it. This is what Paul did when he wrote to Timothy: "Bring the cloak that I left with Carpus at Troas when you come" (2 Timothy 4:13).

In those days, a cloak was an outer garment—the ancient version of the modern overcoat. It was actually more like the Latin American poncho—a thick blanket with a hole for the head to fit through. The cloak had no buttons, and it was "one size fits all." It was likely the only coat Paul owned, and winter was coming.

We can imagine his sense of urgency. Next-day shipping didn't exist, and the process of retrieving the cloak would take weeks. Paul's letter to Timothy would have traveled by sea from Rome to Ephesus. On receipt of it, Timothy would have traveled up the coast of Asia Minor by sea or by foot to Troas to retrieve the cloak, and then he probably would have traveled by sea from Troas to Rome.

Fifteen centuries after Paul's experience in Rome, William Tyndale, the great English Bible translator, made a request similar to Paul's when he was imprisoned for his Bible translation work in Belgium. In 1535 Tyndale wrote a letter to the governor of the castle where he was imprisoned:

> I entreat your Lordship . . . that if I must remain here for the winter, you would beg the commissary to be so kind as to send me, from the things of mine which he has, a warmer cap. . . . I feel the cold painfully in my head. . . . Also a warmer cloke, for the one I have is very thin. . . . He has a woollen shirt of mine, if he will send it.[25]

We can see the importance of having strong connections to dedicated Christians who would go to great lengths to meet our desperate needs. It is also important that we have our antennae out to perceive the needs of our fellow Christians and friends. Empathy stokes the fires of love and compassion.

In his book *Life Together*, Dietrich Bonhoeffer writes that one of the most important services Christians can perform for each other is active helpfulness:

> This means, initially, simple assistance in trifling, external matters. . . . We must be ready to allow ourselves

to be interrupted by God. God will be constantly
canceling our plans by sending us people with claims
and petitions.[26]

Disconnected and isolated people are often in desperate need
of compassion. We may figure their separation is their own fault
and they're "getting what they deserve." But thankfully, God
isn't gracious merely to the deserving—and we'd best be diligent to pass on to others the grace we receive from God. Neither
should we be grudging in compassion and ignore hurting people
because we're preoccupied with "more important" tasks, as was
the priest who ignored the man who had fallen among thieves
(Luke 10). For all we know, the priest may have been praying,
reading Scripture, or going to an important ecclesiastical conference. But that was no excuse. Compassion should overflow from
us as it did from Christ, who looked out upon crowds of strangers, saw sheep without a shepherd, and loved every face He saw.

## We Need Courage

If you have been there, you know that isolation and loneliness
can be scary places. The antidote to fear is courage. But do you
know what builds courage for the Christian? It's not willpower or
a pep rally or the power of positive thinking. The true opposite
of fear is faith. Either we look at the future in fear of what might
happen, or we look at the future with faith directed toward our
sovereign Father-God, who holds all things in His hands. We
have no other options. And the best way to build faith is through
the Word of God.

Paul, facing imminent death in Rome's most dreaded prison,
wanted something even more than the comfort of a cloak.
He writes to Timothy: "Bring . . . the books, especially the

parchments" (2 Timothy 4:13). We are given no clue as to what books and parchments Paul desired. We do know this much: the "books" (Greek *biblos*, from which comes "Bible") were scrolls, probably made of papyrus reeds. The "parchments" would have been scrolls made of thin, specially treated leather.

Even though we don't know the content of these particular scrolls, I seriously doubt that he was asking for recreational reading—Greek philosophers or dramas. It's likely that Paul, a highly trained scholar, owned parchments that contained some or all of the Old Testament writings. The books may have been early Christian writings, such as *The Sayings of Jesus*, that had begun to circulate in his day. Or they could have been blank scrolls to be used for his own writing. I believe Paul wanted to spend his remaining days on earth building his faith—and thus his courage.

I admit that I am reading into Paul's experience from my own here. When I feel my own faith waning, nothing rebuilds it like the Word of God. My heart is always encouraged when I meditate on the promises of God. These promises show God to be faithful even when others forsake or oppose us:

When my father and my mother forsake me,
Then the LORD will take care of me.
PSALM 27:10

He Himself has said, "I will never leave you nor forsake you." So we may boldly say:

"The LORD is my helper;
I will not fear.
What can man do to me?"
HEBREWS 13:5-6

When you find yourself in need of courage, remember that it is your faith, not your spine, that needs strengthening! And your faith will be strengthened when you read the Bible, the only book with proven credibility to give you the courage to heal your disconnections and face your future with hope and confidence.

### We Need Christ

Finally, we learn from Paul a powerful truth about being a Christian: we are never alone. God has promised never to leave us nor forsake us (Hebrews 13:5), and faith is the act of hanging on to that truth even when we don't feel His presence. It's not what we feel that counts; it's what we know. Feelings deceive, but our knowledge of truth leads us to know that though all others may fail us, leaving us abandoned and disconnected, God never will. As His children, we are always connected to Him, even when we don't feel it. Paul knew this, and it was the source of his confidence:

> At my first defense *no one stood with me*, but all forsook me. May it not be charged against them. But *the Lord stood with me and strengthened me*. . . . And the Lord will deliver me from every evil work and preserve me for His heavenly kingdom. To Him be glory forever and ever. Amen!
>
> 2 TIMOTHY 4:16-18, EMPHASIS ADDED

As a Roman citizen, Paul had premium rights but not immunity from prosecution. He did have the right to appeal his arrest to Caesar, which he had done several years earlier. This appeal led to his first house arrest in Rome. After that, he was released. A year or two later, he was rearrested, bringing him to the time of this letter to Timothy. This evangelist of Christ was not likely to find favor with the emperor Nero, a notoriously anti-Christian ruler.

Apparently Paul was brought before some authority to be charged (perhaps Nero himself). This was the incident he referred to as "my first defense." No person stood with him, he said—except God, who provided strength.

Paul knew that God would not forsake him, and that gave him the courage he needed. Everyone we know may turn away, but Christ will be there for us. It's a sacred promise. Jesus tells His disciples, "I am with you always, even to the end of the age" (Matthew 28:20). So when Paul speaks of standing alone, he only means he is without human support. Christ is with us; we can depend on it. In a very real sense, there is no "alone." There is no place we can ever be that is outside the presence of our Lord.

God's tenacious connection with us does not mean we have no need for human connections. The newly created Adam had an intimate relationship with God, yet God says, "It is not good that man should be alone" (Genesis 2:18). And He created Eve. God knows that we need people. Disconnection from others is not good, but when it happens, God uses it to help us make the transition from enjoying the *physical* presence of others to experiencing the *spiritual* presence of God. This reveals an essential difference between our earthly parents and our heavenly One: mothers and fathers know they must someday let go; they can't be with us forever. Not so with God. Once we come to know Him, we need never be separated.

The ideal maturing process involves making this transference of connections. It begins when we're disconnected from the security of the womb. After a few years, we learn to leave the security of our parents for a few hours at a time in preschool, in day care, or with a babysitter. Then for a half day in kindergarten; then for a whole day in elementary through high school. On reaching adolescence, we begin to disconnect socially as we discover our own separate identities as individuals. Going off to college is a huge disconnection, followed by one of the most significant of all: marriage. Let me make it clear that these disconnections, when managed well, are good. They are steps in a positive process toward maturity.

If the process goes according to God's design—if our parents have introduced us to our heavenly Father through Christ—our connection with God supports us through our increasing independence of our family of origin. We don't leave our familial connection behind, of course. But we ultimately have to leave our fathers and mothers and establish an adult relationship with the One who is our ultimate source of security.

I cannot close this chapter without addressing the final disconnection that every human must prepare for: "It is appointed for men to die once" (Hebrews 9:27). Death—whether our own or that of a loved one—is the final disconnection. But, as I will discuss in chapter 9 of this book, we need not fear that event. For the Christian, being disconnected from loved ones in this life is only temporary; we will be reconnected with them in eternity. And we can easily take our own death in stride when we see it as Paul did: "To be absent from the body [is] to be present with the Lord" (2 Corinthians 5:8). We will be eternally connected to the One who has been with us all along.

But what about those who die apart from Christ—those who have rejected the grace of God? Sadly, the Bible says they will remain disconnected from God for all eternity. Just as Adam and Eve, by their sin, were disconnected from God in the Garden of Eden, all their descendants will remain disconnected if they do not embrace Christ's sacrifice for their sin. That disconnection is the only one that gives real cause for fear: "It is a fearful thing to fall into the hands of the living God" (Hebrews 10:31).

Isolation is, in fact, a hellish characteristic. To be cast into "outer darkness" (Matthew 22:13) is to be forever on the outside, permanently isolated from God and possibly from all others. In C. S. Lewis's *The Great Divorce*, souls in hell continue throughout eternity to move farther and farther away from each other, eventually losing all contact with any other being.

When Jesus Christ cried out from the cross, "My God, My God, why have You forsaken Me?" (Matthew 27:46), He expressed the anguished separation from God that awaits all those who die in their sins. Jesus took upon Himself the sins of the whole world and submitted Himself to God's judgment on sin. Even though He died voluntarily, this cry reflected the agony of His separation. His anguished response stands as a stark warning to all who mistakenly believe that being separated from God is not something to fear.

Jesus' separation from His Father was only temporary, of course. After He experienced death on our behalf—death that is the natural consequence of our sin—God raised Him from the dead. As a result, He could announce to the world that death was defeated—that all who place their faith in Christ need not fear being separated from God again.

God doesn't want us to be alone. He has done everything possible to ensure that we can live connected lives in harmonious human relationships. But those relationships are merely a foreshadowing of our eternal relationship with God Himself. God has provided a twofold provision for those who fear loneliness either in this life or in eternity. First, if you find yourself isolated or disconnected from others, you can know you are never alone, simply because Christ has promised always to be with you. Second, you have the security of knowing that when you die, you will be immediately united with Christ in heaven.

The question, then, is this: Are you confident that Christ is always with you and that you will always be with Christ? Placing your faith in Him is the only way to be sure.

# CHAPTER 6

# DISAPPROVAL:
## *The Fear of Rejection*

*In God I have put my trust; I will not be afraid.*
*What can man do to me?*
PSALM 56:11

In her time, she was a superstar of the cinema; they didn't come any more glamorous than Marlene Dietrich. She began her career performing on the stages of Berlin and in the silent films of the 1920s. Her success (and the rise of the Nazi Party in Germany) eventually brought her to Hollywood, where she became a US citizen in 1937. At the height of her career, she commanded $200,000 per film (nearly $2 million in 2013 dollars—small by today's Hollywood standards, but huge in her day). In 1999, some sixty years after her peak of fame, the American Film Institute named her the ninth-greatest female star of all time. But her true story is as heartbreaking as any film in which she ever performed.

In spite of her success and acclaim, Dietrich was a conflicted soul. She lived for the approval and applause of her adoring public. When she invited guests to her home, she often played for them the recorded ovations of the audiences present at her live performances. No music, no words—just the sounds of cheers and applause. Guests—many of them equally famous—were forced to sit and listen as she identified the cities where the applause was recorded.

During her one marriage, she carried on a string of affairs with leading figures in Hollywood and Washington. Going from man to man, she never found the fulfillment and approval she constantly sought. She even passed on to her husband (who had affairs of his own) the love letters from her paramours to show him how much they adored her.

Dietrich's life in the spotlight ended in Sydney, Australia, in 1975 when she fell off a stage and broke her thigh. Then, addicted to alcohol and painkillers, she lived her final eleven years in loneliness and seclusion, bedridden in a Paris apartment, refusing to see anyone except a select few.

Marlene Dietrich's search for approval was amplified by her public visibility, but there was nothing unique about it. Humans are relational beings, and each of us has a built-in longing for approval. It originates deep in the human psyche, where we have embedded the knowledge that we are not what we were created to be. We sense the truth of Romans 3:23, that "all have sinned and [fallen] short of the glory of God." Believing we have lost God's stamp of approval, we search elsewhere for affirmation, which leads to dramatic missteps (like those of Marlene Dietrich).

This longing for approval is so strong that we spend our lives chasing it, often sacrificing our values and priorities in an attempt to secure it. As teens, we encounter peer pressure. As young adults, many of us deal with people pleasing. We've even invented a specialized form of approval seeking called codependency. But it's all roughly the same thing. In every age group, there are people who live in self-imposed slavery to others and their opinions.

We can't write this off as a problem for shy individuals and outsiders either. Nearly everyone is controlled by other people in some way or another. Competitive people, angry people, even superstar athletes live off the high of popular adulation. It comes in all shapes and colors.[1]

The Bible has a name for this need for approval: the fear of man. In the Bible, the word *fear* means more than fright; it's any kind of awe and reverence that causes us to subject ourselves to something or someone else. Biblical counselor Ed Welch explains:

> "Fear" in the biblical sense . . . includes being afraid of someone, but it extends to holding someone in awe, being controlled or mastered by people, worshiping other people, putting your trust in people, or needing people.
>
>   However you put it, . . . the fear of man can be summarized this way: We replace God with people. Instead of a biblically guided fear of the Lord, we fear others.[2]

We are offered the fear of God—a healthy fear—as the key to life; we substitute the fear of man, and things fall apart.

Once we begin chasing approval, we never stop running. It's servitude to a thousand masters, as Andrée Seu points out: "You have a thousand masters instead of one to please. You think fear of God is bad? It's nothing compared to the alternative. Fear of man is a cruel tyranny. It's exhausting, it's complicated, and you're not nimble enough to pull it off."[3]

King Solomon sums it up well in this proverb: "The fear of

man brings a snare, but whoever trusts in the LORD shall be safe" (Proverbs 29:25).

Therein lies the danger and deceitfulness of the fear of disapproval, or the fear of man: it becomes a snare. A snare is a trap set to capture an animal. In this case it is a metaphor for trapping human beings in some moral or spiritual compromise. An animal snare is camouflaged and baited with morsels of food to entice a creature. A moral snare works in the same way. It is not plainly obvious at first, but it is baited with something we humans long for, which is what makes it so terribly effective.

If the bait is an overpowering desire for approval, then we are drawn into the trap by doing whatever it takes to gain approval. And that often means sacrificing our values or standards or priorities, or giving up moral or spiritual ground.

Think of a teenager who is so afraid of disapproval that she gives up her moral convictions to gain acceptance by her school's "in crowd." When the cool kids get what they want from her—submission, money, loyalty, or sex—they may turn their backs and walk away. Even if they don't, she may remain in the snare, held fast by her fear of disapproval.

Yes, to fear other people is a great snare, yet it's our great folly that we keep doing it—just as people did in Bible times. Allow me to offer an example or two:

- Because King Saul shifted his fear from God to man, he lost his throne (1 Samuel 15:24).
- The nation of Israel feared men, though men were as grass; God asked Isaiah why (Isaiah 51:12).
- In the first century, some followers of Christ stifled their expressions of faith because they feared the men of the synagogues (John 12:42-43).

In this chapter we will focus primarily on another biblical character who shows us the danger of fearing man's disapproval: the apostle Peter. The story of Peter disowning Jesus three times is one of the best known in the Bible—even in world literature. It ranks right up there with the parting of the Red Sea, Jonah and the big fish, and Daniel in the lions' den.

We often think of Peter as impulsive, faithless, or excitable. But the root of his weakness, it seems, was fear. That's the case for many of us. Peter feared disapproval so greatly that he let its shadow come between him and Jesus, whom he loved, and in the moment of all moments when he might have stood up for the Master, he denied he even knew Him.

By way of summary, here's what happened: at Jesus' last supper with His disciples, He predicted that Peter would deny Him three times before the rooster crowed. Shortly afterward, a band of soldiers and Jewish officials arrested Jesus in the garden of Gethsemane and took Him to the high priest. Peter and some other disciples followed at a distance. He and another disciple were allowed into the high priest's courtyard to await the outcome. While they waited, three different people asked Peter if he was not one of Jesus' disciples, and each time he denied it. After Peter's third denial, a rooster began to crow, just as Jesus had predicted (Matthew 26:31-35; John 18:12-27).

Peter's disloyalty illustrates just how complex the fear of man can be, how entangling the snare can become. Peter probably denied knowing Jesus because he had just witnessed Jesus' arrest. He didn't want the same thing to happen to him, so he lied to save his own skin. His denial was all about the fear of man.

Had Jesus' predictions about His impending death begun to make sense to Peter? Did he finally get it—that the outcome of Jesus' arrest would likely be His death?

If Peter was putting these pieces together in the crisis of that moment, he could see that Jesus' impending fate could easily be his own. He simply hadn't thought through what his commitment to Jesus might mean. He made the same mistake many of us make: we wait until a crisis to decide what our values are. That's like trying to buckle your seat belt when your car is spinning out of control down an icy mountain road. Seat belts, and commitments about spiritual values, need to be buckled up long before the crisis hits. On the night Jesus was arrested, Peter was not buckled in. He was in self-preservation mode and denied any relationship with this Man whom it could be fatally dangerous to know.

Here it is easy to see how fear of man links up to fear of disapproval. The religious leaders who arrested Jesus disapproved of Him—that is perfectly obvious. But never did Jesus fear their disapproval. In fact, when they arrived in Gethsemane and said they were looking for Jesus of Nazareth, Jesus replied, "I am He" (John 18:5). Those are not the words of a fearful man.

Peter's fear was rooted in the Jewish leaders' disapproval of Jesus and His followers. He feared that their disapproval could easily result in his own arrest. So he lied and denied knowing his leader. His fear of man proved to be a treacherous snare. The crow of the rooster brought home to Peter what he had done, and he "went out and wept bitterly" (Matthew 26:75).

## THE REALITY OF THE FEAR OF DISAPPROVAL

Peter's three denials were addressed to three different individuals or groups, each representing a different dynamic in prompting his fear.

When we interact with people, our perceived standing with them—whether it's based on age, social status, or some other standard—influences our relationships and reactions. You can feel in some way superior, inferior, or equal to others, depending on the group you are in. These rankings may be merely imagined, but we react to them as if they are realities.

With some people you might feel no fear or intimidation at all. Perhaps you are older, better educated, or more experienced than they. With others of your approximate age or standing—either an individual or a group—you may or may not feel intimidated. Your perception of equality, or lack of it, can vary. The most intimidating group is generally the last—those you perceive to have greater power, social class, wealth, ideology, or education.

On the night Jesus was arrested, Peter encountered people representing these three different social dynamics, and he was afraid of them all! It just goes to show that people cannot predict infallibly what they will do in a given situation if they have not firmly set their values beforehand. When unprepared people think they're strong enough to resist any intimidation they may face, they're at great risk for abysmal failure. Pride in one's own strength cannot take the place of spiritual preparation. Discipleship is crucial to our ultimate destiny, but its cost is total commitment. Jesus warned against failing to count this cost before committing (Luke 14:25-33).

Let's look at how Peter responded to the three different social dynamics he encountered in the high priest's courtyard.

### Unexpected Fear

The first person Peter encountered was both younger than he and, in that day, somewhat beneath him in social standing. She was a servant girl at the high priest's house assigned the task of keeping the door (John 18:17). Peter was only a blue-collar fisherman, but that was a step above being a servant. As she brought Peter into the courtyard, she asked him, "You are not also one of this Man's disciples, are you?"

Her question was totally unrelated to her job as doorkeeper. She was being confrontational, and it was not customary in that day for a younger woman to ask an accusatory question of an older man. Caught off guard, Peter mumbled the first thing that came to him: "I am not" (verse 17).

Peter, as the de facto leader of Jesus' disciples, had sworn he would never deny Jesus. And now, only a few short hours afterward, he had already done it! And it wasn't in front of the emperor or someone he might understandably fear. He, a burly, type A fisherman, had just let an unexpected question from a young servant girl intimidate him to the point that he denied his allegiance to Jesus.

This incident shows just how powerful the fear of disapproval can be. It can be stronger than our confidence in our own strength. As Proverbs 16:18 warns us, "Pride goes before destruction, and a haughty spirit before a fall."

But before we condemn Peter too harshly, we should ask ourselves whether we have done the same thing. Perhaps you could have used your age, your standing, your emotional weight, or some other intangible to correct a wrong, yet you failed to speak up. Perhaps someone's unexpected urging intimidated you into committing some immoral or unethical act.

Peter's unexpected fear is a warning: decide in advance that you will stand by your convictions no matter who tries to intimidate you.

### Understandable Fear

Even if you have not been surprised by an unexpected confrontation, most of us have experienced Peter's second encounter:

intimidation by a group. After leaving the servant girl, Peter moved quickly to disappear into a group of "servants and officers who had made a fire of coals" in the high priest's courtyard. "Peter stood with them and warmed himself" (John 18:18).

Let's say this was a group of a dozen or so people standing around the fire, bundled against the cold. There was probably a conversation running about the events of the night. The group was already in place when Peter joined them, so he likely hovered on the periphery. Peter likely knew none of these people except for "the other disciple"—probably John—who had arranged for Peter's access into the courtyard (verse 16). It seemed a perfect place for Peter to catch any news about Jesus while remaining anonymous.

But Peter couldn't catch a break. Suddenly someone in the group saw him and blurted, "You are not also one of His disciples, are you?" (verse 25). The phrase "one of His disciples" would have brought the conversation to a halt as everyone looked up to see whom the questioner was addressing. And when they saw him looking at Peter, all eyes turned and locked on him.

I can imagine Peter wanting to dissolve into the ground. He may not have even looked up, trying to imply that the question couldn't possibly be directed toward him. Fear came over Peter, and he lied a second time, denying his association with Jesus. Peter was caught in the classic peer pressure situation: one person intimidated by a group. That doesn't make Peter's fear or his lie defensible. But it makes them more understandable. We know what it feels like to be one against the world (or at least one against a group).

Flash back to teenage years. You're in a social setting with kids from your school, and they offer you a cigarette, some alcohol, or even a pill. You hesitate, and then the pressure starts: "What are you, afraid? Hey, look, the mama's boy is a goody two-shoes! It's probably past your bedtime, kid. Maybe you should call your mommy to come pick you up." And so on. Everything you've wanted since the second grade hangs on that moment: respect, inclusion, acceptance, and status. If you say yes, you're in. If you stand your ground and say no, then no more invitations will come your way.

This kind of peer pressure is not limited to teens. It can occur in a group at work, in social settings, or even in church. You find yourself being the odd man or woman out, and you find it surprisingly difficult to speak up and say what you really believe. Instead of falling victim to the fear of man, we fall victim to the fear of *men*—to the multiplied intimidation spawned by the pressure of a peer group.

Jesus warns about fearing a group more than we fear Him: "If anyone comes to Me and does not hate his father and mother, wife and children, brothers and sisters, yes, and his own life also, he cannot be My disciple" (Luke 14:26). Here the word *hate* is used to signify preference, not emotional resentment. If we don't prefer Jesus more than we prefer any others—including a group of our peers or even our own families—we cannot be His disciples.

Peter's fear in the face of a group is not excusable. But it is understandable.

### Unsurprising Fear

The third accusation against Peter seems to have been the most threatening and the least surprising. It gives us another window into the nature of fear.

When the Jewish leaders came to Gethsemane to arrest Jesus, armed soldiers accompanied them (John 18:3). Yet Peter showed no fear whatsoever. He slashed one of the party with a sword, cutting off his right ear. The man, a servant of the Jewish high priest, was named Malchus (verse 10). Now, Peter was a fisherman, not a soldier. We even wonder what he was doing with a sword in the first place! Yet he was apparently willing to risk his life for Jesus, maybe intending to hold off the soldiers long enough for Jesus to make a getaway.

But as we know, that wasn't Jesus' plan. He rebuked Peter, telling him to put his sword away (verse 11). He then reached out and healed Malchus's ear (Luke 22:51). All Peter gained by his foray into bravery was an enemy: Malchus.

Now—back to the courtyard of the high priest's house, where Peter stood in a group around a fire. He had just become the center of attention when someone suggested he was one of Jesus' disciples. Suddenly another high priest's servant became very interested—one of Malchus's relatives who had also been in Gethsemane when Peter cut off Malchus's ear: "Did I not see you in the garden with Him?" he asked (John 18:26).

This man had obviously seen Peter with Jesus. And worse, he knew Peter was the man who had chopped off his kinsman's ear! Peter was first confronted by a young servant girl and then by an anonymous group. But now he was confronted by someone with an agenda, someone who would like to see Peter pay for his attack in the garden.

Peter stuck to his lie: "Peter then denied [the accusation] again" (verse 27). Though he must have known better, Peter no doubt felt constrained by his lies to continue the charade. He figured he was in too deep to turn back.

If we are surprised when the world tries to intimidate us because of our faith, then we haven't embraced and internalized the truth of Jesus' words: "If the world hates you, you know that it hated Me before it hated you" (John 15:18).

Peter had not internalized those words—perhaps because the time between their utterance and his confrontations in the courtyard had been so short. But most Christians today have had plenty of time to take Jesus' words to heart. We should not fear or be intimidated by those who disapprove of our allegiance to Him. We should expect it and be prepared for it. We should "be ready to give a defense to everyone who asks you a reason for the hope that is in you, with meekness and fear" (1 Peter 3:15). But leave your sword at home.

## THE REASONS WE FEAR DISAPPROVAL

Fear of disapproval can be unexpected, understandable, unsurprising—or, as in Peter's case, all the above. Those are the dynamics, but what are the causes? Why do we find ourselves in situations where fear seems to rise automatically? Let me offer five reasons.

### We Are Filled with Ourselves

It's clear from the biblical record that Peter was full of energy, optimism, boldness, outspokenness, and confidence. He was the kind of person who thought everyone was entitled to *his* (Peter's) own opinion—including Jesus! Incredibly, he once took Jesus aside and rebuked Him for saying He was going to die in Jerusalem (Matthew 16:21-22). When Peter saw Jesus walking on water, he impulsively jumped out of the boat to try it himself (Matthew 14:25-31). So it's not surprising that Peter boasted that he would never deny Jesus and brashly maimed an enemy with a sword. Peter was impulsive and prideful—an embarrassing calamity waiting to happen. To put it biblically, Peter was full of the pride of self.

Even Satan recognized the potential for Peter's downfall. Just as Satan had asked God for permission to attack Job (Job 1–2), he had asked Jesus for permission to "sift [Peter] as wheat" (Luke 22:31). I believe Satan was allowed access to Peter for a good reason: Peter needed to see his own human weakness in order to learn that his strength was inadequate for following Jesus faithfully. Peter had yet to learn what Paul learned: "When I am weak, then I am strong" in Christ (2 Corinthians 12:10).

Peter needed to learn the lesson that every follower of Jesus must learn: there is no place for pride or self-sufficiency in the Kingdom of God.

### We Fail to Pray

People who depend on themselves rarely feel the need to pray. Why would they? Just after Peter boasted that he would never deny the Lord, Jesus asked him and the other disciples to pray with Him in Gethsemane, saying, "Watch and pray, *lest you enter into temptation*. The spirit indeed is willing, but the flesh is weak" (Matthew 26:41, emphasis added). This occurred immediately after Satan had asked for permission to attack Peter. Jesus was trying to shield Peter by urging him to do the only thing that would protect him: pray.

Prayer is an admission, a confession, of dependence; it involves the recognition that we cannot do this thing called life alone. Prayer is the only way to maintain a constant state of dependence on God. Prideful people don't pray, because they don't sense the need. They think they can handle any challenge quite well, thank you very much.

Was Paul thinking of Peter when he wrote, "Let him who

thinks he stands take heed lest he fall" (1 Corinthians 10:12)? Or maybe he was thinking of himself before he saw the light—a prideful, religious person if ever there was one. Or he could have been thinking of us. When we find ourselves fearful of others' disapproval, it may be because we have not spent enough time in prayer, reminding ourselves of our dependence on Christ.

### We Function in the Energy of the Flesh

How do we know Peter was walking in the energy of the flesh the night Jesus was arrested? The most obvious way is by his attack on the high priest's servant. No one in the high priest's party had attacked Jesus. Yet Peter went on the offensive, making an unprovoked attack with a sword! What was he thinking?

I suggest that Peter was not thinking at all. He was acting by the sheer energy of the flesh. Armed defense against Jesus' arrest was far from the will of God, which is why Jesus rebuked Peter and added, "All who take the sword will perish by the sword. Or do you think that I cannot now pray to My Father, and He will provide Me with more than twelve legions of angels?" (Matthew 26:52-53).

If I had been Peter, I would have turned beet red with embarrassment. Here he was, a lowly fisherman wielding a seldom-used sword, probably rusty, trying to defend Someone who had legions of angels awaiting His command to strike.

Why didn't Jesus give that command? We find the answer in what He said to Pilate: "My kingdom is not of this world. If My kingdom were of this world, *My servants would fight*, so that I should not be delivered to the Jews" (John 18:36, emphasis added). God doesn't need fleshly zeal to defend His interests in this world. As Paul later writes, "Though we walk in the flesh, we do not war according to the flesh" (2 Corinthians 10:3).

If we depend on our flesh for victory, we will be intimidated by those whose flesh seems stronger than ours. But when we live in the power of God's Spirit, we will see the fleshly attacks against us to be as wimpy as that of Pilate acting unwittingly under the shadow of Jesus' massive army of angels.

### We Follow Jesus from Far Off

All humans are double minded. At our lowest level, we are largely motivated by the flesh, which habitually overrides our conscience in order to satisfy our world-centered desires and maintain our pride. At the higher spiritual (Christian) level, we can be filled with the Holy Spirit, who will empower us to think and act within the will of God. Paul writes that the Spirit and the flesh war against one another continually—that the only way not to walk in the flesh is to walk in the Spirit (Galatians 5:16-17).

But we want to have it both ways, just as Peter did: "Having arrested [Jesus], they led Him and brought Him into the high priest's house. *But Peter followed at a distance*" (Luke 22:54, emphasis added). Peter wanted to be with Jesus but not so close that he might also get arrested. He wanted to be faithful ("Here I am, Lord, back here behind You!"), but he didn't want it to cost him anything—like maybe his life.

Peter wanted the *approval* of the followers of Jesus for following the Master, but he didn't want the *disapproval* of the Jews for following too closely. He was concerned about what might happen to Jesus; he just didn't want it to happen to him. So he followed at a distance. That's what double mindedness looks like in someone who fears man.

I recall that struggle as a young Christian in high school. I wanted to be approved by Jesus, but at the same time I wanted to be popular and approved by my peers. With a godly group of peers, that may sometimes be possible. But that's pretty hard to pull off in school. I didn't want to lose my peer acceptance by following Jesus too closely. I soon discovered, however, that it's impossible to be popular with Jesus and popular with the world at the same time. That's why many Christians today do what Peter did (and what I did as a young teenager)—they follow Jesus at a distance.

## We Find Fellowship in the Wrong Place

If we step back from the picture John paints of Jesus' arrest, we see two groups of people: Jesus and His disciples in the garden, and the servants and soldiers of the high priest entering it. The two groups are essentially enemies. Fast-forward maybe an hour, and we find a curious scene: Peter is now standing in the midst of the people who had just arrested his Lord, warming himself by their fire (John 18:18, 25)! How did Peter go from drawing a sword on this group to standing around their fire?

We may assume that Peter was spying or keeping an eye on what happened to Jesus. But should he have been there at all? What did Peter have in common with the enemies of Jesus that would justify his sharing common ground with them?

Charles Haddon Spurgeon was not impressed with Peter's actions:

> Peter was on dangerous ground. When his Master was being buffeted, he was trying to make himself comfortable. We read of the high priest's servants . . . rough servants of ill masters. He was in bad company and he was a man who could not afford to be in bad company—for he was so impulsive and so easily provoked to rash actions.[4]

The great commentator Matthew Henry adds a more philosophical warning: "Those that warm themselves with evil doers grow cold toward good people and good things, and those that are fond of the devil's fire-side are in danger of the devil's fire."[5]

Even if we give Peter the benefit of the doubt, there is a warning here: don't go into the midst of God's enemies without being prepared to declare yourself the friend of God. To do otherwise is to risk succumbing to the fear of disapproval.

## THE RESOLUTIONS TO THE FEAR OF DISAPPROVAL

After the Crucifixion, Peter probably thought his three-year hope of Jesus' becoming Israel's king had failed. Or at least he, Peter, had failed. Even after Jesus' resurrection, Peter probably thought his chances of finding a place in His Kingdom were slim to none. So he and some of the other disciples retreated to Galilee to take up fishing again.

But Jesus went after His disciples. He met Peter and the others on the shore of the Sea of Galilee, and it was there that Peter discovered the Good News. Even though he had miserably failed his test of loyalty, it was possible to be restored. What Jesus communicated to them, coupled with their receiving the power of the Spirit a few weeks later at Pentecost, restored their courage and their resolve. And it can do the same for us.

### Replace Our Fear of Others with His Approval of Us

Jesus did not abandon Peter, He pursued him.

Peter had discovered that following Jesus is the journey of a lifetime, while following at a distance ultimately leads into darkness and confusion. Jesus had returned, just as He said He would, but hadn't Peter disqualified himself from the celebration? Hadn't his rejection in the shadow of the cross cut him off from fellowship by the light of the empty tomb?

As a matter of fact, Jesus decreed, it did not.

God paints beautiful backgrounds for His great canvases of grace. In this case, He chose the beauty of a beach at sunrise—the setting of fishermen at the chores of a typical day, as the first gleams of the sun hit the water, and as birds cried out in the dawn. It was Peter's kind of time and place—optimal conditions for him to receive the most wonderful message of his life: he was forgiven. He was accepted.

Jesus' goal was to replace Peter's fear of men with His own approval.

There would be more intimidation and confrontation to come, and Peter needed something stronger than fear to see him through. And the only thing stronger than the fear of man's disapproval is the approval of God. Once Peter knew that Jesus had forgiven him, he had no reason to fear what others might say or do.

If you live in fear of others' disapproval, that fear can be displaced, just as Peter's was, by knowing how tenaciously God loves and accepts you. As the apostle Paul writes, "If God is for us, who can be against us?" (Romans 8:31).

### Replace Our Fear of Others with Love for Him

There on the shore of Galilee, Jesus initiated a vital conversation with Peter. He asked him the same question three times: "Do you love Me? . . . Do you love Me? . . . Do you love Me?" (John 21:15-17). Just as Peter had verbally denied Jesus three times, Jesus asked Peter three times to verbally declare his love for Him. And Peter did. Each time he was asked, Peter replied, "You know that I love you." And Jesus followed each of Peter's confessions with a slightly varied response: "Feed My lambs. . . . Tend My sheep. . . . Feed My sheep."

Even though Peter was grieved that Jesus persisted with the same question (verse 17), it was necessary. First, it probably had a cathartic effect on Peter to overlay his three denials with three declarations of love. Second, it enabled Peter to understand his coming role as the foundation stone of the church: he was to take care of Jesus' flock. If Peter was to fulfill Christ's commission, love for Jesus would have to be his highest motivation.

No one can say he loves Jesus who fears man more. And no one can fear man who gives all his love to Jesus.

### Replace Our Fear of Others with Love for Others

In his book on fear, Neil Anderson says that phobias are like the coils of a snake—squeezing tighter the more we give in to them.[6] We can't love because fear gets in the way. Worst of all, fear pushes us even further into the ultimate manifestation of sin: self-centeredness.

Before his restorative encounter with Jesus, Peter's life was pretty much all about Peter. He said and did what he wanted, even when it landed him in trouble. But when Jesus recommissioned Peter to care for His followers, He was reminding Peter to replace his fear of others with love for them.

When Jesus told Peter, "Tend My sheep," He was charging him to spend the rest of his life putting the well-being of the sheep above his own. To his rough-hewn personality as a fisherman—which would still be needed to defend the flock against predators—Peter would need to add the gentle hand of a healer and a feeder of the sheep. His fear of others would be displaced by his love for the flock Jesus was entrusting to him.

Fear drains us, while love empowers us. We cannot fear people and love people at the same time. We cannot sacrificially and unconditionally love others if all our energy is directed toward protecting ourselves. When we love others (including those who can harm us), life is no longer about us, and fear of disapproval is driven away.

### Replace Our Fear of Others with Faith in Him

Jesus' new commission for Peter did not mean Peter would never again be afraid. Quite the contrary: "'When you [Peter] are old, you will stretch out your hands, and another will gird you and carry you where you do not wish.' This [Jesus] spoke, signifying by what death [Peter] would glorify God" (John 21:18-19). History indicates that is exactly what happened. Peter's hands were stretched out on a cross when the Roman emperor had him crucified. Peter reportedly asked to be crucified upside down, considering himself unworthy to die in the same manner as his Lord.

Was Peter afraid? Undoubtedly, yes—in the same human way I was afraid after hearing a cancer diagnosis in 1994. And, I believe, in the same way Jesus was afraid as He prayed and wept in the garden over what He was about to endure. It is possible to be humanly afraid without succumbing to fear. It is possible to feel fear and faith at the same time without fear getting the upper hand. It is even possible to experience the fear of disapproval from others while knowing that God approves us totally.

We cannot prevent others from disapproving of or intimidating us, but our faith can prevent us from succumbing to fear. Jesus was honest with Peter about what lay ahead for him. And He is honest with us: "In the world you will have tribulation" (John 16:33). But He doesn't leave us to suffer disapproval, intimidation, or tribulation alone: "But be of good cheer, I have overcome the world" (verse 33).

### Replace Our Fear of Others with the Glory of God

Why did Jesus tell Peter how he was going to die? It's likely that He was saying, "Peter, your life so far has been about glorifying Peter. Henceforth, your life will be about glorifying God. And if dying for God is the best way to glorify Him, then that is what you are called to do—just as I was."

When others disapprove of our walk with Christ, we are called to glorify God. When others intimidate us for standing for biblical values, we are called to glorify God. When we face physical, financial, vocational, or other harm at the hands of others, we are called to glorify God. We may never be called to glorify God with martyrdom. But we are called to glorify Him in everything we do. As the apostle Paul writes, "Whether you eat or drink, or whatever you do, do all to the glory of God" (1 Corinthians 10:31). That includes showing courage in the face of the disapproval of others.

## THE REVERSAL OF FEAR OF DISAPPROVAL

After a Monday night NFL football game in 1990, something happened for the first time in professional football. When the San Francisco 49ers and the New York Giants completed their game, a group of eight players—some from both teams—gathered near the center of the field. They knelt on one knee and prayed together in the name of Jesus Christ.

The practice caught on, and soon other players began gathering on the field to pray after their games.

To no one's surprise, not all fans supported the mixing of faith and football. *Sports Illustrated*, the iconic sports magazine, said the players should pray in private. NFL management considered prohibiting the practice. But the players wouldn't budge, insisting they would continue to pray after the games. Some said they would maintain the practice even if they were fined for it.[7]

What if Peter had been an NFL player (I'm guessing he'd have been a linebacker)? Would he have maintained his faith in the face of media and spectator disapproval? Well, observing his performance in the high priest's courtyard, we would have to say no. But after his lakeside conversation with the risen Jesus and the coming of the Holy Spirit at Pentecost, we would have to change our answer to a definite yes. Peter's fear of disapproval was completely reversed. No longer was he bold for the wrong reasons (pride, ego); he was bold for the right reasons (faith, fearlessness).

After the Holy Spirit came upon the group of 120 of Jesus' followers, everything changed. Instead of cowering in fear of being identified with the resurrected Jesus, believers had a new boldness. And they were led by Peter himself, the apostle who was once afraid to be identified with his Lord.

It was Peter who stood up with the other eleven apostles and preached a powerful message to the massive crowds assembled in Jerusalem for Pentecost (Acts 2:14-40). Quoting extensively from the Old Testament, Peter explained what the crowds had just witnessed—Jesus' disciples speaking in languages they hadn't learned. He explained how God had sent Jesus as the Messiah and verified His identity through miracles. He explained how the Old Testament predicted the resurrection of the recently crucified Christ. And then he concluded by boldly repeating the very assertion that had gotten Jesus killed: "Let all the house of Israel know assuredly that God has made this Jesus, whom you crucified, both Lord and Christ [Messiah]" (Acts 2:36).

Then the crowds cried out, "Men and brethren, what shall we do?" (Acts 2:37). So Peter told them: "Repent, and . . . be baptized in the name of Jesus Christ for the remission of sins" (Acts 2:38). And about three thousand souls did exactly that (Acts 2:41).

Think back to the scene in the high priest's courtyard. Can you imagine Peter now boldly proclaiming the divinity of Christ when before he wouldn't even admit to being a follower of Jesus? Peter was no longer the fearful, intimidated man whose fleshly talents proved insufficient for the pressure of that hour. Instead of letting a dozen or so people intimidate him, Peter now warned a crowd of thousands to "be saved from this perverse generation" (Acts 2:40).

As the church began to grow, the Jewish religious leaders became alarmed as more and more Jews became followers of Jesus. Peter became a lightning rod for their attacks. Soon he and John were thrown in jail for preaching about Jesus. The next day the ruling body of the Jews—the very leaders who had condemned Jesus—brought them in for questioning. Peter jumped on the opportunity to preach to them, and his words left them stunned: "When they saw the boldness of Peter and John, and perceived that they were uneducated and untrained men, they marveled" (Acts 4:13). Nobody had marveled at Peter's boldness the night Jesus was arrested!

The rulers, fearing the disapproval of the people if they harmed Peter and John, released them with a warning to cease their preaching. But Peter did not even consider putting on the brakes. Not long after, the rulers again ordered them to quit preaching Jesus. "Peter and the other apostles answered and said: 'We ought to obey God rather than men.' . . . When [the rulers] heard this, they were furious and plotted to kill them" (Acts 5:29, 33).

The tables had turned. Now who was afraid of whom? Who was no longer controlled by the fear of men but by love for

God? Peter was a changed man. He had undergone a spiritual reversal—his fear had been replaced by faith.

The same reversal can happen in the life of anyone who fears being identified as a follower of Jesus. There's no formula we can write on a spiritual prescription pad: "Do this and this, and you'll never fear the disapproval of man again." But we can learn from the example of Peter by identifying some major turning points in his life.

First, his fleshly strength failed him. His charismatic personality was insufficient for the demands of a critical moment. He came to the end of himself and realized he was not who he thought he was.

Second, he went through a dark period of introspection, not unlike what Saul of Tarsus went through after his encounter with Christ on the Damascus road. For three days Saul (Paul) sat alone in a house in Damascus calling into question everything he had believed. Peter went through a similar valley of despair, forced to think about what it really meant to follow Jesus.

Third, Peter experienced the unconditional love of the same Christ he had denied just days before. He was called back into Christ's service as a newly humbled and now-forgiven follower.

Fourth, Peter experienced the power of the Holy Spirit. Nothing else can explain his radical transformation.

And fifth, Peter came to the realization—by the grace of God—that it is better to fear God than to fear man.

We cannot duplicate Peter's journey, but I've never seen anyone conquer the fear of disapproval without traveling through spiritual stages similar to his. God orchestrates that journey and those transitions in His own way and time.

And we can tell God that, as our world grows increasingly hostile to Christianity, we want to lose our timidity about revealing our faith. We can ask for the boldness of the post-Pentecost Peter. We can ask God to lead us to desire His approval so intensely that the disapproval of men will mean nothing to us.

In his book *Charles Kuralt's America*, the veteran CBS television journalist recounted a town meeting he attended in the small town of Stafford, Vermont. Such meetings displayed democracy in action: each citizen was allowed to voice his or her opinion on matters of concern to the town. When all viewpoints were heard, the moderator announced, "I'm going to ask for a standing vote. All those in favor, stand up and be counted."[8]

When it was time for Peter to stand up and be counted for Jesus on that terrible night in Jerusalem two thousand years ago, he failed. And many of us have failed just as he did. But those days can be over. We know how strong Jesus stood for us. We know that he cared for no man's approval, but only the approval of the Father. That's the bottom line. It is more than enough to give us the boldness to stand and be counted for Him.

# CHAPTER 7

# DANGER:
## *The Fear of Sudden Trouble*

*Do not be afraid of sudden terror, nor of trouble
from the wicked when it comes.*

PROVERBS 3:25

When the *Andrea Gail* left Gloucester Harbor in Massachusetts on September 20, 1991, and headed into the North Atlantic, no one could have known that this fishing boat would never be seen again. Only a bit of debris ever turned up, and the six crew members vanished forever.

In his book *The Perfect Storm*, author Sebastian Junger immortalized the fate of the *Andrea Gail*. A film followed, featuring George Clooney and Mark Wahlberg. But these stars, big as they are, played only supporting roles. The real star was the storm itself—a terrifying, relentless oppressor born of fierce wind and mountainous waves.

It was meteorologists who named this cataclysmic tempest "the perfect storm." I might not tend to use the word *perfect* to describe something so terrible, but once you understand the meteorologist's usage, "perfect storm" makes perfect sense. It is merely a vivid way of saying "worst-case scenario." In the case of the *Andrea Gail*, it was the simultaneous convergence of the toughest weather conditions possible.

Three deadly elements came together in October of 1991: a front moving from Canada toward New England; a high pressure system building over Canada's east coast; and the dying remnants of Hurricane Grace, churning along the eastern seaboard of the United States. Strong weather was coming from three of the four points on the compass, all of it converging on the little *Andrea Gail*.

On their own, warm air, cold air, and moist air are hardly noticeable. But when wind patterns force them together, the result can be lethal. The last radio transmission of Billy Tyne, the captain of the fishing boat, came at 6:00 p.m. on October 28, 1991. He reported his coordinates to the captain of his sister ship, the *Hannah Boden*, saying, "She's comin' on, boys, and she's comin' on strong."[1]

The popular book and movie brought the term "perfect storm" into common usage, but the concept is as old as humanity. People have always had to deal with the convergence of multiple rough circumstances. So much can go wrong so quickly that we shake our heads and say, "When it rains, it pours."

We've all been there, haven't we? Your child gets sick, and your car breaks down on the way to the doctor. All the while it's pouring rain, and your spouse isn't answering the cell phone because it's being charged. One or two of these difficulties aren't so bad, but when they arrive together, they can form quite a storm.

As frustrating as such storms can be, much worse can happen. Today, in our faster, more crowded, and more complex world, a few little squalls can quickly become "the perfect storm." When multiple conditions converge and threaten critical areas of our lives, such as finances, relationships, jobs, and health, we question how much more we can endure. Somewhere there's a cutoff at which we reach critical mass. Once there, we wonder whether we will stay afloat or go under like the *Andrea Gail*. Knowing that could happen strikes fear into us.

The fate of the *Andrea Gail* demonstrates two specific kinds of fear that we all experience. The first is that gut-level, adrenaline-drenched fear that the crew felt in the midst of the storm. They were afraid because their lives were on the line. This kind of fear is beneficial; it's a necessary instinct for survival. No doubt the fishermen of the North Atlantic feel a little surge of that fear every time they leave port. One poor decision in the face of threatening weather could mean death. But that doesn't stop these men and women. Reasonable fear is a healthy, normal part of the job description. If they couldn't handle it, they'd be in some other line of work.

But there's another kind of fear that can immobilize us completely: the fear of fear itself. Fear in the midst of the storm is instinctive and beneficial. Fear of a storm that *could* happen is not. It's an intrusive emotion that can lead us to a greatly diminished life. The imagined fear becomes so vivid that we no longer distinguish it from reality, and for some of us, that fear becomes so debilitating we can hardly get out of bed in the morning. Though the sky is clear, we're devastated by thoughts of rain. Inside a storm, at least we can look the beast in the eye. But with the fear of fear, the imagined monster is always just on the other side of the door, looming large, even though it doesn't exist. It's like the fear educator William Hughes Mearns expressed in his poem:

*Last night I saw upon the stair*
*A little man who wasn't there*

*He wasn't there again today*
*Oh, how I wish he'd go away.*[2]

As our nation was recovering from the Great Depression, President Franklin D. Roosevelt attempted to encourage us, saying, "The only thing we have to fear is fear itself—nameless, unreasoning, unjustified terror which paralyzes needed efforts to convert retreat into advance."[3]

Everyone must face fear, but for the believer, its fangs are drawn in because we are protected by an overarching umbrella of hope. Nonbelievers must contrive coping mechanisms, all of which are ineffective. Fatalism ("we're all doomed") doesn't work. Existentialism ("we're all clueless") leads nowhere. Optimism ("hey, it's all good") lets us down because it's a lie. It's *not* all good. There are things in life worth fearing.

We need a perspective on fear that takes into account the perfect storms of life but also reassures us that there's a safe harbor within reach. We can't put away all fear, but we need not live as its slaves.

That's where Jesus Christ comes in. As we follow Him, this world and its emotions look different in the light of His goodness, power, and wisdom. Fear is simply a fact we must deal with in a fallen universe, but in the Bible we learn that fear can be managed. In God's Word there is a wealth of guidance on dealing with storms, perfect and imperfect.

## THE PROBABILITY OF STORMS IN OUR LIVES

When evening had come, [Jesus] said to them, "Let us cross over to the other side." Now when they had left the multitude, they took Him along in the boat as He was.

And other little boats were also with Him. And a great windstorm arose, and the waves beat into the boat, so that it was already filling.

MARK 4:35-37

Matthew, Mark, and Luke all relay the story of a perfect storm in the lives of Jesus' disciples. On that night a quiet boat ride turned into a terrifying brush with death. While Matthew (8:23-27) and Luke (8:22-25) cover the basic facts, Mark's version of the event is the most detailed (4:1, 35-41).

The Gospels record that Jesus was near exhaustion, and His twelve disciples were reeling from the rigorous training He'd been giving them. The crowds had been overwhelming. Sick people, craving His healing touch, had flocked to Jesus on every street. The disciples stood in awe of their Master's miracles and were astonished that He expected them to perform miracles too. Their lives were being turned inside out.

Now Jesus was speaking near the shore of the Sea of Galilee. The crowds began to press in so hard that He was almost shoved back into the water. He climbed into a boat, pushed out a few feet, sat down, and continued teaching (Mark 4:1). By the time He had finished, it was evening. Since Mark devotes almost thirty verses to the event, it must have been a significant teaching session, lasting several hours. Jesus must have been exhausted. The crowd, however, was not about to leave. Desperately needing rest, Jesus and the disciples simply remained in the boat and set sail for the eastern shore, where Jesus sought to minister next.

The elements of a perfect storm were gathering. First, Jesus was utterly exhausted (Mark 4:38). Second, the disciples, too, were tired and emotionally befuddled by their extraordinary experiences with Jesus. Third, it was already nighttime—late to be setting out to cross the sea. Fourth, a small flotilla of eager followers was trailing them, meaning that when they landed, rest would remain elusive.

Then there was the sea itself. The Sea of Galilee is like a bowl of water nestled nearly seven hundred feet below sea level. It is both fed and drained by the Jordan River, which enters at the northern end and exits from the southern end. Mountains flank nearly every side, forming valleys and gullies that set the stage for howling winds. When the cool air from the mountains swoops through the valleys and collides with the warm, moist air hovering over the sea, violent storms can erupt in a matter of minutes.

And that is just what happened. "A great windstorm arose, and the waves beat into the boat, so that it was already filling" (Mark 4:37). Mark uses a Greek word for *windstorm* that can be translated "furious squall" or "hurricane." Matthew describes the storm as a "great *seismos*," or earthquake—as if the sea were being shaken by the winds (Matthew 8:24).

Fatigue. Confusion. Darkness. Tempest. The perfect storm had arrived. It was as if all their fears had combined and crystallized. As fishermen, they had a deep, fearful respect for the turbulent water. As men, they had a deep but relatively untested respect for Jesus. But now this Jesus—the One they had left everything to follow—had led them right into the storm. To make matters worse, He had dozed off, having no apparent concern for their safety or the disaster that now seemed inevitable. They must have wondered whether they had taken the right step in following Him. There was a lot they still didn't know about this man. Could He even deliver them from the disaster that now seemed inevitable?

Just as sudden storms are inevitable on the Sea of Galilee, sudden storms can descend upon our lives as well. When this happens, the disciples' predicament becomes ours: How is it possible to trust a God who allows perfect storms to assail us?

## THE PARADOX OF STORMS IN OUR LIVES

The disciples were following Jesus wherever He went, assisting Him in all His ministries. They were listening to His Word and helping Him preach the Gospel, yet they found themselves being tossed up and down by a storm and in real danger of drowning. The disciples were learning a difficult lesson—one every believer must learn: we can find ourselves in the middle of God's perfect will and in the middle of a perfect storm at the same time!

When author Gary Thomas and his wife considered buying a house, they prayed diligently for God to guide them. If it wasn't His will, they figured He would close the windows of opportunity.

The window did not close, so they proceeded with their purchase. Five years passed, during which they enjoyed their home and the blessing of God. Then the economy entered a tailspin, and the house was suddenly worth less than they had paid for it. They wondered why God hadn't stopped them from making a bad investment. They had prayed. They had listened. They had not heard "no."

As Gary's wife was seeking God one day, she heard His answer: *Have you considered the possibility that I wanted you in that neighborhood to minister rather than to bolster your financial equity?* That insight caused them to rethink their questions about God's guidance. They realized it was all about lives touched for Christ rather than value earned from holdings. Now the question was, did they trust God enough to follow Him down a path with no financial profit, but with great spiritual profit?[4]

Christ doesn't ask us to take up our portfolios and follow Him; He says to take up our crosses. Comfort is not a factor. But He does promise that the way to grow into the image of Christ is by trusting and obeying in all circumstances.

As in the case of Gary and his wife, the will of God is not always crystal clear. But on that day by the Sea of Galilee, God's will couldn't have been clearer to the disciples: Jesus had said, "Let's go!" They didn't call a meeting to deliberate; they didn't pray; they didn't seek counsel from others. God's will had been right there in front of them, so without hesitation, they got into the boat. And now the thing that loomed right in front of them was death.

This unexpected peril was something new for the disciples. So far, following Jesus hadn't been overly costly—little more than quitting their jobs and getting a bit of carping and criticism from local religious leaders (Mark 3:22). But they had faced nothing life threatening. In fact, it had been just the opposite; they were close associates of the most popular person in Galilee. They'd been welcomed in small towns as heroes. This movement of God was working, and all systems were go.

Then came the perfect storm. It certainly raised some questions.

Many people believe faith is some kind of insurance against high blood pressure and heartache. *Trust God and you'll have no worries.* But a great paradox of Christianity is that trusting Christ doesn't keep the storms away. In fact, sometimes it pushes us into deep and turbulent waters.

Jesus faced a perfect storm when He rode into Jerusalem on the back of a donkey. He knew what He was about to face—unthinkable torture and death—and He dreaded it. In the garden He cried out, "O My Father, if it is possible, let this cup pass from

Me; nevertheless, not as I will, but as You will" (Matthew 26:39). He was fully aware of the storm He was heading into.

The disciples in their tossing boat weren't cognizant of these underlying spiritual issues. Fear gripped them, pushing aside all concerns about being in the will of God. But they were about to learn a priceless lesson: there is security in the heart of God's will. Storms are not punishment for lack of obedience; oftentimes they are the *result* of obedience! Those men were in that storm because they had jumped in the boat when Jesus said, "Let's go!"

You will follow Jesus into a storm someday. And you will learn that, although it may be overwhelming, it's the safest of all harbors.

## THE PRESENCE IN THE STORMS OF OUR LIVES

He was in the stern, asleep on a pillow. And they awoke Him and said to Him, "Teacher, do You not care that we are perishing?"

MARK 4:38

Juan Carlos Ortiz is a well-known preacher, evangelist, and author originally from Argentina. He once related a conversation he had with a circus trapeze artist about the security a safety net provides. The performer said yes, the net does the obvious—it keeps performers from being injured should they fall. But it does much more. "Imagine there is no net," he said. "We would be so nervous that we would be more likely to miss and fall. If there was not a net, we would not dare to do some of the things we do. But because there's a net, we dare to make two turns, and once I made three turns—thanks to the net!"

Ortiz saw an application for Christians: "We have security in

God. When we are sure in His arms, we dare to attempt big things for God. We dare to be holy. We dare to be obedient. We dare, because we know the eternal arms of God will hold us if we fall."[5]

The disciples had yet to learn the nature of their "net." If they'd realized the full power and authority Jesus held, they would have laughed and shouted at the wind, "Bring it on!" Facing a storm is exhilarating when we are protected by something even more powerful.

Our degree of fear is a gauge of our degree of faith. When we've trusted Jesus and come through the storm, we become more fearless. If we've never really done that, the storm will reduce us to quivering jelly, as it did those disciples.

Some people do believe in the power of God, but they're not sure about His presence. That's a significant deficiency in one's faith. *Will He really be there when I'm in a crisis? Does He care about me?* We can believe in a powerful God who can create a universe, but if He is absent when needed, how does that belief make a difference? Isn't His absence basically the same as if He didn't exist at all?

This was the crisis the disciples faced. They knew that Jesus was there, but apparently they didn't realize He was God. This meant they were unaware of God's presence. Thus, they didn't know what Jesus could and would do. As I witness the fearful lives of many Christians, I'm convinced that the disciples aren't the only ones in that boat, so to speak.

Remember, the Twelve knew the story of Moses and the Israelites crossing the Red Sea. They knew that God could take control over the winds and the seas. But was that same God with them here and now? They did not yet realize that Moses' God and their Master were one and the same. They truly had *Immanuel*, "God with us" (Matthew 1:23).

John Paton was a nineteenth-century Scottish missionary who labored for a lifetime among murderous natives of the New Hebrides Islands. He often faced danger as various tribesmen sought to kill him. He wrote, "Without that abiding consciousness of the presence and power of my dear Lord and Saviour, nothing else in all the world could have preserved me from losing my reason and perishing miserably."[6]

He said that it was in those most dangerous of moments, when he faced the weapons of men, that he saw the face of Christ most clearly.

On one occasion Paton hid within the branches of a tree as the men below searched for him. He heard their murderous threats, yet he knew he was safe in the arms of Jesus. "Alone, yet not alone!" he recalled. "My comfort and joy sprang from the promise, 'Lo, I am with you always.'"[7]

On the Sea of Galilee, an exhausted Jesus slept on a cushion in the rear of the boat with the waves crashing all about Him. The image is striking. How did the disciples view Him? Apparently, they saw Him as a man much like themselves, even though He possessed the supernatural power to heal the sick and feed the hungry, and—as they would soon find out—the power to calm the wind and the waves.

## THE PEACE IN THE STORMS OF OUR LIVES

He arose and rebuked the wind, and said to the sea, "Peace, be still!" And the wind ceased and there was a great calm.

MARK 4:39

The disciples must have wondered how Jesus could possibly nap with the waves crashing and the wind howling. They shook Him, yelling for Him to wake up: "'Do You not care that we are perishing?' Then He arose and rebuked the wind, and said to the sea, 'Peace, be still!' And the wind ceased and there was a great calm" (Mark 4:38-39). The crisis was at an end. No doubt one could hear the pounding heartbeats of twelve shocked men.

The passage tells us that Jesus rebuked the wind, just as a parent would rebuke an unruly child. He dealt with demons in the same way—He rebuked them (Luke 4:35). And the wind obeyed Him just as demons did. He had power over both the natural and the supernatural.

This enormous display of miraculous power should have quelled any remaining doubts in the minds of the disciples as to who Jesus was. Only God has such authority. The Old Testament tells us that He has power over nature: "He calms the storm, so that its waves are still" (Psalm 107:29; see also Psalm 89:9; 93:4). Before His disciples' eyes, Jesus demonstrated that He possessed power that could emanate only from God. Apparently they hadn't grasped this fact until they saw Him halt a storm in its tracks. Some things must be seen to be believed.

During their three years of following Jesus, these men witnessed ever-greater displays of God's power through Him. They believed, not because they were taught, but because they were shown. The disciples were like newborn spiritual babes whose eyes were slowly opening to the true identity of this Man they followed.

God is committed to developing our spiritual sight as well. And He often uses the storms of life to show us that we can trust Him—His power, love, and wisdom. In his book on the Gospel of Mark, Pastor Tim Keller explains:

You could argue that this world is just the result of a monumental "storm"—you're here by accident, through blind, violent forces of nature, through the big bang—and when you die, you'll turn to dust. . . .

However, if Jesus is who he says he is, there's another way to look at life. If he's Lord of the storm, then no matter what shape the world is in—or your life is in—you will find Jesus provides all the healing, all the rest, all the power you could possibly want.[8]

Joni Eareckson Tada illustrates how drawing on the power and peace of Jesus transforms her life:

"O God," I often pray in the morning, "God, I cannot do this. I cannot do this thing called quadriplegia. I have no resources for this. I have no strength for this—but you do. You've got resources. You've got strength. I can't do quadriplegia, but I can do all things through you as you strengthen me [Phil. 4:13]. I have no smile for this woman who's going to walk into my bedroom in a moment. She could be having coffee with another friend, but she's chosen to come here to help me get up. Oh, God, please may I borrow your smile?"[9]

Our loving heavenly Father is kind and patient with us when the storms of life overwhelm us and fill us with anxiety. He is gracious to show us His power even when we are beginning to wonder if He is asleep or absent, even when our cries to Him for help are permeated with doubt. But we can face whatever circumstances await us with courage if we just reflect on God's faithfulness and place our confidence in His great power and loving purpose for our lives.

## THE PURPOSE OF STORMS IN OUR LIVES

Did Jesus bring about this storm simply so He could calm it and build His disciples' faith? The Bible gives no direct answer, but I'm inclined to say no. He had no need to create new storms to demonstrate His true nature, because this fallen world stirs up more than enough trouble on its own. He builds our faith by using the storms that are already there. So I see no reason to believe that Jesus went to sleep for any other purpose than to catch some much-needed rest. Yet He was quick to use the storm as a teachable moment. The storm brought Him their full attention, and the lesson would never be forgotten.

Since you are a human being, I think I'm safe in saying you have no shortage of storms in your life. As someone has said, we're always in one of three places: heading into a storm, in a storm, or emerging from a storm. Because we live in a fallen world, trouble of some kind is woven into the fabric of life. Until these storms hit, we live with "delusions of adequacy," as someone put it. We think we have it all under control—until suddenly we don't. Storms cut us down to size and cause us to fear what we cannot control.

Although God does not create the storms in our life, He does what Jesus did that night on the Sea of Galilee. He uses the churning seas to demonstrate His power and strengthen our faith in Him.

C. S. Lewis explains it like this:

God, who has made us, knows what we are and that our happiness lies in Him. Yet we will not seek it in Him as long as He leaves us any other resort where it can even plausibly be looked for. While what we call "our own life" remains agreeable, we will not surrender it to Him. What then can God do in our interests but make "our own life" less agreeable to us, and take away the plausible source of false happiness?[10]

God knows we need Him, and He knows we forget how much we do. Sometimes He allows the storms to rage so they will send us scurrying to Him, as did those disciples in that tossing boat.

David, the psalmist, discovered the value of the storms God allowed him to go through:

Before I was afflicted I went astray,
But now I keep Your word.
PSALM 119:67

It is good for me that I have been afflicted,
That I may learn Your statutes.
PSALM 119:71

In his book *If God Is Good*, Randy Alcorn writes that we see uncured diseases and unprevented tragedies and wonder why God didn't glorify Himself by acting. How we yearn for Him to crush every manifestation of evil and difficulty in our lives. "But power isn't his only attribute," Alcorn writes. "He is also glorified in showing his wisdom."[11] The power of God is an immediate crowd pleaser, but to appreciate the wisdom of God requires patience and discernment. One day we will be with God, praising Him for "his wisdom in not preventing certain evils that he used, in ways we could never have imagined, for our ultimate good."[12]

Jesus allowed the winds to rage in order that His disciples would learn to trust Him. Through the storms of life, our Lord teaches us many precious lessons. He reminds us of our own emptiness and our total dependence on Him. He teaches us to fear God with astonished reverence and not to fear the storms.

## THE PRODUCT OF STORMS IN OUR LIVES

> [Jesus] said to them, "Why are you so fearful? How is it that you have no faith?" And they feared exceedingly, and said to one another, "Who can this be, that even the wind and the sea obey Him!"
>
> MARK 4:40-41

Jesus was gentler with His disciples than He was with the wind. While He rebuked the wind, He only asked His disciples two questions: "Why are you so fearful? How is it that you have no faith?" (Mark 4:40). With these questions, Jesus reveals a key spiritual truth: the opposite of faith is not unbelief; the opposite of faith is *fear*. Belief breeds confidence, while unbelief breeds fear. Essentially, Jesus was saying, "Why are you afraid? Do you not yet trust God, whose power is present in Me?"

The book of 1 Kings tells about the prophet Elijah challenging the prophets of Baal to a duel of faith on top of Mount Carmel. From morning till noon, the prophets of Baal called upon their god to send down fire and consume the sacrifice on the altar. But nothing happened—not even a flicker. Elijah mocked them with stinging sarcasm: "Cry aloud, for he is a god; either he is meditating, or he is busy, or he is on a journey, or perhaps he is sleeping and must be awakened" (18:27).

Of course the nonexistent idol-god was indifferent toward his prophets. The disciples apparently assumed that Jesus was just as indifferent to their plight. They cried, "Teacher, do You not care that we are perishing?" Elijah's suggestion that Baal might have been asleep is precisely the complaint the disciples leveled at Jesus: "You're sleeping while we're drowning! Wake up!"

Lamar Williamson Jr. reminds us that our storms make us wonder whether God even knows what we're feeling:

> We cry out to God in the midst of our storms, "Don't you care?" We try to wake God up to take care of us. At such times the text speaks to our condition. It pictures Jesus in the boat with his disciples, present with us and concerned for us even when we do not perceive his care.[13]

Maybe there's a specific fear claiming your attention today. Whatever that fear is, it will only be amplified by failure to trust in God. He is not sleeping. He is here; He knows every thought in your mind, every feeling in your heart. While you stare with apprehension or even terror at the dark skies, He focuses on the person He is forming you to be. He sees those storms as growing pains—part of the formation process. He knows that a storm may be the very thing that awakens you to deep faith in Him.

What really intrigues me about this account is that Jesus replaced their fear with *more fear*! After gaping in awe at the suddenly calm and windless sea, "they feared exceedingly, and said to one another, 'Who can this be, that even the wind and the sea obey Him!'" (Mark 4:41). Several Bible translations say, "They were terrified." They suddenly realized they were in the presence of a power they had never imagined—a power residing in a Person mightier than the violence of a stormy sea.

But as to coming to full belief that this Man was God on earth, the disciples weren't quite there yet. Matthew tells us that in their awe they asked, "What kind of *man* is this?" not "What kind of God is this?" (Matthew 8:27, NIV, emphasis added). They were still focused on His humanity, although they were beginning to realize that He was something more than mere flesh and blood. They were on their way toward that great confession Peter made later: "You are the Christ, the Son of the living God" (Matthew 16:16).

At this point, the disciples were still learning the extraordinary truth the apostle Paul later expressed in Colossians 1:16: "By Him all things were created that are in heaven and that are on earth." It never entered the disciples' heads that Jesus actually *created* the Sea of Galilee, that the winds and waters are *His*. The disciples in that boat-shaped classroom were beginning to recognize that Jesus was greater—and more fearsome—than anything or anyone they could imagine.

The disciples' fear made a critical transition from being self-centered to being Christ-centered. They no longer worried about drowning; now they were in awe of Jesus and felt a new sense of security in Him. Debilitating fears were being replaced with the empowering fear of God, whom they dimly began to realize was present in the Man before them.

Jesus wants us to be overcome with awe and wonder at His power so we're never deeply frightened again. If He has to use every storm that tears at our sails, He will do it because He's determined to bring us to maturity.

## THE PROMISES FOR THE STORMS IN OUR LIVES

Imagine that you hold a key post in the US Department of State. On March 1, you meet with the secretary of state, who reminds you of a London meeting planned for the last day of the month. As the briefing concludes, the secretary says, "I'll see you in London on the thirty-first." The State department will see that you won't

DANGER: THE FEAR OF SUDDEN TROUBLE

miss the meeting. They will provide the jet to get you there. Your activities during the weeks before that date, however, are more flexible. As you attend to your usual responsibilities, your schedule will undergo all kinds of changes to meet unexpected crises. But on the thirty-first, there's no question about where you will be. You'll be in London; the secretary will see to it.

Something similar happened to the apostle Paul. When he was almost lynched by a Jewish mob, Roman soldiers arrested him for his own safety. "The following night the Lord stood by him and said, 'Be of good cheer, Paul; for as you have testified for Me in Jerusalem, so you must also bear witness at Rome'" (Acts 23:11).

This vision told Paul two things. First, he was heading to Rome. Second, he wasn't going to die in Jerusalem, because God would see that he got to Rome. The time between was more uncertain. Acts 23–28 fills in the details. Paul spent two years defending himself before Roman governors and King Agrippa. When he was shipped to Rome, a storm dashed the ship on the rocks at Malta. Paul survived the wreck and, after that, a poisonous snakebite. He simply wasn't going to die before he got to Rome. Paul had a command performance ahead, and God would see that he got there.

The disciples were given similar assurance before setting out on the Sea of Galilee. Jesus had said, "Let us cross over to the other side" (Mark 4:35). If Jesus named a destination, it was certain they would reach it. Could there be a storm? Certainly. Would it be a comfortable voyage? No assurance of that. The disciples could have worried about seasickness, but they didn't need to worry about drowning. Jesus had told them where they were going.

It's really no different for us. From our point of view, the days ahead are uncertain. We don't know their content or their count. But we know our destination. We've been told that Jesus has gone ahead to prepare a place for us (John 14:1-3). The Word of God is filled with such promises, and to grasp them is to have the cure for fear.

### God's Word Assures Us of a Safe Landing

Notice what Jesus said to the disciples as they began their journey: "On the same day, when evening had come, He said to them, *'Let us cross over to the other side'*" (Mark 4:35, emphasis added). Now consider what the text says about the end of the journey: "Then they came *to the other side* of the sea, to the country of the Gadarenes" (Mark 5:1, emphasis added).

God's Word assures us of a safe landing: we will make it to the other side. There are two kinds of destinations that deserve our attention: temporary destinations and our ultimate destination. God assures us that we will arrive at our ultimate destination—life in His eternal Kingdom. That promise alone should dispel all manner of fear—fear of storms and the fear of fear itself. If God says that those in Christ will be saved, they will be saved.

But are we guaranteed passage through every storm en route to that ultimate destination? No. Think of all the saints who died as martyrs. I find it significant that, once death was certain, many of these heroes of the faith died without fear. They could do so only because they had complete faith in God's assurance of their ultimate destination.

Could you die like that? If your day were today, would you feel the joy of knowing you were going to reach the farther shore? In Christ, death loses all power to terrify.

Jesus offered these words of encouragement to His disciples, and He offers the same promise to us: "My sheep hear My voice, and I know them, and they follow Me. And I give them eternal life, and they shall never perish; neither shall anyone snatch them out of My hand. My Father, who has given them to Me, is greater than all; and no one is able to snatch them out of My Father's hand. I and My Father are one" (John 10:27-30).

### God's Word Alerts Us to Expect Stormy Seas

I find it illuminating that the apostle James, the half brother of Jesus, used the metaphor of a stormy sea when he talked about trials (James 1:2-8). He says we will encounter storms in this life, and without faith we will be "like a wave of the sea driven and tossed by the wind" (James 1:6).

"My brethren," James writes, "count it all joy *when* you fall into various trials" (verse 2, emphasis added). Note that he doesn't say *if* but *when*. Clear skies are never promised in the Bible, though some struggle to embrace that idea. Even Jesus, who lived a perfect life, was given no exemption from storms. Hebrews 5:8 tells us that He was allowed to suffer, and Romans 8:32 explains why, telling us that God "did not spare His own Son, but delivered Him up for us all." God allowed His Son to suffer so that we might be spared the punishment we've earned and go on to enjoy every good gift God gives us.

If Jesus had to suffer, why would we think ourselves exempt? After all, as He explained, "a disciple is not above his teacher, nor a servant above his master" (Matthew 10:24). Then He told them not to fear the storms that inevitably would assail them (verse 26).

The Bible is filled with accounts of God's people enduring and overcoming storms. Hebrews 11 is a collection of such stories. Paul recounts his own stormy weather experiences in 2 Corinthians 6 and 11—and he's not just speaking metaphorically. This man endured at least four shipwrecks! We must not dismiss these heroic examples as special cases; they remind us that ordinary Christians like us can also be overcomers. That's God's promise. But we're never promised that when the storm comes, we are guaranteed to dodge the raindrops. Peter writes,

> Beloved, do not think it strange concerning the fiery trial which is to try you, as though some strange thing happened to you; but rejoice to the extent that you partake of Christ's sufferings, that when His glory is revealed, you may also be glad with exceeding joy.
>
> 1 PETER 4:12-13

Jesus gives us the key to surviving storms in His story about two houses: one built on the sand, the other on solid rock. The sand represents the shallow, shifting, and unreliable values of worldly culture. The rock represents the unshakable truth of God (Matthew 7:24-27). As the storm rages, the first house quickly topples into the sand and washes out to sea. The other stands firm, withstanding the force of the most violent winds. In decades of ministry, I have often seen the truth of this parable vividly demonstrated. People who place their trust in God withstand every storm because they have built their lives on the only foundation that cannot be moved.

### God's Word Announces That the Savior Is on Board

The disciples were too inexperienced with Jesus to have a faith devoid of fear. Perhaps you're the same way. You identify with Christ, but you draw no assurance as the clouds roll in. When the sky darkens, you might wonder whether you should step into the boat with Jesus or stay ashore in hopes of avoiding the storm. The problem with that choice is that it's a false one. You can run, but you cannot hide. The storms will find you. You don't get to decide whether the rain is coming; you only get to decide whether to carry an umbrella.

"But He is sleeping," you say. "He doesn't care." Don't let His seeming silence lead you to conclude that He isn't with you. He says, "I will never leave you nor forsake you" (Hebrews 13:5). As He told His disciples, "Lo, I am with you always, even to the end of the age" (Matthew 28:20).

Those are promises, and He has yet to break a promise. That He will be with you is the most certain fact of your life. What's uncertain is your grasp of that fact—your ability to trust and to build your house upon that truth. It's the only storm-proof foundation in existence.

Adoniram Judson was America's first foreign missionary. He devoted his life to God's service, and yet he lost his wife and then, three months later, their infant daughter, Maria. Judson was overcome with grief. He had been away, doing his Father's business, during his wife's illness, and he found it nearly impossible to forgive himself. He wrote, "God is to me the great Unknown. I believe in him but I find him not."[14]

God's deepest and wisest servants have felt that way. C. S. Lewis, the most influential Christian writer of the twentieth century, was grief stricken when his wife died. He could not feel God's presence. He wrote, "Go to Him when your need is desperate . . . and what do you find? A door slammed in your face, and a sound of bolting and double bolting on the inside. After that, silence."[15] In spite of these anguished expressions of aloneness, neither Judson nor Lewis had lost his faith. Sometimes the rains pound hard enough to drown out all other voices, and we struggle to hear Christ calming the storm. But that doesn't mean He isn't calming it. The storms pass, as they did for these two Christians, and we hear the voice of God once again—this time through a new wisdom tempered by our struggles. And we realize that He was there all the time.

> God is our refuge and strength,
> A very present help in trouble.
> Therefore we will not fear,
> Even though the earth be removed,
> And though the mountains be carried into the midst of
>     the sea;
> Though its waters roar and be troubled,
> Though the mountains shake with its swelling.
> PSALM 46:1-3

### God's Word Affirms That Faith Drives Out Fear

As we noted earlier, when the terrified disciples awoke Jesus in the midst of the storm, He asked them to choose between fear and faith (Mark 4:40). This is what He asks us. But why do we still fear, knowing what we do about the love and power of Jesus? I think the answer is often that our faith has not grown to full maturity.

Charles Spurgeon uses two biblical examples to show how one's faith can grow to be stronger and more complete. The first is David, who says, "Whenever I am afraid, I will trust in You" (Psalm 56:3). The second example is Isaiah, who says, "I will trust and not be afraid" (Isaiah 12:2).

Charles Spurgeon compares the faith of these two men to medicines, with Isaiah's being the stronger brand. He tells about a man who got the chills but gave thanks for the prescription that helped him through them. A neighbor said, "Thankful for that? I have something that would keep you from getting the chills in the first place!" If you have a faith that helps you deal with fear, said Spurgeon, good for you. But why not go after a higher-grade faith that is fear resistant?[16]

When the disciples stepped into the boat with Jesus, they did not even have the first kind of faith. They didn't trust in Jesus, so their fear escalated to sheer terror. When Jesus awoke and calmed the storm, the dawning realization of who He really was ratcheted their faith to a new level. Later we learn that they became utterly fearless, proclaiming the truth of the Kingdom in the face of all kinds of storms. Had they possessed mature faith that day in the boat, they could have curled up and napped with Jesus with no regard for the storm raging about them.

No matter what your trouble is, you can call on God in the midst of it, and He will calm the storm. But deep is the joy of the one who calls on God *before* the storm, for he will find that his faith drives out all fear.

# CHAPTER 8

# DEPRESSION:
## *The Fear of Mental Breakdown*

*Fear not, for I am with you; be not dismayed, for I am your
God. I will strengthen you, yes, I will help you, I will uphold
you with My righteous right hand.*

Isaiah 41:10

Alice Metzinger felt closed in, smothered. Life for her was a deep,
dark pit with no way out. There was no future, no present. But
there was certainly a past—a past that would not recede, with its
questions of the life that might have been. Alice wasn't anything
she appeared to be. She wasn't even Alice.

She was actually Katherine Power, a fugitive from the law for
nearly a quarter of a century. The real Alice Metzinger had died
as an infant, owning nothing but a name, and that name was
stolen in a moment of desperation by Katherine.

She had attended Brandeis University at the height of the
Vietnam War protest era. In 1970, she led a radical organization called the National Student Strike Force. Intoxicated
with the idea of fighting the establishment, Katherine's group
was set on supplying firearms to the Black Panther Party. The

Panthers would then overthrow the government—or at least that was the idea.

Somehow the Strike Force broke into the National Guard armory and got their hands on four hundred rounds of ammunition and a few weapons. Then they set fire to the building.

Three days later, the Strike Force robbed a bank in Brighton, Massachusetts. Katherine, at the wheel of a getaway car, watched as a policeman was gunned down by one of her accomplices. Things got out of control; all the dissenters were captured and arrested except for Katherine and a friend. They vanished into thin air with new identities until the friend was captured in 1975.

Katherine eluded authorities by changing her name, moving from town to town, lying low—lying about everything. She wondered what it would be like to live free and clear, without an alias—to be a real next-door neighbor without secrets. She had followed the path of student unrest, and now unrest was all she had.

Eventually she landed in Oregon, where she managed to find a job in the restaurant business. She became a mother and then a wife. Maybe she had finally outrun the dark cloud that had followed her since her youth. But the depression became darker, no matter what she did to erase her past.

One day Katherine simply knew she'd come to the end of the road. She had to step away from the lie of a lifetime, the lie called Alice Metzinger. She understood now that the core issue wasn't what she had done—it was about who she was, or wasn't, inside. Depression and its twin, despair, were suffocating her. Katherine turned herself in to the Boston police.

She pled guilty to armed robbery and manslaughter, and headed for prison. For her, it was just another way to be the prisoner she'd always been.

In 1999, at the age of fifty, she was released after six years behind the prison walls. She told a reporter she was "learning to live with openness and truth, rather than shame and hiddenness." She had finally faced her guilt and her depression. Katherine now devoted herself to education and philosophy, and eventually became a professor. After all the years of running a losing race against a relentless foe—clinical depression—she now felt as if she were stepping out of the deep shadow and into an April day.[1]

Life wasn't perfect, but it held one essential thing: *meaning*.

Depressed people don't always carry shocking secrets. But they do carry an overwhelming burden of despair. They can move, they can change jobs, they can change spouses, but the dark cloud never changes; in time, it simply defines the sky.

Depression is a long, twisting road through the blackness with no landmarks, no scenic vistas, and no clear destination. It leads through discouragement, despair, and despondency, and onward to death. At least that's how it feels. Those who suffer from it see no exit ramps, no route of escape. Depression is a withering illness of the spirit.

I have occasionally experienced discouragement in my life, but to the best of my knowledge, I have never crossed the line into depression. I have, however, been pastor to some who have, and I've read about the experiences of others. As I've counseled with the depressed, I've heard common themes in their accounts: empty hearts, lifeless spirits, a sadness that recurs like cancer. The dust of death comes through the words of depressed people, and I know there is no deeper disease of the soul. One counselor has described it as "a day-in, day-out, night-in, night-out, almost arterial level of agony."[2]

Fear is one of depression's evil associates. "When depression is at its most severe, paranoia is one of its cardinal features. It is fear run amok. It can feel as if both you and your world are falling apart, and you are certain there is nothing you can do about it."[3]

When our fears are identifiable, we can defend ourselves against them. But with most depression, the fears cannot be grasped and expelled. They have captured their target and won't let go.

Depressed people suffer not just in spirit but also in body, because we are holistic people. They become ill more often. They lose the energy they need for everyday life and fall into lethargy or escape into sleep—when it can be found. They struggle to think clearly or to care about anything around them.

Over the centuries, writers have described depression in bleak terms, even comparing it to hell or death. J. B. Phillips characterized it as an "almost unendurable sense of terror and alienation."[4] Author William Styron labeled depression as "hell's black depths."[5] And in Dante's *The Divine Comedy*, entrance into hell is equated with the hopelessness of despair: "Abandon all hope, ye who enter here," reads Dante's inscription over the entrance to hell.[6]

Depression soaks through flesh and bone, saturates the mind, and finally quenches the human spirit.

## THE EPIDEMIC OF DEPRESSION

Let's crunch the numbers:

- The lifetime risk of developing major depression is about 17 percent.
- Nearly seventeen million American adults and two million teens report major depression in a given year.
- Depression is now the leading cause of disability in the United States.

- The disease costs $55 billion in lowered productivity and workplace absenteeism each year.
- Antidepressant use has soared nearly 400 percent since 1988. Antidepressants are now the most common medication for young adults.[7]

These statistics lead to another question: Is the United States the world's saddest nation? The World Health Organization and Harvard Medical School suggest it could be true. They found that 9.6 percent of Americans experience bipolar disorder, major depressive disorder, or chronic minor depression over the course of a year—the highest among fourteen major nations polled.[8] The nations that received better scores than the United States included countries suffering from war, unemployment, and poverty, such as Lebanon, Mexico, and Nigeria.

If the numbers are to be believed—and I think they are— then we all know someone struggling with depression, or we may struggle with it ourselves at some point in our lives. We must realize that depression is the spiritual equal to cancer or any other terrible illness. The difference is that depression comes from within, so we often fail to recognize it. We only know that we're puzzled by the gradual changes in ourselves or our loved ones.

That's why I believe this fear needs to be discussed. I know it's a tough subject—what could be more depressing than depression? But we're no longer talking about some rare and unlikely situation. We know now that depression is a silent killer—a parasite of the heart and mind. We must be vigilant when it shows up in our own lives; we must be compassionate when it comes into the lives of those we love.

There are things we can do to keep our spirits healthy, just as there are exercises to help us keep our bodies healthy. And let's recognize up front that sometimes, despite our best of efforts, we need to reach out for help. Still, our journey toward healing is more effective when we proactively care for our souls.

The first course of action is to know the enemy. We see an array of characters in the Bible who show us what it is to be depressed—and what it requires to be healed.

## THE EXPERIENCE OF DEPRESSION

To "depress" something simply means to make it lower than it normally is. In this sense, everybody has experienced some form of depression at some point in life—thinking and functioning at a level below the norm. In fact, depression (feeling "low") has been called the common cold of the soul because most people, sooner or later, catch it.

Depression is a *human* thing—not just a non-Christian thing. A number of Christian heroes through the ages have suffered from bouts of depression, so it's dangerous to be spiritually arrogant. Rain falls on the righteous and the unrighteous, and so does depression. We are fallen creatures because we've rebelled against God, and therefore we're open to depression along with countless other bitter fruits of the Fall. The Bible testifies to that fact with its many case studies.

Listen, for example, to Moses, who was tasked with leading a whining nation of Israelites on an aimless journey through the desert (a metaphor for depression, if there ever was one). Moses cries out to God, "I am not able to bear all these people alone, because the burden is too heavy for me. If You treat me like this, please kill me here and now—if I have found favor in Your sight—and do not let me see my wretchedness!" (Numbers 11:14-15).

The "kill me now" mentality recurs in the story of Elijah, when the prophet was hounded and pursued by the wicked Queen Jezebel. "It is enough!" he prays in despair. "Now, LORD, take my life, for I am no better than my fathers!" (1 Kings 19:4).

And yet, here's what you need to know about Moses and Elijah: Jesus met these same two on the Mount of Transfiguration (Matthew 17:1-13). J. Oswald Sanders makes this point: we should be comforted that two men who reached the depths of melancholy would rise to the height of earthly glory.[9]

Yet, in depression there are no mountaintops, and transfiguration seems unimaginable. The most eloquent expressions of heartfelt despair can be found in the Scriptures. Listen to David as he expresses his fear of depression:

My tears have been my food day and night,
While they continually say to me,
"Where is your God?"
PSALM 42:3

When I kept silent, my bones grew old
Through my groaning all the day long.
For day and night Your hand was heavy upon me;
My vitality was turned into the drought of summer.
PSALM 32:3-4

Many prominent church leaders have struggled through a dark night of the soul. On a Sunday morning in 1866, the famous British preacher C. H. Spurgeon shocked his five thousand listeners when he got up in London's Metropolitan Tabernacle to begin a sermon from Isaiah 41:14. We can see why his listeners were shocked by this spiritual giant's words:

I have to speak to-day to myself; and whilst I shall be endeavoring to encourage those who are distressed and down-hearted, I shall be preaching, I trust to myself, for I need something which shall cheer my heart—Why I cannot tell, wherefore I do not know, but I have a thorn in the flesh, a messenger of Satan to buffet me; my soul is cast down within me, I feel as I had rather die than live; all that God hath done by me seems to be forgotten, and my spirit flags and my courage breaks down. . . . I need your prayers.[10]

For some in Spurgeon's audience, it was incomprehensible that the world's greatest preacher would confess to such despair.

Martin Luther, considered by many to be the father of the Protestant Reformation, was subject to such fits of darkness that he would hide himself away for days, and his family would remove all dangerous implements from the house for fear he would harm himself. In the midst of one of these times, he wrote, "For more than a week I was close to the gates of death and hell. I trembled in all my members. Christ was wholly lost. I was shaken by desperation and blasphemy of God."[11]

The Scottish reformer John Knox prayed, "Lord Jesus, receive my spirit and put an end to this miserable life."[12]

John Bunyan, who gave us the classic allegory *Pilgrim's Progress*, wrote, "Sometimes I should be assaulted with great discouragement . . . fearing that I should not be able to speak a word at all of edification . . . at which times I should have such a strange faintness and strengthlessness seize upon my body that my legs have scarce been able to carry me."[13]

You can see why I say that depression is a human condition that respects no one's spiritual stature. Depression is one more result of our fallen status—but also one more opportunity for God to be glorified.

## THE EXPRESSION OF DEPRESSION

While there are many expressions of depression in church history and in the Bible, none are more poignant than the account recorded in Job 3.

As the chapter begins, Job stands empty handed before his God. We learn in chapters 1 and 2 that everything he owned was destroyed, including his children and his health. His wife has remained, but her spirit has turned poisonous. She believes her husband should "curse God and die!" (Job 2:9). Here is a woman urging her man toward suicide.

In Job 2:11-13 we find an appraisal of the depths of Job's pain. Three of his friends come for a visit—that's what friends are for, right? When they see Job, they are shocked by his appearance and begin to weep. They proceed through the rituals of mourning (tearing their robes, sprinkling dust toward heaven) and sit in silence for seven days. Job is in visible torment, and they're afraid to speak. He's also covered with boils as part of the devil's attack. But what is on his skin is measurably less devastating than what is in his heart—the sheer blackness of despair and depression, the absence of hope.

In Job 29–30, Job talks about how far he has fallen, contrasting his present condition with his blessed life before his afflictions began. He remembers a time when life was simple. God was his friend, a part of his home who blessed him with children and prosperity and every good thing. In town, the movers and shakers applauded Job, and the young men emulated him. But all that is gone. Now he is a punch line for local comedians, a target for the cruel, a cautionary story that makes others feel better about their own lots.

The glow of divine favor in Job's life has become the dry rot of depression, and prayer has become an empty monologue delivered to a vacant sky.

Yet Job gets over the physical losses rather quickly. He worries most about the lack of answers—the sheer *why* of his bitter misfortune. What are God's purposes? What bothered Job is what most often troubles those who are depressed: no answers, no explanation, no light at the end of the tunnel—and worst of all, the silence of God.

The late pastor Ray Stedman wrote, "Few things are harder to bear than meaningless suffering. If we could see some reason for what we have to go through, we could more easily endure it. But pointless trouble is corrosive to our souls."[14] Like Jesus' disciples (John 9:1-2), Job associated suffering with sin. But Job was "blameless and upright, and one who feared God and shunned evil" (Job 1:1). So he wanted an explanation. Why did God allow everything in his life to be taken away?

What started as the collapse of Job's external life—wealth, family, health—became a battle to prevent his inner life from collapsing. As long as one maintains faith and hope, losses can be restored. But when depression sets in, faith and hope are often cut loose. With those anchors of the soul gone, it is hard for those suffering from deep despair to rise up and reverse their situations. That's why Job was paralyzed—unable to do anything except profess his innocence and ask, "Why?"

In Job 3, we see a bold display of Job's humanity as he pours out three laments. Let's explore each of them.

### *"Why Did I Arrive?" (Job 3:1-10)*

Job doesn't curse God, but he does curse the day of his own birth:

> May the day perish on which I was born,
> And the night in which it was said,
> "A male child is conceived."
> May that day be darkness;
> May God above not seek it,
> Nor the light shine upon it."
>
> JOB 3:3-4

These are obviously the words of a man who sees no future for himself.

Job later admits that his words have been rash (Job 6:2-3). For now, though, it's plain, ugly honesty—a wounded soul talking. We all know what it's like when deep anguish finds its voice in us. When life becomes irrational, our point of view follows suit, and we say things we might never have imagined.

### *"Why Did I Survive?" (Job 3:11-19)*

If Job regrets his very birth, he must also question the life made possible by his birth. "Why did I not die at birth?" he wonders. "Why did I not perish when I came from the womb?" (Job 3:11).

When life is good, we think, *Ah, this is what it's all about.* Rewarding work, healthy family, the enjoyment of God and His gifts. This is living. But what happens to that definition when the joys are systematically stripped away? Job wonders why God would let such a heartbreaking life continue.

Abraham Lincoln, another great figure tortured in the shadows, once said,

I am now the most miserable man living. If what I feel were equally distributed to the whole human family, there would not be one cheerful face on earth. Whether I shall ever be better, I cannot tell; I awfully forebode I shall not. To remain as I am is impossible; I must die to be better, it appears to me.[15]

The isolation of depression speaks in a commanding whisper: "You are alone. No one feels like you, and it's never going to get better." Abraham Lincoln, who had to reconcile a divided nation, first had to reconcile his own chaotic soul.

Despite his suffering, Job believed there had to be some solution; he knew the sum total of his sin could not translate to this level of affliction. He was sure there must be an answer, and God would reveal it someday. Still, in the third chapter, despair has the upper hand, and Job wonders why he must live through such a moment.

### "Why Am I Alive?" (Job 3:20-26)

Job's third lament is a very common one today. He is essentially saying, "Since I had to be born and I didn't die in childbirth, why can't I just die now?"

> Why is light given to him who is in misery,
> And life to the bitter of soul,
> Who long for death, but it does not come,
> And search for it more than hidden treasures;
> Who rejoice exceedingly,
> And are glad when they can find the grave?
> JOB 3:20-22

Six times in Job 3, Job asks, "Why?" This should tell us clearly that it's no sin to ask why. As He is dying on the cross, Jesus asks His Father, "Why have You forsaken Me?" (Matthew 27:46). But even Jesus received no answer. It's okay to ask the question as long as we don't get the idea that God owes us an answer. Job asked, "Why?" but God was silent.

At least six biblical figures took their own lives: Samson, Saul, Saul's armor bearer, Ahithophel, Zimri, and Judas. There is a fine line between wanting to end one's life and actually doing it. And here we must give Job credit: he never crossed that line, even though his wife suggested it (Job 2:9). His thoughts about death did not lead him to take his own life. He knew his life belonged to God and not to himself. His question to God was, "Why are You keeping me alive to endure this agony when, for all practical purposes, I am dead?"

William Barclay writes that this is Job's greatness—the courage and tenacity of belief right in the midst of the storm:

> The very greatness of Job lies in the fact that in spite of everything which tore at his heart, he never lost his grip on faith and his grip on God. Job's faith is no groveling, passive, unquestioning submission; Job struggled and questioned and sometimes even defied, but the flame of faith was never extinguished in his heart.[16]

Veterans of despair have a place in the Kingdom; we must simply hold on to the faith we have, as Job did, knowing that God has an eternal purpose for us, even if we are assailed by troubles now.

## THE EXPLANATIONS FOR DEPRESSION

As Job's drama plays out, we have the benefit of a backstage pass. We understand more than Job himself does about why these things are happening. We've been clued in to the spiritual under-currents that have brought on the storm in his life.

If only we could do the same in our own situations. We can't know the details of the spiritual warfare that ensues, or sometimes even the chemical or purely emotional founda-tions of depression. Sometimes the night clutches its mysteries tightly. But we can spend some time getting to know the terri-tory. We can learn the most common reasons people become depressed.

### Sometimes There Are Situational Causes

Put yourself in Job's sandals. You've done everything you know to live a life pleasing to God. Suddenly, you look around and find yourself worse off than people who wouldn't give God the time of day if they were standing next to a grandfather clock. Such a situation could devastate a godly person like Job. Depression doesn't always happen in the wake of disastrous circumstances, but it often does.

Job's depression was based on his situation: he had lost every-thing he valued. Some of David's depression was circumstantial as well, caused by oppression from his enemies (Psalm 42–43). For Elijah it stemmed from a sense of isolation (1 Kings 19:10).

In our own lives, there are sometimes links between what is happening to us and how we are feeling. The circumstances of life are a good place to start in searching for the cause of depres-sion. What's been going on that might explain our downcast spirits?

### Sometimes There Are Systemic Causes

I don't know who deserves credit for this observation, but I believe it is true: our souls and our bodies live so close together that they catch each other's diseases.

Dr. Martyn Lloyd-Jones was a British medical doctor who became a prominent preacher. For thirty years he served as pastor of Westminster Chapel in London. He wrote,

> There are certain physical ailments which tend to promote depression. . . . Take that great preacher who preached in London for nearly forty years in the last century—Charles Haddon Spurgeon—one of the truly great preachers of all time. That great man was subject to spiritual depression, and the main explanation in his case was undoubtedly the fact that he suffered from a gouty condition which finally killed him. . . . And there are many, I find, who come to talk to me about these matters, in whose case it seems quite clear to me that the cause of the trouble is mainly physical. Into this group, speaking generally, you can put tiredness, overstrain, illness, any form of illness. You cannot isolate the spiritual from the physical for we are body, mind and spirit. The greatest and the best Christians when they are physically weak are more prone to an attack of spiritual depression than at any other time and there are great illustrations of this in the Scriptures.[17]

### Sometimes There Are Satanic Causes

Satan attacked Job in two ways: he destroyed Job's possessions and family, and he afflicted him with boils all over his body. That is the clearest instance in Scripture of an attack of Satan leading someone into despair.

A similar attack, but with a different outcome, occurred in the life of the apostle Paul. He found himself under some kind of attack that he called "a thorn in the flesh . . . , a messenger of Satan" (2 Corinthians 12:7). We don't know who or what the "messenger" was. But we do know that God gave Paul grace to endure the attack (verse 9). We can safely say that God's grace preserved Job as well. The difference in their responses was due to the fact that Job didn't understand the satanic cause of the affliction, while Paul did.

Sometimes the devil is at the tip of the spear in the attacks we receive; other times he waits in ambush, when we're suffering from some negative but ordinary event of life. We feel disappointment or pain or rejection. We've received harsh words. It is at precisely that point that Satan attacks—when we are vulnerable and he can do the most damage.

Although Satan does not hesitate to destroy property or wealth or even our bodies, those attacks are only steps toward his ultimate target—our faith in God. If he can cause us to question God's goodness, love, fidelity, and purposes, his destruction of our property or health has accomplished his purpose.

That's why the most dangerous time for a Christian is not the moment a disastrous or disruptive event occurs. It is the hours and days after that event, when we are in the throes of confusion, pain, and frustration. That's when faith can turn toward doubt, and our *questions for* God can turn to *demands on* God. That's when a test of faith makes us vulnerable to the breakdown of faith.

When Satan attacked Jesus in the wilderness, our Lord effectively countered those attacks with truth from the Word of

God (Matthew 4:1-11). The Word of God, our sword, is the one offensive weapon in the Christian's spiritual armor. In times of spiritual warfare, it is the only way to counter the lies Satan always tells (John 8:44; Ephesians 6:17).

### Sometimes There Are Spiritual Causes

An old preacher said it this way: "God sometimes puts His children to bed in the dark."

Does God allow suffering? Yes He does, but He never concedes control. He never allows things to happen without purpose, and we can always rest in the knowledge that He is just and compassionate.

Through his suffering, Job learned an important lesson that the Bible makes abundantly clear: God is in charge. Job's suffering was more spiritual than physical—his depression stemmed more from his unanswered questions than from his loss of property, children, and health. And God never did answer Job's questions; this was part of Job's learning process. Job returned to a place of peace and prosperity because he gained a proper perspective of God. He decided to let God be God.

Here is one of the greatest lessons from the life of Job: we cannot view God as a cosmic machine into which we insert the coin of good works or sacrifice to receive a prize. That would be a simple and comfortable system—or would it? Would we really wish to receive strictly what we deserve and reap precisely as we sowed?

Job thought he was managing the system by living a conscientious life toward God. Fearing that either he or his children might offend God in some way, he regularly offered sacrifices in an attempt to maintain their ritual purity (Job 1:4-5). He assumed that his blessings from God resulted from his standing before God.

It was when God began to act in an unfamiliar way that Job didn't know what to do. Job's depression was not just because of his skin disease or even because he feared he would soon be dead, but rather because he couldn't comprehend the sovereign plan God was working for his good.

Depression might arise for any or all of the four reasons I've just named, or for other reasons. The good news is that we need not understand the darkness to recover the light. Job never got the answers he asked for. The extent of the explanation he received was that God is God and Job was not.

The mystery endured. Scripture isn't concerned with solving mysteries but with aligning paths to lead to God.

## THE EXPECTATIONS OF DEPRESSION

Someone described spiritual depression in nautical terms: "The height of the wave determines the depth of the trough that follows it."

Biblical examples certainly prove this point. In Elijah's dramatic confrontation with the prophets of Baal on Mount Carmel, God worked a mighty miracle in response to Elijah's prayer, and the pagan prophets were routed. Yet within hours of this victory, he was running for his life from Queen Jezebel. When he could run no more, he collapsed under a broom tree and said he wanted to die. On the mountain, Elijah stood strong. After the victory, he fled in fear and wished for death.

Jesus experienced a high point at the beginning of His ministry. At His baptism, He received God's anointing by the Spirit and was divinely proclaimed as God's own Son. Immediately after that mountaintop event, Satan confronted Jesus in the wilderness and attempted to get Him to renounce His allegiance to God.

The plunge from the most beautiful mountaintop is always steep and treacherous.

Over the years I've learned to expect a spiritual challenge after times of special joy or celebration. Trial always follows triumph, and to know that is to be armed and ready. But the opposite is also true. Sometimes the depth of the valley is a promise of the height of the blessing to come. We can anticipate that the path through a dark valley rises toward an elevated scene—a place where God will bless us. Valleys are defined by the high places that surround them.

Charles Haddon Spurgeon discovered that depression often came before an outpouring of God's blessing on his life:

> Before any great achievement, some measure of the same depression is very usual. . . . Such was my experience when I first became a pastor in London. My success appalled me; and the thought of the career which it seemed to open up, so far from elating me, cast me into the lowest depths. . . . Who was I that I should continue to lead so great a multitude? I would betake me to my village obscurity, or emigrate to America and find a solitary nest in the backwoods, where I might be sufficient for the things which would be demanded of me. . . . This depression comes over me whenever the Lord is preparing a larger blessing for my ministry; the cloud is black before it breaks, and overshadows before it yields its deluge of mercy. Depression has now become to me as a prophet in rough clothing.[18]

When those times of darkness come, we can find great comfort in understanding what King David and Charles Spurgeon learned. We may now be in the valley, but valleys wouldn't be valleys without surrounding mountains to ascend, and God promises to lead us upward. It will calm our anguished souls if we wait patiently on Him, "that we may obtain mercy and find grace to help in time of need" (Hebrews 4:16).

## THE ELIMINATION OF DEPRESSION

I am not a psychiatrist with a prescription pad or a plan guaranteed to remove depression. I am a pastor who has tended some of God's flocks for nearly five decades. I've ministered to people who were discouraged and, yes, at times, depressed. I've learned a few biblical principles that can help us avoid the tendency toward deep, lasting emotional distress. And in many cases, these principles will help to deal with depression once it comes.

### Reveal Your Depression

First, be honest when you are facing depression. Job is a superb model of transparency. He fills the ears of his friends with his questions and his feelings: "I will not restrain my mouth; I will speak in the anguish of my spirit; I will complain in the bitterness of my soul" (Job 7:11).

In his book *The Gospel according to Job*, Mike Mason writes,

There is a point at which any man simply throws in the towel. He does not abandon his faith, necessarily; he just gets thoroughly sick and tired of trying to put a good face on things, when things he is facing do not have anything good about them at all. This is not sin; it is just plain honesty. . . . Job is a forthright and plainspoken man, the sort of person who is not afraid to say what is on his heart, and . . . we need grudgingly to acknowledge that such uncommon honesty may be one of the greatest virtues a saint can possess.[19]

Our greatest error in the face of depression is to privatize our pain. When we make our despair known to those who care about us, we join the company of saints who have found deliverance—in part through their authenticity.

### Resist Your Depression

Jesus asked the man who was lame lying by the pool at Bethesda, "Do you want to be made well?" (John 5:6). It wasn't a rhetorical question. None of us want to be depressed, but we need to consider how intent we are to be healed. Depression distorts every feeling and stifles every desire, including the yearning for wholeness. Distress can become "the new normal," so we lose any vision of ordinary happiness. Don't put down roots when you visit depression.

One pastor who is recovering from depression writes,

You must see depression as your enemy, to be killed and buried and replaced. It is not your friend. It has come to feel comfortable and comforting, even friendly.

So what I'm calling you to see is that you need to *battle* depression, as surely as you would battle temptation to immorality or violence or theft. [Depression] is equally your enemy; it is not your friend.[20]

The good thing about the battle with depression is that, with God as our defender, it's winnable.

### Research Your Depression

Dr. Karl Menninger once took questions from an audience after speaking on the topic of mental health. Someone asked, "What would you advise a person to do if that person felt a nervous breakdown coming on?" Everyone expected the great psychiatrist to say, "Make an appointment with a psychiatrist immediately."

But he didn't. Dr. Menninger said, "Lock your house, go across [town], find someone in need and do something for him."[21]

I think Menninger's point was this: when you are in a depressed place in life, don't do what you naturally feel like doing. Don't withdraw, don't isolate, don't hunker down and "be sick." Instead, do the opposite. As best as you are able, with Christ's help, don't let the way you *feel* control you. If you don't feel the presence of God, then pursue your Christian life *by faith*. Pray, give, worship, study, serve, encourage, minister, and all the rest. We Christians walk by faith, not by sight (2 Corinthians 5:7). And that applies even when—*especially when*—we don't feel like it. It's not how we feel that counts; it's whom we trust. When you trust Him, at times you may *feel* down, but you won't be *let* down.

Other valuable kinds of research include counseling, medical checkups, and evaluation of your circumstances. "Research" your Christian life and see if you have slowly, imperceptibly, stopped doing the things that healthy Christians do. And begin doing them again—by faith. Don't dismiss this as a "mind over matter" issue or a "power of positive thinking" approach. It is nothing of the kind. It is self-examination like that of the psalmist when he says, "Why are you cast down, O my soul?" (Psalm 43:5).

## Replace Your Depression

If it makes sense to engage with people rather than avoid them, how much more should we lean into God rather than away from Him?

When your emotions are low or muted, the important question is not "What have I done wrong?" but "Whom should I turn to?" Some turn inward; others to friends; the wisest turn to God.

It has been my experience that as we tell God what we *want*, He gives us what we *need*. We frequently don't know what to pray for, but He is gracious and kind, holding higher standards for us than we have for ourselves. Job wanted answers; Paul wanted relief. But God had the grace to give them what they truly needed—more of Himself. He will do the same for you. The blessing is seldom what we expected, but it's always better than we could have dreamed.

Humility says, "God owes me nothing. He is not my servant; I am His. God is God, and I'm only me. The wisest thing I can do is to place my trust in Him." This humble understanding is the gift God gave Job at the end of his spiritual quest.

Job started by questioning God and ended up being questioned by God. After hearing God's fatherly but unanswerable questions, Job was humbled before Him. He realized the vast difference between the holy, almighty God and himself:

> Job answered the LORD and said:
> "I know that You can do everything,
> And that no purpose of Yours can be withheld from You. . . .
> I have heard of You by the hearing of the ear,
> But now my eye sees You.
> Therefore I abhor myself,
> And repent in dust and ashes."
> JOB 42:1-2, 5-6

We all question God at some point; in the end, what matters is His questioning of us. Job, with deepening insight, said, "Behold, I am vile; what shall I answer You? I lay my hand over my mouth" (Job 40:4). His breath was taken away as he saw things as they really were. Who was he, one tiny man, to question the ways of the almighty God?

To face God is to be humbled. With humility comes wisdom; with wisdom comes the strength to wait upon the Lord.

A man on vacation went swimming in the ocean. It was a glorious day, and he lost all track of his location. When he opened his eyes, he was shocked to find he was twice as far from shore as he'd thought. He was in severe danger of drowning because he was already tired from swimming, and what little strength he had left wasn't enough to get him to the beach. His spirit cried out to God for a miracle, and the answer came to him—so simple, so wonderful.

In his own strength, by flailing toward shore, he would exhaust himself and go under for good. But if he relaxed and floated, the tide would carry him toward the sand. Rather than drown him, the seas would bring him home, if he simply cooperated with their flow. It was all about trusting and waiting.

If you feel the undertow of depression slowly pulling you out into the depths, don't rage at the heavens; don't wear yourself out trying to recover. Wait on God, rest in Him, and let Him pull your spirit homeward. All the tides of this world move toward Him.

Mike Mason summarizes the impact a chapter like Job 3 can have on us:

Just the presence in Scripture of a book so dark, chaotic, and thoroughly eccentric as Job should come as an immense comfort to any suffering believer. For the book says, in effect, "This is what faith is often like. Do not be surprised if you find yourself confused, doubting, afflicted, all but crushed. It does not mean you have lost favor with God."[22]

## THE EFFECT OF DEPRESSION

Even before his testing was over, Job expressed confidence in the end result:

> He knows the way that I take;
> When He has tested me, I shall come forth as gold.
>
> JOB 23:10

After his suffering was over, Job realized his quest had been for the wrong thing. He didn't need to know *why*; he needed to know *whom*. He needed a clearer vision of how God works: "I have heard of You by the hearing of the ear, but now my eye sees You" (Job 42:5). Instead of getting what he wanted, he got what he needed—a deeper vision of God's grace and strength in his life.

Author Ed Welch points out that it's the ending that makes the story. *Romeo and Juliet* is a lovely romance until it all comes to a tragic conclusion. Some stories are almost painful until everything comes together in a happy ending. We stay on the edge of our seats at a movie because we're uncertain what will happen. A hopeful conclusion delights us.

But what if we go back to see that film again? Now we know the plot. The complications and misunderstandings and entanglements don't fool us—we know where it's all headed. It looks gloomy right now, but just wait! The faces in the seats around us are filled with worry, but we wear confident smiles. We *know*.

Life is like that for those who know God. We've read the Book. We know the ending. And though there are plot entanglements and complications, though we have our laughs and we shed genuine tears, we know how it all works out. We can't lose. God's love has the victory. Those who trust Him live happily ever after. End of story.

So yes, there will come times of deep sorrow. We will find ourselves lost and wandering occasionally, and the sky will grow dark. Even then, in the most difficult moments, we remember: *We know this plot.*[23]

Christ has the last word. And it's all right to cry, knowing that at the end of the road, He waits to dry every tear.

## CHAPTER 9

# DEATH:
## *The Fear of Dying*

*Yea, though I walk through the valley of the shadow of death,*
*I will fear no evil; for You are with me.*

PSALM 23:4

In the mid 1970s, high-tech workers in Los Angeles began constructing a new generation of spaceships. The first to be launched was the Space Shuttle *Columbia*, the flagship of NASA's new fleet.

*Columbia* blasted off April 12, 1981, and orbited the earth thirty-six times. Twenty-seven missions followed, but *Columbia*'s final trip was a flight to tragedy. While reentering earth's atmosphere at nine o'clock (EST) on the morning of February 1, 2003, the shuttle broke apart. A piece of insulating foam the size of a small briefcase had peeled off during launch sixteen days earlier and punctured one of the vessel's wings. The intense heat of reentry caused gases to penetrate the wing, triggering the catastrophe that killed the seven astronauts. Debris fell across large parts of Texas and Louisiana as thousands of people gazed upward in horror.

Several years later, a poignant report emerged about the destruction of *Columbia*. While the mission was in progress, NASA specialists studying the punctured wing questioned whether the damage was fatal. Wayne Hale, the space shuttle program manager, recalls these words of flight director Jon Harpold: "You know, there is nothing we can do about damage to the TPS [thermal protection system]. If it has been damaged it's probably better not to know. I think the crew would rather not know. Don't you think it would be better for them to have a happy successful flight and die unexpectedly during entry than to stay on orbit, knowing there was nothing to be done, until the air ran out?"[1]

Harpold's question was a speculative one—should the crew be told *if* it was determined that the damage meant doom. Further analysis, however, led mission control to conclude that Columbia's reentry would be safe. The crew was given a full report of NASA's conclusion, and no one on the ship or on the ground had any expectation that the damage would prove fatal.

So neither NASA nor the *Columbia* crew ever knew the situation was hopeless before their spacecraft broke apart 207,000 feet above Texas. Evidence shows that even in the final moments of the flight, the crew was still desperately trying to regain control of the ship and safely reenter the atmosphere.

But the hypothetical question raised by Jon Harpold remains a haunting one. What would you do if you knew the crew was doomed? Would you tell them, causing indescribable mental anguish but giving them time to say their good-byes, reflect on life, and perhaps make peace with God? Or would you remain silent, making their final hours a time of exhilaration and anticipation of reunion with their loved ones?[2]

In a way, the plight of *Columbia* resembles our own: we're flying through space on a spinning planet, and every person is subject to sudden death at any moment. None of us will escape. The difference is, we all know we are going to die, and we have the opportunity to prepare!

## OUR ATTITUDES TOWARD DEATH

*Death.* Your favorite subject? It's not mine, either. I'm not trying to cloud up your day, but I want to point out that for many people, death is the ultimate fear and the ultimate confusion. When someone dies, I hear a lot of people saying, "He's in a better place," even though before the death they tried with all their might to pray him away from that place.

Woody Allen once said, "It's not that I'm afraid of dying, I just don't want to be there when it happens."[3] Apparently he has given the matter some thought, because this comment is also attributed to him: "I don't want to achieve immortality through my work. I want to achieve immortality through not dying. I don't want to live on in the hearts of my countrymen; I would rather live on in my apartment."

We treat death as the ultimate obscene word. Rather than simply saying, "He died," we plug in an endless supply of euphemisms: "Passed on." "Went to a better place." "Was called home." "Went to sleep." "Departed this life." Or if Shakespeare is your thing, "shuffled off this mortal coil." An Internet page lists two hundred ways of saying death without saying *death*.[4] The poet John Betjeman wanted to know, "Why do people waste their breath inventing dainty names for death?"[5]

In his book *The Hour of Our Death*, historian Philippe Aries notes that death used to be taken more casually as a part of life.

Young people weren't shielded from it. Folks died at home, and the body was put on display there. People came by to weep and mourn their loss, but no one pretended a death hadn't occurred, as we often do today when we gather in little groups in the parking lot after funerals and nervously tell jokes.[6]

Because of our discomfort, we airbrush the whole experience. We pretend people aren't going to die, and we change the subject when they wish to discuss it. Then we dispatch them from this life in white, sterilized hospital corridors, cutting them off from home and the familiar. Most of us go to great lengths to avert our eyes from the reality of death.

Joseph Bayly says that death is the great leveler of the mighty and the lowly. It plays no favorites and cuts no deals:

> Dairy farmer and sales executive live in death's shadow,
> with Nobel Prize winner and prostitute, mother,
> infant, teen, old man. The hearse stands waiting for the
> surgeon who transplants a heart as well as the hopeful
> recipient, for the funeral director as well as the corpse he
> manipulates. Death spares none.[7]

Right about now, you may be thinking about skipping to the next chapter, hoping it will address a more "manageable" fear. I feel your trepidation, my friend, but just hear me out. What if I promised you that we could forever change the way you look at death—perhaps move it out of the fear category entirely? Isn't it taking up too much space in your anxiety closet? It's the idea of facing the unknown that frightens people. So let's take on this subject and, with the Bible as our guide, pull death out of the terrifying darkness once and for all.

## THE FACT OF DEATH

The Bible isn't afraid to speak of death: it calls it what it is. Words such as *die* and *death* occur nearly nine hundred times in the New King James Version of the Bible. The biblical terms for death are often graceful and poetic: "gathered to my people" (Genesis 49:29); "gather[ed] . . . to your fathers, . . . gathered to your grave in peace" (2 Kings 22:20). Who isn't moved by the image of "the valley of the shadow of death" (Psalm 23:4)? I consider the following to be the most beautiful verse in the Bible concerning the death of God's people:

Precious in the sight of the LORD
Is the death of His saints.
PSALM 116:15

From the time of Adam's fall, death in the Bible is presented as a part of life. The writer of Hebrews sums it up succinctly: "It is appointed for men to die once, but after this the judgment" (Hebrews 9:27). The countdown to death begins at birth. You and I are dying at this very moment. Given that fact, how is it possible that the Bible can treat the death of believers so lightly?

The answer lies in a paradox: though death begins when we are born, life begins when we are born again by the Spirit of God through faith in Christ. Many Christians have the mistaken notion that eternal life begins when they die. But that is not biblically accurate. Eternal life begins when we are born again into the Kingdom of God. Jesus Himself defines eternal life this way: "This is eternal life, that they may know You, the only true God, and Jesus Christ whom You have sent" (John 17:3).

If you know God through Jesus Christ, then you are

experiencing eternal life right now even though you haven't physically died. And if you are experiencing eternal life right now, death is no more than a brief interruption to that which you are already experiencing—life that has no end.

The New Testament is filled with passages conveying this positive, transitional perspective on death:

- Jesus refers to death as being "carried by the angels to Abraham's bosom" (Luke 16:22).
- Jesus tells the repentant thief who died beside Him, "Today you will be with Me in Paradise" (Luke 23:43).
- Paul describes death as being "absent from the body and . . . present with the Lord" (2 Corinthians 5:8).
- More than a dozen times death is described as "sleep"— the temporary status of the body from which it will be awakened in resurrection at the end of the age (John 11:11; Acts 7:60; 1 Thessalonians 4:13).
- Paul says to die is gain since we'll be with Christ, and he calls death "far better" than being on earth (Philippians 1:21, 23).
- When we die, our bodies (our "earthly house, this tent") will be destroyed, but we will inherit "a building from God, a house not made with hands, eternal in the heavens" (2 Corinthians 5:1).
- Death is "the last enemy that will be destroyed" (1 Corinthians 15:26).
- Those who die are "blessed" and have the ability to "rest from their labors" (Revelation 14:13).
- Jesus describes the separation of death as merely temporary: "A little while, and you will not see Me," he says. "And again a little while, and you will see Me" (John 16:16).

The Bible, then, gives us the full truth about death. It isn't something to fear, but a journey begun at birth, culminating in our final destination: being conformed to the image of Christ for all eternity (Romans 8:29).

## THE FACES OF DEATH

The word *death* means "separation." The Bible speaks of three kinds of death: physical death, which is separation of the spirit and soul from the body; spiritual death, the separation of the human spirit from God in this life; and second death, the separation from God for eternity.

James describes *physical death* in this way: "The body without the spirit is dead" (James 2:26). The death of Rachel, the wife of the Old Testament patriarch Jacob, is expressed as "her soul . . . departing" (Genesis 35:18). Solomon describes the separation this way: "The spirit will return to God who gave it" (Ecclesiastes 12:7).

While on the cross, Jesus confirmed this separation between the spiritual and the physical as He experienced it, saying, "Father, 'into Your hands I commit My spirit'" (Luke 23:46). Matthew 27:50 adds that Jesus "yielded up His spirit."

We also see the distinction between physical death and spiritual death in the account of the church's first martyr: "They stoned Stephen as he was calling on God and saying, 'Lord Jesus, receive my spirit'" (Acts 7:59). When Stephen's spirit left his body, his body fell into the state we call physical death—which isn't the cessation of one's existence, as we can see by the heavenly reception of his spirit.

In physical death, the spirit and the soul leave the body and move either into the presence of God or into isolation from God.

There are no exceptions; the statistics regarding death are 100 percent—except for Christians who are alive at the moment of the Rapture (1 Thessalonians 4:16-17). As the saying goes, death is still the number one killer in the world.

*Spiritual death* refers to our separation from God. Because of our sin, we have fallen short of the glory of God. We are separated from Him. Even though we are alive physically, we experience a separation the Bible describes as death: "The wages of sin is death" (Romans 6:23). When sin entered the world through Adam, it spread to everyone, so that all unregenerate men and women are dead spiritually—separated from God (Romans 5:12).

The last form of death, *second death*, is the final banishment from God—the final misery of the wicked in hell following the Great White Throne Judgment (Revelation 20:11) at the end of the Millennium. John describes this second death in the book of Revelation:

> The sea gave up the dead who were in it, and Death and Hades delivered up the dead who were in them. And they were judged, each one according to his works. Then Death and Hades were cast into the lake of fire. This is the second death. And anyone not found written in the Book of Life was cast into the lake of fire.
>
> REVELATION 20:13-15

I have tried to bring understanding to this subject by using a little mathematical formula: if you have been born only once, you will have to die twice. But if you have been born twice, you will have to die only once (and you may even escape that one death if Jesus returns to the earth during your lifetime).

All of us are born once (our physical birth), but if we are not born again through the Spirit and the Word of God (John 3:3-8; 1 Peter 1:23), we will die twice: once physically, when our bodies expire, and again at God's final judgment. However, if we are born the second time through trusting in Jesus Christ as our Savior, we will die physically, but then we will never die again. This is what our Lord means when He says, "I am the resurrection and the life. He who believes in Me, though he may die, he shall live. And whoever lives and believes in Me shall never die" (John 11:25-26).

I must note here that death also brings about another kind of separation—the separation from loved ones, which we feel physically, spiritually, and emotionally. The psalmist writes,

> Loved one and friend You have put far from me,
> And my acquaintances into darkness.
> PSALM 88:18

Some years ago, I confronted cancer and the possibility of my own death. My greatest fear was that I'd leave my wife and my children alone. I could see the fear and worry in their faces, and that grieved me. By the grace of God, that separation didn't come. But for some people, the pain of loss in this life is only a foretaste of the greater pain to come when believing and nonbelieving loved ones are separated forever.

In his book *Chasing Daylight: How My Forthcoming Death Transformed My Life*, Eugene O'Kelly describes his diagnosis of terminal brain cancer at age fifty-three. In 2002 he was the CEO of KPMG, one of the largest accounting and financial services companies in the world. He received his terminal diagnosis in 2005 and died four months later, leaving behind his wife and two daughters. Yet he had reflected very deeply on this eventuality when his first child was born, years before the diagnosis:

> On the day my daughter Gina was born, the nurse placed her in Corinne's arms. I moved closer to my wife and baby girl, awed by what lay before me. My newborn daughter was staggeringly beautiful. . . . Before I could touch her, she reached out, startling me, and grabbed my finger. She held on tightly.
>
> A look of shock darkened my face.
>
> That day and the next I walked around as if in a fog. Corinne picked up on my odd, distracted behavior. Finally, she confronted me.
>
> "What's wrong?" she demanded, "You're acting very strange."
>
> I looked away.
>
> "What is it?" she asked. "Tell me."
>
> I couldn't hide it any longer. "The moment she grabbed my finger," I said, "it hit me that someday I'll have to say good-bye to her."[8]

The believer, however, has a radically different perspective. We grieve, of course. We miss our loved ones with every fiber of our being, and our suffering is real. But we also know that the separation is not what it seems, that life consists of more than the visible. Deep in our mourning, our souls are kindled by the eternal hope of reunion with those we have lost, after which there will be no more parting.

Non-Christians only meet to part again; Christians only part to meet again.

There's a vast chasm of difference between those two outlooks.

As Paul points out, we need not "sorrow as others who have no hope" (1 Thessalonians 4:13). Dr. S. I. McMillen and Dr. David E. Stern observed the truth of this in their book *None of These Diseases*: "After sitting beside hundreds of deathbeds, we have seen this recurring pattern. People with a strong faith tend to die in peace. People without faith tend to die in terror and torment."[9]

In his book *Fear Not!: Death and the Afterlife from a Christian Perspective*, Ligon Duncan explains that believers are animated by a hope that affects positively this life as well as the one to come:

> The apostle Paul says emphatically, "If in this life only we have hope in Christ, we are of all people most to be pitied" (1 Cor. 15:19). "If the dead are not raised, 'Let us eat and drink, for tomorrow we die!'" (verse 32b). . . . He is not simply trusting in Christ so that this life might be more full or more prosperous; instead, he is trusting in Christ for this life and forevermore. . . . Christian hope is a hope that not only controls our present living, but also our anticipation of what will come to be beyond this life.[10]

## THE FEAR OF DEATH

I heard a story about a man who goes to the doctor for his annual physical. As he leaves, the doctor promises to call with the results. A couple of days pass before the call comes. The doctor says, "Are you seated? I'm afraid I have some bad news for you."

The man turns pale and tells the doctor to continue.

"Well," the doctor says, "you've got forty-eight hours to live."

"What?" the man stammers.

"Now for the worst," the doctor says.

"How could anything be any worse than that?" the man shouts.

"Well, it's just that I've been trying to call you since yesterday."

Calls like this happen only in bad jokes. But doctors make similar calls bearing fatal news every day. While life has no two-minute warning, time does run out. Don't we want to have our lives, our homes, and our eternal souls in order when that moment comes?

We say we want to be ready, but the problem is, death is high on our fear list. We'd rather not talk about it. So in this section of the chapter, I want to present biblical reasons that death should not be feared. If you are a Christian who remains apprehensive about death, even a little bit, I want this section to encourage you to replace your fear with biblical hope and assurance. I pray that the biblical truths presented here will move you toward faith in Christ so that His life, not your death, brings you to joyful anticipation of the future.

There are only two ways to face the future: with fear or with faith. Those who live by faith in the Son of God (Galatians 2:20) will find all their fears—especially the fear of death—consumed by the security of His person and the certainty of His promises.

### The Prince of Death Has Been Defeated

The author of the book of Hebrews declares that Jesus conquered death by death, freeing us from the fear of death:

> Inasmuch then as the children have partaken of flesh
> and blood, He Himself likewise shared in the same, that
> through death He might destroy him who had the power
> of death, that is, the devil, and release those who through
> fear of death were all their lifetime subject to bondage.
> HEBREWS 2:14-15

From the Garden of Eden until Jesus' sacrificial death, the devil used death to gain the upper hand and enjoy the last laugh. Satan stirred in people the desire to violate God's laws and then watched them reap death—the reward of their sin. Paul writes that "the sting of death is sin, and the strength of sin is the law" (1 Corinthians 15:56). It was quite a system. We failed to be obedient, and we died for it—every time.

In His death and resurrection, the Son of God played the devil's own trump card. Just as David took the sword of Goliath and cut off his head with it, Jesus took the weapon of Satan and defeated him with it. The Cross must have seemed like the ultimate victory for Satan, but it was precisely the opposite. When Christ by His own death paid the penalty for sin, He took the sting out of the devil's condemnation.

When Jesus stepped from the open tomb on Resurrection Sunday, Satan's defeat was certain. His weapon of death had been destroyed. He is still alive and active, but his failure is a foregone conclusion. He must settle for winning the smaller battles, because the war he started has been lost forever.

Satan's last hope is to convince you to live as if the victory of Christ never happened. He would love for you to be enslaved to the fear of death. The first-century Jewish philosopher Philo wrote that "nothing is so calculated to enslave the mind as fearing death."[11] The author of Hebrews, undoubtedly a learned Jewish Christian, may have been aware of Philo's words, for he expresses the same sentiment, saying those who fear death "were all their lifetime subject to bondage" (Hebrews 2:15). If you do fear death, your fright is based on a lie. It is God's truth that will set you free (John 8:32).

Steve and Ann Campbell of Hampton, Tennessee, were sitting in their breakfast room one day, reading and relaxing. Their little dog, Gigi, a Maltipoo (Maltese and poodle mix), was asleep on the bench in the bay window. Suddenly a jolt rocked the room and toppled Gigi from the bench. Nothing was hurt but the little dog's pride. The couple wondered what had caused all the commotion. They couldn't find any clues until they spotted a large hawk outside lying beneath the bay window. The bird had swooped down, talons out, to get Gigi with no regard for the protective pane of glass. A few minutes later, the hawk shook off its stupor and vanished into the sky, minus its canine snack.

The devil wants to get his talons into us. The power of the Resurrection, however, provides a pane of protection that cannot be broken. Satan may knock himself out trying, but he can't claim us. Because Christ died, we have lives that are *forgiven*; because Christ rose, we have lives that are *forever*.

### The Power of Death Has Been Destroyed

The prophet Isaiah, in an outburst of hope, predicts a day when the Lord will destroy death and restore His people:

> He will swallow up death forever,
> And the Lord God will wipe away tears from all faces;
> The rebuke of His people
> He will take away from all the earth;
> For the Lord has spoken.
> ISAIAH 25:8

Hosea, a contemporary of Isaiah, also foretells Christ's victory over death:

> I will ransom them from the power of the grave;
> I will redeem them from death.

O Death, I will be your plagues!
O Grave, I will be your destruction!

HOSEA 13:14

These two prophecies are the first in the Bible to declare that death itself would die. The New Testament leaves no doubt as to the meaning of these words:

When this corruptible has put on incorruption, and this mortal has put on immortality, then shall be brought to pass the saying that is written: "Death is swallowed up in victory."

"O Death, where is your sting?
O Hades, where is your victory?"

The sting of death is sin, and the strength of sin is the law. But thanks be to God, who gives us the victory through our Lord Jesus Christ.

1 CORINTHIANS 15:54-57

In the book of Revelation, the apostle John describes what life will be like in heaven when these prophecies are fulfilled: "God will wipe away every tear from their eyes; there shall be no more death, nor sorrow, nor crying. There shall be no more pain, for the former things have passed away" (Revelation 21:4).

The apostle Paul reminds Timothy that through His resurrection, Christ has "abolished death and brought life and immortality to light through the gospel" (2 Timothy 1:10).

And in one of the most poignant passages in the New Testament on the inviolability of God's love for His children, Paul includes death in the list of realities that will never separate us from that love:

> I am persuaded that neither death nor life, nor angels nor principalities nor powers, nor things present nor things to come, nor height nor depth, nor any other created thing, shall be able to separate us from the love of God which is in Christ Jesus our Lord.
> ROMANS 8:38-39

Jesse Irvin Overholtzer, the founder of Child Evangelism Fellowship (CEF), was growing old. He knew he had few remaining years in this life. He and his wife, Ruth, invited a young nurse from India to stay with them while she attended classes at the nearby CEF Institute. When Overholtzer suffered a seizure, she was up with him throughout the night. Yet at dawn she took off for classes as if she'd gotten a full night's sleep.

"Isn't it wonderful to be young and full of life?" Ruth said to her husband.

"Yes," Overholtzer answered, "but it is more wonderful to be old and ready to go to heaven!"[12]

### The Process of Death Has Been Described

An eleven-year-old wrote to Pope John Paul with this question: "What is it like when you die? Nobody will tell me. I just want to know, but I don't want to do it."[13] Jesus tells a story in Luke 16:19-31 that offers a penetrating view of what happens after death. In fact, this story tells us more about life after death than we might expect.

His parable concerns two men—one rich and one poor. The pauper's name is Lazarus (though not the same man Jesus raised from the dead). We don't know the rich man's name, but we know his lifestyle. He wears the finest clothing and eats the finest cuisine. He has the best of everything, and he lets everyone know about it—even Lazarus, the beggar at his gates, who hopes to be thrown a few crumbs from the bountiful table. Lazarus is not only hungry but also very ill, covered with sores that the town dogs lick. His is a miserable existence.

Lazarus, however, possesses one thing that no one can take away: his love for God. The rich man possesses one thing he cannot keep: his life. Both men die. On the other side of the gate that separates this life from eternity, the beggar Lazarus is carried by heavenly angels to the bosom of Abraham. Now he is kissed by angels rather than licked by dogs.

So it will be for you and me. We won't simply be "beamed up" to heaven. We will be carried there by angels. This passage provides one of the euphemisms we employ for death: "The angels took him." It may sound like a cliché from a Victorian greeting card, but it is biblical truth as applied to believers in Christ. On the day when you wait for the curtains to be drawn on this life, God's messengers stand ready to bear you away on life's ultimate journey. The great hymn writer Isaac Watts expressed it in fine poetry:

> Lord, when I leave this mortal ground,
> And thou shalt bid me rise and come,
> Send a beloved angel down,
> Safe to conduct my spirit home.[14]

In his children's book *Somewhere Angels*, Larry Libby suggests that God sends angels so we won't have to make that journey alone. Great voyages need great companions, and God says, "When it's your time to come, I'll send someone to bring you.

You won't need to fear; you won't need to find your own way. And the person I will send knows the way very well."[15] At the moment when you first set eyes on your forever home, an angel will be there to share your joy. As you realize you've now been made perfect, with every ailment gone, an angel will be there to laugh with you, to hear your shouts of triumph.

On that journey, Christians will experience none of the travel worries we face now—no getting lost, no missing the bus, no waiting for the next plane. God has an angel assigned to bring you home. In the face of such assurance, how can we fear?

### The Picture of Death Has Been Developed

On December 7, 1941, Rev. Peter Marshall was speaking to the cadets at Annapolis. A "day of infamy" was unfolding at Pearl Harbor, which now lay in the flames of an enemy attack. The room was filled with young men who would soon sacrifice their lives for their country. He told them the story of a dying child—a little boy with a disease who asked his mother, "What is it like to die? Does it hurt?" The mother thought for a minute, then said, "Do you remember when you were smaller, and you played very hard and fell asleep on your mommy's bed? You awoke to find yourself somehow in your own bed. Your daddy had come along, with his big, strong arms and lifted you, undressed you, put you into your pajamas as you slept. Honey, that's what death is like. It's waking up in your own room."[16]

Like this little boy, most of us are curious about the process of death. Perhaps no single verse of Scripture gives us a more comforting picture of it than the widely quoted Psalm 23:4:

Yea, though I walk through the valley of the shadow of
   death,

> I will fear no evil;
> For You are with me;
> Your rod and Your staff, they comfort me.

The sheer beauty of the passage never fails to move us, of course. But the power of this truth hits us at a deep level in times of suffering. When we face death—our own or the death of a loved one—this verse should be held close to our hearts. Its poetic phrases teach us several things.

### DEATH IS A JOURNEY, NOT A DESTINATION

> I walk through the valley. . . .
>
> PSALM 23:4

Pastor and author Leith Anderson tells of a woman who buried her husband after he lost a battle with cancer. A short time later, she found that the same disease had come for her. She could only await her reunion with the husband she had loved and lost.

When she knew she had only a few days left, the woman invited Anderson and his wife to her home. They sat with deep emotion, holding her hands as she spoke casually of the reality of death and anticipating her joy in the presence of God. She talked about her children and wanted to know all about the Andersons' kids. You'd have thought she was preparing for a cruise instead of a departure from this life.

A constant stream of friends came to comfort her, but it was the other way around. They left deeply blessed. And those who couldn't visit heard encouragement from her on the phone. Through it all, she never thought of herself. Everything she did illustrated her concern and love for others. Her hope for the afterlife enabled her to use death as an opportunity to reach out and bless as many people as possible.[17]

Most of us speak of hope for the afterlife. But the way we approach death shows what we really believe. Those committed to a biblical perspective have no reason to treat death as their greatest enemy. They see it as another journey that calls for preparation. They say their good-byes, they get their affairs in order, and they prepare their spirits for the joy of a new existence.

As we know, many people today believe this life is all there is—that physical death and spiritual death are one and the same and that their entire existence will come to an end. For people who believe this way, it's perfectly reasonable to fear death. They think it's the final curtain. Believing this life to be all there is, they clutch it tightly. To these people, life must be a source of deep frustration and even despair because it has so many limitations, so much disappointment. You come into the world, you're young and strong, then you reach the top of the hill and begin a long, sad descent—and at the bottom lurks nothing but darkness.

Christians, however, live in a brighter now because everything in life has a reason. The ups and downs point to an eternity that will fulfill all our hopes and repay all our frustrations. Poor Lazarus had reason for hope. He knew what other hurting believers know—that this world was never their home anyway. They are citizens of heaven, ambassadors of a bright reality.

We must remember that for believers and nonbelievers alike, death is not the end. We are all eternal creatures. The distinction is whether one's eternity will be brighter than a billion suns or darker than the imagination can conceive.

In the "Shepherd Psalm," David sees death not as a destination but as a journey through a dark country—a journey we make with God's hand in ours. My friend Pastor Rob Morgan describes how this journey reveals the transitory nature of death:

> Psalm 23:4 does not speak of a cave or a dead-end trail. It's a valley, which means it has an opening on both ends. . . . The emphasis is on *through*, which indicates a temporary state, a transition, a brighter path ahead, a hopeful future. For Christians, problems are always temporary and blessings always eternal (as opposed to non-Christians, whose blessings are temporal and whose problems are eternal). Valleys don't go on forever, and the road ahead is always bright for the child of God, as bright as His promises. There are no cul-de-sacs on His maps, no blind alleys in His will, no dead ends in His guidance.[18]

Paul speaks of being "absent from the body and . . . present with the Lord," indicating that the two conditions are one and the same (2 Corinthians 5:8). As James M. Campbell observed, death is an exit gate and heaven is an entrance. But the two are arranged so closely that one opens as the other shuts. When one person says that a dying person is "lying at the gates of death," another could say that, no, he is "lying at the gate of heaven." And both would have it right.[19]

### DEATH IS A SHADOW, NOT A REALITY

The valley of the shadow of death . . .

PSALM 23:4

When I was a young boy, my father was the pastor of a church in Toledo, Ohio. During his eleven-year pastorate there, the church relocated to a property that had once been a luxurious mansion.

The mansion was restored and an auditorium was built on one end of it, and that became our new church.

Behind this mansion was a huge ten-car garage. The parsonage was on the second floor of the garage in what had formerly been the servants' quarters. One of my nightly chores was to carry out the trash to containers located outside the cavernous garage. When I waited until after dark to do my chores, I had to carry the trash through the eerie, dimly lit garage. At night it was a foreboding place, filled with eerie shadows that seemed to hide unthinkable horrors. In my terror, I ran through those shadows, possibly setting new speed records for trash-and-carry.

During daylight hours I could clearly see that I was in no danger—no monsters lurked in that garage. But darkness does something to a place, doesn't it? It distorts. It becomes a canvas for the imagination. The good news is that shadows are only the deflection of light. They can frighten, but they can do no harm.

As Dr. Donald Grey Barnhouse was driving home from the funeral of his first wife, he and his children were overcome with grief. As he sought some word of comfort for his kids, a huge moving van passed them, and its shadow swept over the car. Dr. Barnhouse said, "Children, would you rather be run over by a truck or by its shadow?"

"The shadow, of course," one of the children said. "It's harmless."

"Two thousand years ago," the father said, "the truck ran over the Lord Jesus . . . in order that only its shadow might run over us."[20]

For the Christian, death is but a shadow. No longer is it the true substance of our fear; it's just a momentary obscuring of the light. Jesus' promise to every believer is this: "Because I live, you will live also" (John 14:19). He also says, "I am the resurrection and the life. He who believes in Me, though he may die, he shall live. And whoever lives and believes in Me shall never die" (John 11:25-26).

## DEATH IS LONELY, BUT YOU ARE NEVER ALONE

You are with me. . . .

PSALM 23:4

Something strange but subtle happens in Psalm 23:4. You may not have noticed, but an editor would. The narrative mode changes: *He* becomes *You.* In the first three verses, we've seen the Lord referred to in the third person: "*He* makes me to lie down; *He* restores; *He* leads me . . . for *His* name's sake." Very abruptly, however, third person becomes second person, and David says, "*You* are with me." He stops talking *about* the Shepherd and begins talking *to* Him. It's as if he has been talking about God, and then in the midst of the shadows he realizes that God is right there: "I will fear no evil; for *You* are with me." An essay becomes an intimate conversation.

It all makes beautiful sense if you've ever walked through that valley. You think about God, and suddenly you find yourself caught up in a conversation with Him. His presence suddenly changes your whole line of thought. Over the years, I've spoken to many people who were traveling their darkest roads, and they've often told me that they were never more aware of the presence of the Shepherd than when they were walking in that shadow.

Corrie ten Boom once ran into an old friend who was only going to be in town for the day. So they dispensed with small talk and had a substantial conversation together. Corrie asked him, "Are you afraid to die?"

Yes, he was, he admitted. Corrie was surprised, knowing that her friend had a deep faith in God. She asked, "Why are you afraid? You've been a believer for as long as I've known you. Surely you know Jesus won't leave you alone for one moment."

He explained that he was afraid because death was the unknown for him; he didn't know what to expect. So they began talking about Jesus and how death was also unknown to Him when He went to the Cross. He had never died before. Surely He, too, had to confront fear. But now Jesus knows all about death. He has been there. He has conquered it. And He promises never to leave or forsake us. He says He will be with us always, and the journey through death is no exception.

The old man smiled, at peace, and thanked God for the conversation.[21]

I've counseled with many people as they sat in death's waiting room, and experience has proved to me that God makes His presence known as they walk through the valley. He reaches for their hands. He whispers words of comfort and promise. And it's not limited just to the dying people themselves; it's also for those who grieve for them. They, too, walk through the valley, and God reaches to them as well.

The Bible is filled with comforting promises such as these:

God is our refuge and strength,
A very present help in trouble.
Therefore we will not fear.
PSALM 46:1-2

He Himself has said, "I will never leave you nor forsake you."
HEBREWS 13:5

Indeed, the darkness shall not hide from You,
But the night shines as the day;
The darkness and the light are both alike to You.

PSALM 139:12

We never have to walk that road alone. The Shepherd appears at our shoulder, and as we reach the gate, angels are there to attend us and usher us into the wonderful surprises that await us.

This life seems like the "real" one, but it is only a preface, and we have yet to see the first chapter. As Hungarian composer Franz Liszt expressed in the introduction to his symphonic poem *Les Preludes*, "What else is our life but a series of preludes to that unknown Hymn, the first and solemn note of which is intoned by Death?"[22] We think the story ends with death, but the truth is, death is only the beginning. The Bible assures us that what follows is too wonderful for us to understand now.

In the seven books of C. S. Lewis's Chronicles of Narnia series, four children explore another world, ruled by Aslan the Lion. In the first six books, Aslan sends them back to their home in England after each adventure. As the final book draws to its close, the children find themselves in a brilliantly enhanced Narnia, and they don't want to leave. Their own world seems pale by comparison. But Aslan has a surprise. He reveals that the railway accident that brought them to Narnia this time was a real one, and they have, in earthly terms, died and left their everyday world for the last time. "The term is over," Aslan says. "The holidays have begun. The dream is ended. This is the morning."

The great Lion then begins to transform into something that is—like the adventures facing the children—too wonderful to write about. Their lives on earth and in the old Narnia were only "the cover and the title page," and now they are truly beginning the first chapter of the real story. It is a story that "no one on earth has read: which goes on forever: in which every chapter is better than the one before."[23]

Born in 1800, a century before Lewis, John Todd also saw the significance and hope of death. Todd was a Vermont boy who at the age of six lost both parents. He lost his siblings, too, when they were divided among relatives. John was taken in by a kindly aunt. He lived with her for fifteen years until he left to study for the ministry. The years passed, and he became an effective pastor. One day he received a letter from the aunt who raised him. She was dying, and she had the same questions we all ask: "What awaits me in death? Is this the end?" John could feel her anxiety in every line she wrote.

John loved his aunt, and he sat down to answer her letter. He began with the story of a little boy of six who waited for the arrival of the woman who would become a mother to him:

> I can still recall my disappointment when instead of coming for me yourself, you sent your servant, Caesar, to fetch me.
>
> I remember my tears and my anxiety as, perched high on your horse and clinging tight to Caesar, I rode off to my new home. Night fell before we finished the journey, and I became lonely and afraid.
>
> "Do you think she'll go to bed before I get there?" I asked Caesar anxiously.
>
> "Oh no," he said reassuringly. "She'll sure stay up for you. When we get out of these here woods, you'll see her candle shining in the window."
>
> Presently we did ride out in the clearing, and there, sure enough, was your candle. I remember you were

waiting at the door, that you put your arms close about me—a tired and bewildered little boy. You had a big fire burning on the hearth, a hot supper waiting on the stove. After supper you took me to my new room, heard my prayers, and then sat beside me until I fell asleep.

Someday soon God will send for you, to take you to a new home. Don't fear the summons, the strange journey, or the dark messenger of death. God can be trusted to do as much for you as you were kind enough to do for me so many years ago. At the end of the road you will find love and a welcome awaiting, and you will be safe in God's care.[24]

John Todd painted for his aunt a picture of new life as beautiful as any person could hope for. But I can assure you that it is only a dim shadow compared to the magnificent beauty and joy awaiting us when we finally close this gate and open the new one into God's presence.

# CHAPTER 10

# DEITY:
## *The Fear of God*

*The LORD takes pleasure in those who fear Him.*

PSALM 147:11

In C. S. Lewis's Narnia book *The Silver Chair*, the schoolgirl Jill finds herself alone and desperately thirsty in an unknown wood. She knows nothing of Aslan, the Christ figure in these stories, but when she comes upon a stream, she sees the great Lion between her and the water. Though her thirst is overpowering, Jill freezes in her tracks, too petrified with terror to either advance or run.

"If you are thirsty, you may drink," the Lion says.

The terrified Jill, afraid she will be eaten, doesn't move. She says, "Will you promise not to—do anything to me, if I do come?"

"I make no promise," the Lion answers.

"I daren't come and drink," Jill replies.

"Then you will die of thirst," the Lion tells her.

Jill says she will go find another stream, but the Lion responds, "There is no other stream."[1]

Throughout the Bible God's people are admonished to fear God. Is this fear to be equated with Jill's—that of a child quivering in unmitigated terror at an all-powerful being who forces hard choices and may do anything to anyone at any time?

Harold S. Kushner, the popular rabbi and author of *When Bad Things Happen to Good People*, seems to equate the fear of God with this kind of terror. As a result, he doesn't like the idea of fearing God. In his 2009 book *Conquering Fear: Living Boldly in an Uncertain World*, he wrote,

> If there is one phrase I would like to see banished from theological discourse, it is the four words "the fear of God." I don't think much of a religion that tries to control its adherents by frightening them. . . . Where the phrase "the fear of God" occurs in the Bible, I don't believe it refers to being afraid of God. I take it to refer to the sense of awe that overwhelms us when we contemplate the greatness and majesty of God.[2]

I happen to admire Rabbi Kushner. I find his works refreshing and provocative. But on this subject, I couldn't disagree more. I think these assertions concerning the fear of God contain two mistakes.

First, Kushner seems to believe we talk far too much about the fear of God, chasing people out of churches and synagogues with this "medieval" idea. But I would assert that the opposite is true. The fear of God has been absent from any theological discourse I've heard recently. I would counter that it's the *lack* of this discussion that contributes to the mess into which this world is rapidly descending.

In his book *The Secret of the Lord*, Charles Crismier makes this very claim. He pinpoints the 1960s as the time in which "the fear of the Lord" began to embarrass people. The expression used to be common and complimentary, but today the idea appears to be almost incomprehensible to our culture. The phrase is now more likely to be mocked than respected.[3]

A. W. Tozer, a great twentieth-century pastor, also lamented this cultural change. He observed,

> The self-assurance of modern Christians, the basic
> levity present in so many of our religious gatherings,
> the shocking disrespect shown for the Person of God,
> are evidence enough of deep blindness of heart. Many
> call themselves by the name of Christ, talk much about
> God, and pray to Him sometimes, but evidently do not
> know who He is. "The fear of the Lord is a fountain of
> life," but this healing fear is today hardly found among
> Christian men.[4]

The fifty-year span between the writings of A. W. Tozer in 1961 and Charles Crismier in 2011, both lamenting the loss of a fear of God, shows that Rabbi Kushner need not worry about overemphasizing this fear. We weren't teaching it half a century ago, and we're not teaching it now. We can't wear it out when this generation hasn't even worn it *in*.

I believe the rabbi's second mistake is in his restricted definition of the word *awe*. Most people would agree that the fear of God includes awe, but it's more than that. As we explore the occurrences of this phrase throughout the Bible, you will likely be amazed to discover how ingrained the concept is in all of Scripture. I think you will agree that the definition extends far beyond the emotion of awe.

I realize Rabbi Kushner is not a follower of Christ; thus, we can't expect him to look to the New Testament as he develops his ideas. But those of us who are believers can read the book of Hebrews—perhaps the most "Jewish" of the New Testament letters—as a compelling reference that shows the fear of God as something more than mere awe.

The same God who invites us to come boldly into His presence (Hebrews 4:16; 10:19) also expects us to "serve God acceptably with reverence and *godly fear.* For our God is a consuming fire" (Hebrews 12:28-29; emphasis added).

As one who lives in Southern California and has seen consuming wildfires up close and personal, I can say that fear is an apt description of the emotion they produce. Do they also produce a sense of awe? Yes—one cannot help but be awed by flames shooting hundreds of feet in the air and consuming everything in their paths. But is it awe that causes my neighbors and me to flee for safety when these fires are on the loose? No, it is fear of dying in their presence—not because the fire has any intent of harming us, but because fire has an innate nature that can harm us if we don't respect it. So when the author of Hebrews says "our God is a consuming fire," I am not surprised to read that I should serve Him with "godly fear." Yes, God inspires overwhelming awe. But just as fire acts according to its nature, so does God. He operates according to His providential intent for His world, and we had best align ourselves with that intent to keep from getting burned.

## TWO WAYS TO FEAR GOD

Biblical references to the fear of God fall into two distinct categories. The first is awesome dread, and the second is astonished devotion. Let's explore the meaning of these two terms.

## Awesome Dread

The term *awesome dread* seems to indicate something to avoid rather than embrace. And I realize that I have been guilty of avoiding the topic myself at times because it's so easy to stress the love of God and how Jesus is a friend of sinners. But that is only one side of the equation. Unless we balance our perspective, we end up with the idea that "there's no need to be afraid of our good buddy God."[5]

So when we go to the Bible to adjust that perspective, do we discover that *fear* is just a synonym for *awe* and *reverence*? As a matter of fact, no. In Genesis, where the word *fear* is first used in the Bible, we read about God walking in the Garden just after Adam and Eve had eaten the forbidden fruit. Apparently God made a practice of enjoying fellowship with them "in the garden in the cool of the day" (Genesis 3:8). But after Adam and Eve sinned and God drew near, Adam hid himself from God's presence. He explains, "I heard Your voice in the garden, and I was afraid because I was naked; and I hid myself" (Genesis 3:10).

I assure you that what Adam felt at that moment was much more than awe and reverence for his Creator. He was stone-cold afraid—exactly as he should have been. God had warned him that if he ate of the forbidden tree, he would die (Genesis 3:3).

Christian author and philosophy professor Peter Kreeft explains:

> Terror is a bond, however primitive, between us and God. . . . It is supposed to be there because we are born original sinners, and the sinful self is naturally and rightly terrified of the goodness of God, which is sin's enemy.[6]

A few chapters after the incident in Genesis 3, we find the phrase *the fear of God* for the first time. Genesis 20 tells the story of Abraham's second lie concerning his wife, Sarah. On both occasions, he has claimed that Sarah is his sister. The problem is that he's among some dangerous people, and he has a beautiful wife. He thinks it possible that the king, Abimelech, would kill to add such a wife to his harem. So Abraham lies, hoping the deception will save his skin.

Sarah is saved from dishonor only because God comes to Abimelech in a dream and reveals her true identity. Abimelech is angry; he wants Abraham to explain this deception. *Why, Abraham?* Abraham answers: "Because I thought, surely the fear of God is not in this place" (Genesis 20:11).

We don't fear what we don't know. That's why little ones touch hot stoves once. People who are without God are without fear of Him, so they don't hesitate to act in immoral ways. In Romans 3, Paul the apostle gives us a long list of complaints about ungodly people, and in verse 18 he concludes it by quoting Psalm 36:1: "There is no fear of God before [their] eyes."

But those who know God fear Him. They find this fear so overwhelming that they cannot stand on their feet in His presence. We read that,

- Abraham "fell on his face" (Genesis 17:3).
- Moses "hid his face, for he was afraid to look upon God" (Exodus 3:6).
- Balaam "bowed his head and fell flat on his face" (Numbers 22:31).
- Joshua "fell on his face to the earth and worshiped" (Joshua 5:14).

- Gideon and Manoah cried out in alarm lest they should die (Judges 6:22-23; 13:20-22). Isaiah felt that he was undone (Isaiah 6:5).
- Ezekiel fell on his face (Ezekiel 1:28).
- Daniel felt like a man who had been drained of all his strength (Daniel 10:8).
- The three disciples who saw Jesus' face shining like the sun "fell on their faces and were greatly afraid" (Matthew 17:6).
- Saul of Tarsus fell to the ground and was left blind (Acts 9:4-9; 22:11).

Many Christians today seem to think the Incarnation eliminated the need for any fear of God. In Jesus, God came to earth in the form of a man, giving us an accessible God, one we could love and relate to as a friend. Those who adopt this mind-set as the whole truth often describe Jesus as a gentle, compassionate, loving person. He was (and is) all that, but this is not the entire picture. Forgotten is the fearsome Jesus who took a whip and single-handedly drove from the Temple a mass of thieving merchants. You can be sure that those around Him felt fear. Later, Jewish leaders came to arrest our Lord, saying they were looking for Jesus of Nazareth. "When [Jesus] said to them, 'I am He,' they drew back and fell to the ground" (John 18:6). You can be sure that these men also felt fear.

It is in the book of Revelation that we witness some of the most terrifying depictions of our Lord. For example, when John saw the risen Christ, he fell at His feet as dead (Revelation 1:17). This was not a voluntary act of worship but an instinctive reaction of fear. Even though John knew this Jesus personally and had laid his head upon His chest (John 13:25), it is not a surprise that he fell at Jesus' feet as dead. He was overwhelmed by the majesty of the glorified Son of Man.

The apostle Peter gives us what is perhaps the primary reason for our awe and dread of God. After a night of unsuccessful fishing, Peter was discouraged. Then Jesus performed a miracle that suddenly overloaded Peter's nets. "When Simon Peter saw it, he fell down at Jesus' knees, saying, 'Depart from me, for I am a sinful man, O Lord!'" (Luke 5:8). Awe and dread are natural responses of the imperfect to the perfect, of the marred to the beautiful, of the contaminated to the pure, of the powerless to the powerful.

I believe we have lost our sense of how far our sin separates us from God. As a result of sin, Paul tells us in Romans 5, we have actually become God's enemies. As imperfect, marred, contaminated, powerless sinners, we cannot imagine what it will be like to stand—or more accurately, to try to stand—in the august presence of the most beautiful, perfect, pure, and powerful being in the universe. It's a little like having a sagging, aging, blemished body and having to stand naked before the most beautiful person in existence.

That, I believe, is the feeling that washed over Peter in his fishing boat that day. Even though he loved Jesus dearly and knew that Jesus loved him and had his best interests at heart, Peter's awe and dread came from his realization of the enormous difference between his sinfulness and Jesus' perfection.

The prophet Isaiah puts it this way:

The LORD of hosts, Him you shall hallow;
Let Him be your fear,
And let Him be your dread.
ISAIAH 8:13

## Astonished Devotion

If awe and dread are appropriate responses to God, how do we reconcile that with Paul's confident statement in Romans 8:1? "There is therefore now no condemnation to those who are in Christ Jesus." As believers in Christ, we know we can live with absolutely no fear of the wrath of God. That's an assurance engraved in eternity.

This brings up an important question. If Christ has removed the need for fear of God's wrath, do we really need to fear God at all? Paul answers by telling us that fear still has its place. He instructs his friends in Philippi to "work out your own salvation with fear and trembling" (Philippians 2:12). Peter also affirms the role of fear when he admonishes us, "Conduct yourselves throughout the time of your stay here in fear" (1 Peter 1:17). Why should we continue to fear God if His grace removes the consequences of His wrath?

We find the explanation in the Bible's second conception of fear. For active followers of Jesus Christ, this understanding is the most meaningful for everyday living. We fear God by honoring, reverencing, and cherishing Him. His greatness and majesty reduce us to an overpowering sense of awe that is not focused only on His wrath and judgment but also on His transcendent glory, which is like nothing else we can confront in this world. It leaves us all but speechless.

But wait—isn't this the position of Rabbi Kushner, with whom I disagreed at the beginning of this chapter?

No. Rabbi Kushner rejects out of hand the need to ever fear God's power or judgment, while I contend that such fear is the healthy basis for all other fears (such as awe and respect) that we have for God. It is God's omnipotence, His consuming holiness, and His right to judge that make Him worthy to be feared. But when you add to these character traits those that are warmer and more appealing by human standards—His love, compassion, grace, mercy, and patience—we stand in astonishment at the revelation of His character.

Though He had every right to judge the human race, in astounding mercy He sent His own Son to stand in judgment for us. So to fear only God's power with trembling and dread without fearing (or respecting) His astonishing love is an incomplete response that diminishes our experience and enjoyment of Him. Pastor and scholar Sinclair Ferguson describes this fear as "that indefinable mixture of reverence, fear, pleasure, joy and awe which fills our hearts when we realize who God is and what He has done for us."[7]

As he so often does, A. W. Tozer has just the right words to describe this fear: "I believe that the reverential fear of God mixed with love and fascination and astonishment and admiration and devotion is the most enjoyable state and the most satisfying emotion the human soul can know."[8]

According to theologian John Murray, "the fear of God . . . is the fear which constrains adoration and love. It is the fear which consists in awe, reverence, honour, and worship, and all of these on the highest level of exercise. It is the reflex in our consciousness of the transcendent majesty and holiness of God."[9]

When we truly fear God, our fear of other things and other people begins to wane. Big fears make little fears go away. We can spend our days worrying about a host of daily challenges, but let the word *cancer* be mentioned in the same sentence with our name, and all our daily anxieties disappear into the cloud of a bigger fear. God, of course, is not a malevolent force like cancer. This means that when our smaller fears are absorbed by fear of

Him, our lives gain security rather than become debilitated by the terror of an uncertain future.

God is the biggest fear of all. In fact, God is referred to as "the Fear" twice in Genesis 31: "Unless the God of my father, the God of Abraham and the Fear of Isaac, had been with me . . . And Jacob swore by the Fear of his father Isaac" (verses 42, 53). "The Fear" is a figure of speech here in which the emotion is personified as the person Himself—in this case, God.

It is when other fears take precedence over God that we get into trouble. This is what happened to the Israelites who lived during the time of Isaiah. Listen to God's words to them:

> Of whom have you been afraid, or feared,
> That you have lied
> And not remembered Me,
> Nor taken it to your heart?
> Is it not because I have held My peace from of old
> That you do not fear Me?
> ISAIAH 57:11

In losing their fear of God, the nation of Judah had become unduly afraid of false pagan gods. They no longer felt "astonished devotion" because they had lost the wonder of who God is.

Vance Havner tells us how easily we, too, can slip into Judah's error:

> It is easy to lose the wonder. The spirit of the age is
> against us. Iniquity abounds and the love of many waxes
> cold. We know too much. We have tried all the thrills.
> . . . A lot of religious activity today has lost the wonder.
> We engage in shoptalk about men and methods and

movement, but we do not exult in the wonderful news that Christ died and rose again.[10]

Ravi Zacharias said, "The older you get, the more it takes to fill your heart with wonder, and only God is big enough to do that."[11] No matter how old we are, we all need astonished devotion, which is the exhilarating element we find in the fear of God.

## WHY WE SHOULD FEAR GOD

I have summarized the two kinds of fear of God as awesome dread and astonished devotion. Now I want to combine those two characterizations into a unifying theme by asking *why*. Why should we fear God? We will look at three reasons: because of who He is, because of what He has done, and because of what He continues to do today.

### We Are to Fear God because of Who He Is

The very nature of God—His unequaled majesty, His unparalleled magnificence, His unmeasured beauty—should cause us to fear Him. There is no one like Him, and this is the primary reason He should inspire awe in us. Psalm 89 asks, "Who in the heavens can be compared to the LORD? Who among the sons of the mighty can be likened to the LORD?" The psalmist's answer is an implied "no one," meaning God is to be "held in reverence by all those around Him" (verses 6-7).

The prophet Jeremiah set up this truth as a premise and drew a logical conclusion: since there is no one like God, therefore all people should fear Him—in other words, dread His power and be devoted to His person (Jeremiah 10:6-7). As Peter Kreeft explains, "The 'fear of the Lord' is something that takes its specific character from its object, from the Lord. It is awe. It is worship. It is wonder. It is absolute adoration."[12] And it is due to the Lord simply because of who He is.

### We Are to Fear God because of What He Has Done

When we fear God for who He is, it won't be long until we fear Him for what He has done.

When the Israelites were liberated from Egyptian bondage, they "saw the great work which the LORD had done in Egypt; so the people feared the LORD, and believed the LORD and His servant Moses" (Exodus 14:31). Along with Moses, they sang a song of worship and gratitude:

> Who is like You, O LORD, among the gods?
> Who is like You, glorious in holiness,
> Fearful in praises, doing wonders?
> EXODUS 15:11

Perhaps the most spectacular demonstration of God's work in the past is Creation itself. The psalmist reminds us that the created world gives us additional cause to fear the Lord for what He has done:

> By the word of the LORD the heavens were made,
> And all the host of them by the breath of His mouth.
> He gathers the waters of the sea together as a heap;
> He lays up the deep in storehouses.
> Let all the earth fear the LORD;
> Let all the inhabitants of the world stand in awe of Him.
> For He spoke, and it was done;
> He commanded, and it stood fast.
> PSALM 33:6-9

Evidence of God's power in creation exists all around us. Paul Thigpen has written of standing behind Niagara Falls for the first time. He could hardly cope with the colossal scale of the natural wonder—the unleashed energy, the ear-splitting tumult of the waters plummeting and crashing into the rocks below. Why did he feel such fear? He was well protected from any possibility of falling in. Rationally, he knew he was perfectly safe. Yet his heart pounded. It was impossible for him to avoid thinking of what *could* happen if his body were hurled downward by that flood. He would be crushed, obliterated. His imagination pushed everything from his mind but the awesome fear those falls evoked.

And yet Niagara wouldn't make God's top-ten list of spectacular creations. Those tons of plummeting water are less than a drop in the bucket compared to the galaxies He has tossed throughout the heavens. Thigpen asks,

> How much more should our hearts pound with fear in
> His presence? We're only grains of sand on the shore
> of His infinity, fleeting seconds in His eternity. He is
> utterly greater than all the greatness we've ever witnessed,
> fantastically more powerful than all the powers we've
> ever encountered, inconceivably more intelligent than
> all the most brilliant minds we've ever known or known
> about.[13]

Yes, we are redeemed and rescued in Christ. We stand on sure footing with God, even as a man stands on the rock and watches Niagara. Yet our fear of His power is utterly appropriate. If our mind is awake to His hand in the formation of the universe, fearful awe of what He has done is the only natural response.

## We Are to Fear God because of What He Is Doing

Israel witnessed firsthand what God was doing when they camped before Mount Sinai to receive the law. They heard thunder rumbling across the horizon. They saw lightning slash violent gashes across the firmament. The mysterious sound of trumpets blared as smoke rose from the mountain toward heaven.

How would you have responded? The people, quaking with fear, were terrified at what God was doing. They pleaded with Moses to go up the mountain, speak with God, and bring His Word back to them. They were convinced that to hear the voice of a God with such power would surely be their death. Moses replies, "Do not fear; for God has come to test you, and that His fear may be before you, so that you may not sin" (Exodus 20:20). In other words, God was showing them His power in order to focus their attention on the need to obey Him and the law He was about to give them.

The psalmist says, "Come and see the works of God; He is awesome in His doing toward the sons of men" (Psalm 66:5). What is He doing among us today that should inspire such awe or fear? We could make an endless list, but let's focus on one work that is vital to us: forgiveness.

If you wonder why forgiveness should move us to fear, consider what God is doing for us compared to what He could have done. As the prophet Joel says, "Return to the LORD your God, for He is gracious and merciful, slow to anger, and of great kindness; and He relents from doing harm" (Joel 2:13). Clearly, God, who is perfect, could have resorted to deadly anger at us for our sin. But instead, "He relents from doing harm." His continuing love for us is the only thing that sustains us and moves

Him to offer forgiveness instead of our deserved destruction. As another psalm tells us,

> If You, LORD, should mark iniquities,
> O Lord, who could stand?
> But there is forgiveness with You,
> That You may be feared.
>
> PSALM 130:3-4

These verses point us toward 1 John 1:9, a verse we tightly embrace as believers: "If we confess our sins, He is faithful and just to forgive us our sins and to cleanse us from all unrighteousness." That's not the equivalent of sending a bit more dirty laundry to the cleaners; it's a miracle that shakes the fabric of the universe. It should shake you and me.

Forgiveness is a work that God is doing in our lives right now, putting our sins away from us and remaking us into His own image. Paul says we can be "confident of this very thing, that He who has begun a good work in you will complete it until the day of Jesus Christ" (Philippians 1:6).

How many times have you prayed for and received forgiveness of your sins? Many, I would hope. But the question is this: How much *astonishing devotion* does forgiveness generate in your heart? Has the incredible reality of Christ's work ever moved you to tears, or do you simply move on without giving it a second thought? Have you, like Paul Thigpen at the waterfall, ever thought with fear how you could have been plunged into the depths of hopelessness and eternal loss without God's miracle of forgiveness?

The gracious forgiveness God offers ought to make our devotion to Him grow and our humility deepen so that we see even more of the magnificence of God. I'm talking about an ever-growing awareness that "in Him we live and move and have our being" (Acts 17:28). Every breath we take is a precious gift of God's sustaining grace. And for that sustenance, God deserves our fear—our never-ending devotion.

## IS IT POSSIBLE TO LOVE GOD AND FEAR HIM AT THE SAME TIME?

> There is no fear in love; but perfect love casts out fear, because fear involves torment. But he who fears has not been made perfect in love.
>
> 1 JOHN 4:18

This verse from the New Testament raises a perplexing question. Is it possible to love God and fear Him at the same time? The Bible says it is. In several places, the Old Testament commands us to both love God and fear Him. For instance: "Now, Israel, what does the LORD your God require of you, but to fear the LORD your God, to walk in all His ways and to love Him, to serve the LORD your God with all your heart and with all your soul?"(Deuteronomy 10:12).

This mingling of love and fear captures our response to two attributes of God: mercy and judgment. Paul addresses both in this passage from Romans: "Consider the goodness and severity of God: on those who fell, severity; but toward you, goodness, if you continue in His goodness. Otherwise you also will be cut off" (Romans 11:22).

The psalmist finds no contradiction in the simultaneous acts of love and fear. In Psalm 118, we are given this reason to love God: "Let those who fear the LORD now say, "His mercy endures forever'" (verse 4). And Psalm 76 shows how God is to be feared: "You, Yourself, are to be feared; and who may stand in Your presence when once You are angry?" (verse 7).

On many occasions throughout my forty years of ministry, people have questioned me about the subject of God's judgment. Often they say something like this: "My God would never send anybody to hell or punish someone for doing evil. My God is a God of love."

I usually answer by telling them that their God does not exist. There is a God to love and there is a God to fear, and He is one and the same! Did He not judge His own Son as a demonstration of His love for the world? And did He not then show His love for the Son He judged by raising Him from the dead? How silly to think that if He is a loving God, He cannot also be a fearsome God. The two attributes complement each other.

For one of the best depictions I've read of the ability to both love and fear God at the same time, we must journey back through the wardrobe to C. S. Lewis's Narnia. In his tale *The Lion, the Witch, and the Wardrobe*, a group of children hear about Aslan, the great Lion who symbolizes Christ. He is no cuddly, fairy-tale animal, for the children are told that few can stand before him without their knees knocking. One of the children asks, "Then he isn't safe?"

Mrs. Beaver, who knows the Lion well, replies that he isn't safe but he's *good*. He is a mighty king—a fearsome and loving one. When the children meet the Lion, their fear is nothing like the quaking, unmitigated terror of Jill, whom we met at the opening of this chapter. Lewis tells us that people often "think that a thing cannot be good and terrible at the same time. If the children had ever thought so, they were cured of it now."[14]

We, too, need to be cured of our weak conceptions of a tame

and innocuous God—a God with all the power to bless but none to terrify.

Another way to understand the relationship between fearing God and loving Him is to think of a father who instructs his little daughter not to play in the street. When she ventures into the street, she quickly learns that her father's discipline is swift and strict. As a result, she stays in her yard out of fear of him. As she grows older, she realizes that her father's sternness is for her own protection—a result of his love. Thus her fear dissolves, and she loves her father all the more.

Deep down, we want a God we can fear. We want Him to be a powerful Father, an overcoming Father—one with the power to keep us safe, one who loves us with the fury of a lion.

## PROMISES FOR THOSE WHO FEAR GOD

When we consider both dimensions of the fear of God— awesome dread and astonished devotion—we discover that the Bible promises abundant benefits for those who hold these fears. The following list of seven promises summarizes why it is wise to fear God. I present them mostly without comment, because I believe they will minister to your heart in their raw beauty and blessing.

### The Promise of Provision

Oh, fear the LORD, you His saints!
There is no want to those who fear Him.
The young lions lack and suffer hunger;
But those who seek the LORD shall not lack
    any good thing.

PSALM 34:9-10

### The Promise of Protection

Behold, the eye of the LORD is on those who fear Him,
On those who hope in His mercy,
To deliver their soul from death,
And to keep them alive in famine.

PSALM 33:18-19

### The Promise of Purity

As far as the east is from the west,
So far has He removed our transgressions from us.
As a father pities his children,
So the LORD pities those who fear Him.

PSALM 103:12-13

Having these promises, beloved, let us cleanse ourselves
from all filthiness of the flesh and spirit, perfecting
holiness in the fear of God.

2 CORINTHIANS 7:1

According to these verses, godly fear is a necessary ingredient in sanctification. The fear of God is not only the key to our knowledge of God, it is also essential to our maturity as believers.

### The Promise of Prosperity

Blessed is every one who fears the LORD,
Who walks in His ways.
When you eat the labor of your hands,
You shall be happy, and it shall be well with you.
Your wife shall be like a fruitful vine
In the very heart of your house,
Your children like olive plants
All around your table.

Behold, thus shall the man be blessed
Who fears the LORD.

PSALM 128:1-4

### The Promise of Prolonged Days

The fear of the LORD prolongs days,
But the years of the wicked will be shortened.

PROVERBS 10:27

### The Promise of Privilege

The prophet Malachi says that God keeps the words of those who fear the Lord in a special book of remembrance:

Those who feared the LORD spoke to one another,
And the LORD listened and heard them;
So a book of remembrance was written before Him
For those who fear the LORD
And who meditate on His name.

MALACHI 3:16

### The Promise of Perpetuity

Oh, that they had such a heart in them that they would fear Me and always keep all My commandments, that it might be well with them and with their children forever!

DEUTERONOMY 5:29

The mercy of the LORD is from everlasting to everlasting
On those who fear Him,
And His righteousness to children's children.

PSALM 103:17

These are only a sampling of the outpouring of promises the Bible gives to those who fear the Lord. They certainly undermine any notion that God is simply a power-hungry tyrant, riding roughshod over the human race to satisfy some galaxy-sized divine ego.

It's true that there is a consequence for not fearing God, but it's not as if God is a shylock exacting a pound of flesh for our failure. Instead, we face the consequence of missing the blessings described above. It's more like the consequence of a child missing out on Christmas morning. Who would want to forgo the spiritual treasures of fearing God?

Yet He leaves the choice to us.

## LEARNING TO FEAR THE LORD

When we begin to understand the blessings that can be ours by fearing God, we will want to begin doing it. Is it possible to learn how to fear God? The Bible tells us we can. In fact, the following verses show that God is eager to teach us to fear Him. As He is preparing to give His law to Israel, He instructs Moses, "Gather the people to Me, and I will let them hear My words, that they may learn to fear Me all the days they live on the earth, and that they may teach their children" (Deuteronomy 4:10).

King David writes,

Come, you children, listen to me;
I will teach you the fear of the LORD.
PSALM 34:11

Teach me Your way, O LORD;
I will walk in Your truth;
Unite my heart to fear Your name.
PSALM 86:11

Every king who took the throne of Israel was required to learn the fear of the Lord, write out God's law, keep it in a priestly book, and hold it by his side for life. He was instructed to maintain a humble heart and be true to the commandments. If he did these things, he was promised that his days and the days of his people would be lengthened (Deuteronomy 17:18-20).

How do we learn to fear God? Like the hopeful king, we begin by reading and obeying the Word of God.

Praise the LORD!
Blessed is the man who fears the LORD,
Who delights greatly in His commandments.
PSALM 112:1

The fear of the LORD is the beginning of wisdom;
A good understanding have all those who do His
     commandments.
His praise endures forever.
PSALM 111:10

And it wasn't just Israel's leaders who were expected to learn the fear of the Lord. God commanded all the people to gather every seven years for a special public reading of the law (Deuteronomy 31:12-13).

One of God's great generational teaching tools was the use of memorials. For example, when Israel crossed the Jordan River and entered Canaan for the first time, the Lord instructed the people to commemorate the event. It was quite a moment: the Lord had rolled back the waters, creating a dry riverbed to facilitate the crossing. After they made their way across, God had Joshua appoint twelve men, one from each tribe, to select a stone and carry it on his shoulders to Gilgal on the west side of the river. There Joshua set up the stones as a monument and announced that in future times when children asked their fathers about the stones, the great story of God's faithfulness could be told, "that all the peoples of the earth may know the hand of the LORD, that it is mighty, that you may fear the LORD your God forever" (Joshua 4:24).

I wonder if we are losing the fear of God in our churches and in our culture because we have no "memorial" stories to share with our children and grandchildren. Do we tell them how God has blessed us as we have lived a God-fearing life? Do we have any miracles that we can communicate to the next generation?

## THE CONCLUSION OF THE WHOLE MATTER

Solomon spent his life questing for meaning and significance, and he concludes that it was wrapped up—yes—in "fearing God."

Let us hear the conclusion of the whole matter:
Fear God and keep His commandments,
For this is man's all.
ECCLESIASTES 12:13

The last words that someone speaks before his death are often considered highly significant. With that in mind, consider the last words of David the king:

He who rules over men must be just,
Ruling in the fear of God.
2 SAMUEL 23:3

And the final words of Joshua:

Fear the LORD, serve Him in sincerity and in truth, and
put away the gods which your fathers served on the other
side of the River and in Egypt. Serve the LORD!
JOSHUA 24:14

Did you realize the Bible has so much to say about the fear of
God? Would it surprise you to know that this fear has played a
large role throughout church history? Times of spectacular spiritual revival have always been sparked by a renewal of the fear of
God. The best example is the preaching of Jonathan Edwards
during the First Great Awakening. During that era, Edwards,
George Whitefield, and others preached on God's judgment,
which brought a sense of terror over the audiences. It's hard for
us to imagine today how Edwards's famous sermon "Sinners in
the Hands of an Angry God" brought on moaning and weeping
and prompted listeners to grip tightly to pews and posts to keep
themselves from tumbling to the floor.

Reverend Joseph H. Weber, a Methodist evangelist who witnessed a revival in the town of Algona, Iowa, wrote, "It seems
as if many more sinners are moved by fear than love."[15] Scottish
evangelist Duncan Campbell said, "It is an entire town gripped
by the fear of God, causing an awareness of God coming over the
whole community."[16] During the Irish revival of 1857, a thirty-
four-year-old man fell to his knees in the street, crying out in
deep agony. People came rushing to his aid, asking who had
attacked him. But he would only cry out, "Unclean! Unclean!
God be merciful to me, a sinner!"[17]

Wesley L. Duewel, in his book *Revival Fire*, said that the fear of
God was so sudden and so powerful in these times of revival that

whole communities came to Christ. Hardened men began weeping. Miracles occurred. Addicts were made clean, homes were restored, and local crime was all but wiped out. The fear of God changed everything. Duewel goes on to record this quote: "They were first affected with awe and fear—then they were bathed in tears—then filled with love unspeakable."[18]

It's a sad fact that something so well established in the history books is so difficult for us to visualize today. As a culture, we have no fear of God; so, as Dostoyevsky said, "All things are permissible." We see no miracles. We are flooded with addictions; broken homes; and rampant, uncontrollable crime. Yet some Christians say we need less "fear of God" in our teaching, though they're all for "love of God" talk. But as we have seen, the road to love leads right through the fear of God.

I will close with a passage from pastor and author John Piper, who imagines a scenario from nature to illustrate what it means to fear God's power and protection:

> Suppose you were exploring an unknown glacier in the north of Greenland in the dead of winter. Just as you reach a sheer cliff with a spectacular view of miles and miles of jagged ice and mountains of snow, a terrible storm breaks in. The wind is so strong that the fear rises in your heart that it might blow you over the cliff. But in the midst of the storm you discover a cleft in the ice where you can hide. Here you feel secure. But, even though secure, the awesome might of the storm rages on, and you watch it with a kind of trembling pleasure as it surges out across the distant glaciers.
>
> At first there was the fear that this terrible storm and awesome terrain might claim your life. But then

you found a refuge and gained the hope that you would
be safe. But not everything in the feeling called fear
vanished from your heart. Only the life-threatening part.
There remained the trembling, the awe, the wonder, the
feeling that you would never want to tangle with such a
storm or be the adversary of such a power.

And so it is with God. . . . The fear of God is what
is left of the storm when you have a safe place to
watch right in the middle of it. . . . Hope turns fear
into a trembling and peaceful wonder; and fear takes
everything trivial out of hope and makes it earnest and
profound. The terrors of God make the pleasures of his
people intense. The fireside fellowship is all the sweeter
when the storm is howling outside the cottage.[19]

I am thankful that my God is a fearsome God. My love for
Him is all the deeper for the fear that His love has answered. The
storm rages all around, but I am safe and secure. I love my God.
And I fear Him. And I love Him because I fear Him.

# Epilogue

What are *you* afraid of?

In this book I've addressed nine of the most common human fears. But recently I discovered one fear that pretty well encompasses them all. I found it on an Internet site where people were invited to share their deepest fears. Here is what one man wrote: "Life, it's my biggest fear, it frightens me. . . . Where are we headed? If we go on, I hate to think where we'll be, in ten years' time!"[1]

That just about sums it up, doesn't it? When we're afraid of life itself, we're pretty much afraid of everything.

From a certain perspective, the man has a point. As I have said many times in this book, in this world we cannot avoid fearful situations. It's a fallen world, and that means evil has a foothold in every corner of it. And from a human perspective, that can be frightening. Not only does the world's fallen status affect people's hearts, darkening their motivations and contaminating their love, it also affects the entire scope of the world—its weather, its flora and fauna, and its subjection to disease and decay.

What do we mean when we say it's a fallen world? Why would God create such a world in which pain, decay, hate, disease, and death run rampant? The answer is simple: God didn't create that world. The world He created was perfect and utterly free from anything evil or fearful. It was man and woman, to whom God paid the incredible compliment of freedom, who caused the fall of the world by their own rebellion against Him.

As a result of their disobedience, the world was invaded with all the evils we now see and experience—disease, disaster, death, and fear. This is the world we inherited from our primeval parents. We're sleeping in the bed the human family has made.

In addition to these evils, the Fall inflicted on us one more thing: guilt. Something in our hearts retains the knowledge of how things should be—the ideal, the perfection God intended for us. We feel it every time our angry words hurt a friend, when we fail to help someone in need, when we lie or cheat or steal. That bothersome thing called conscience stings us with the mental pangs of guilt. Conscience is not a perfect guide—even it can be misshapen and misdirected. But it still points close enough to moral true north to tell us there is a standard of rightness over-arching the universe, and we are out of step with it.

We would like to do better; we would like to improve ourselves so we no longer do bad things. But the harder we try, the more we realize that we can't get there on our own. Doing or even thinking perfectly is out of our fallen reach. This produces guilt, and guilt produces the greatest fear of all—the fear that we are separated from the perfect and most holy God.

This fear explains why ancient peoples were terrified by

lightning, thunder, fires, floods, and storms. They instinctively felt their misalignment and sensed that there were powers above them that needed to be appeased. Even today, we feel this sense of misalignment. Somewhere deep in our hearts we realize that our actions and thoughts offend the only One who matters—God.

Amazingly, the God we offend still loves us deeply. It's hard to find words to express how much He loves us. No earthly comparison quite hits the mark. He loves us as a parent loves a child, as an artist loves his creation, as a lover loves his beloved. I know these comparisons seem inadequate, but they are not totally off the mark. The Bible uses these human images, and more, to help us know and feel how much God loves us.

The greatest evidence of God's love is the fact that, even though we rebelled and deserved death, He didn't want us to die. It's hard to imagine why, but He longs for us to share all eternity with Him. So He found a solution to the doom our sin had brought upon us. He offered to take the pain of the death we deserve upon Himself. So the second member of the Godhead, Jesus Christ, came to earth and represented us by living a perfect human life. He then allowed Himself to be brutally crucified on a Roman cross. But God resurrected Him, showing us that love and life are more powerful than sin and death. That is how much God loves us. Because Jesus died for us and lives again, God can accept Christ as our substitute and offer us His life throughout all eternity.

As overwhelming as this gift of eternal life is, God will not force it upon you. To receive it, you must repent of your rebellion, confess your sins (agree with God about them), and place your confidence in the life, death, and resurrection of Jesus Christ. This is what is often called "accepting Jesus into your heart."

Accepting this amazing gift from God is the only way to free yourself from fear. Yes, the same problems will still ravage the earth, and they will still touch your life. But you need no longer fear them. No matter what happens to you on this planet, you can live with the promise that you are safely in the hands of God, whom to know is to trust. Then you can embrace fearlessness just as the apostle Paul did: "I know whom I have believed and am persuaded that He is able to keep what I have committed to Him until that Day" (2 Timothy 1:12).

If you live with a fear of life, I encourage you to replace your fear of life with faith in new life through Christ our Lord.

# Acknowledgments

Writing this book was like writing ten books. Every chapter was a project of its own. It has taken everything I had to give, and without the support of my wife, Donna, my "everything" would not have been enough. My older son, David Michael, has become a strong partner in the publishing arm of our ministry, and I wish to thank him for his help. Paul Joiner and his creative team continue to be the best in the business. Thank you for the countless hours you spent dreaming and planning for the release of this book. Diane Sutherland stands at the door of my life and graciously protects the resources of my time and energy. She and Barbara Boucher deserve more credit than they ever get for dealing with the increasing demands that are placed upon our offices.

Along with the personal side of publishing, there is also a

more public side. I am very grateful for Sealy Yates, my agent and confidant. I am delighted to be working with Ron Beers and Tyndale House Publishers. I am indebted to William Kruidenier, Rob Morgan, Rob Suggs, and Tom Williams, who have invested their gifts in this project.

Finally, thank you to Beau Sager, who worked so many hours checking and chasing down quotes, working with editors, and making many valuable suggestions about the substance and sequencing of the material.

To do what we do each year would be beyond impossible without you, and I thank you, each one!

# Notes

**INTRODUCTION**

1. Don Wyrtzen, *A Musician Looks at the Psalms* (Grand Rapids, MI: Zondervan, 1991), 10.
2. Linda Lyons, "What Frightens America's Youth?" Gallup.com, March 29, 2005, www.gallup.com/poll/15439/What-Frightens-Americas-Youth.aspx
3. Neil T. Anderson and Rich Miller, *Freedom from Fear* (Eugene, OR: Harvest House Publishers, 1999), 25.

**CHAPTER 1   DISASTER: THE FEAR OF NATURAL CALAMITY**

1. Dinesh D'Souza, *What's So Great about Christianity* (Washington, DC: Regnery Publishing, 2007), 274.
2. George H. Smith, *Atheism: The Case against God* (New York: Prometheus Books, 1979), 81.
3. Allan Laing, "Wave That Beggared My Belief," *The Herald* (Glasgow, Scotland), January 4, 2005.
4. C. S. Lewis, *Mere Christianity* (New York: The Macmillan Company, 1952), 31.
5. Erwin Lutzer, *Where Was God?: Answers to Tough Questions about God and Natural Disasters* (Carol Stream, IL: Tyndale House Publishers, 2006), 100.
6. D'Souza, *What's So Great about Christianity*, 278.
7. James Montgomery Boice, *Romans Volume 2: The Reign of Grace* (Grand Rapids, MI: Baker Book House, 1992), 906.
8. Donald Grey Barnhouse, *God's Heirs: Romans 8:1-39* (Grand Rapids, MI: Wm. B. Eerdmans Publishing Co., 1959), 153.
9. Annie Johnson Flint, quoted in Mrs. Charles Cowman, *Streams in the Desert* (Grand Rapids, MI: Zondervan Publishing House, 1966), 148–149.
10. "The American Colony in Jerusalem," Library of Congress, December 1, 2008, www.loc.gov/exhibits/americancolony/amcolony-family.html.

11. Lutzer, *Where Was God*, 104.
12. Mark Mittelberg, *The Questions Christians Hope No One Will Ask* (Carol Stream, IL: Tyndale House Publishers, 2010), 137.
13. Adapted from Ray Stedman, *Let God Be God: Life-Changing Truths from the Book of Job* (Grand Rapids, MI: Discovery House Publishing, 2007), 69–70.
14. D'Souza, *What's So Great about Christianity*, 279.
15. Hannah Whitall Smith, *The God of All Comfort* (London: James Nisbet and Co., Limited, 1906), 252–253.

CHAPTER 2   DISEASE: THE FEAR OF ILLNESS
1. David Jeremiah, *When Your World Falls Apart* (Nashville: Thomas Nelson, 2000), 38.
2. Isobel Kuhn, *In the Arena* (Singapore: OMF Books, 1960), 225–232.
3. Centers for Disease Control and Prevention, "FastStats: Leading Causes of Death," January 11, 2013, www.cdc.gov/nchs/fastats/lcod.htm.
4. Ezra Klein, "21 Graphs That Show America's Health-Care Prices Are Ludicrous," *The Washington Post*, March 26, 2013, www.washingtonpost.com/blogs/wonkblog /wp/2013/03/26/21-graphs-that-show-americas-health-care-prices-are-ludicrous.
5. KaiserEDU.org, "U.S. Health Care Costs," www.kaiseredu.org/Issue -Modules/US-Health-Care-Costs/Background-Brief.aspx.
6. C. S. Lewis, "The Efficacy of Prayer" in *The World's Last Night and Other Essays* (New York: Harcourt, Brace & World, 1960), 9.
7. Randy Alcorn, *We Shall See God: Charles Spurgeon's Classic Devotional Thoughts on Heaven* (Carol Stream, IL: Tyndale House Books, 2011), 298.
8. Kuhn, *In the Arena*, 225–232.
9. Amy Carmichael, *Gold by Moonlight: Sensitive Lessons from a Walk with Pain* (Fort Washington, PA: CLC Publications, 2013), chapter 10.
10. Ed Dobson, *Prayers and Promises When Facing a Life-Threatening Illness* (Grand Rapids, MI: Zondervan, 2007), 56.
11. Thomas Watson, *A Divine Cordial: Romans 8:28* (La Vergne, TN: Lightning Source, Inc., 2001), 20.
12. Kuhn, *In the Arena*, 252–232.
13. Ibid.
14. Adapted from Robert J. Morgan, *From This Verse* (Nashville: Thomas Nelson, 1998), August 13.
15. Robert J. Morgan, *Real Stories for the Soul* (Nashville: Thomas Nelson, 2000), 1–3.
16. Ibid.
17. Author unknown, quoted by Curtis C. Thomas, *Practical Wisdom for Pastors* (Wheaton, IL: Crossway Books, 2001), 102.

CHAPTER 3   DEBT: THE FEAR OF FINANCIAL LOSS
1. www.statisticbrain.com/home-foreclosure-statistics/.
2. Henry David Thoreau, *Walden* (New York: Barnes and Noble Books, 2004), 74.
3. John Wesley, *Selections from the Writings of the Rev. John Wesley* (New York: Methodist Book Concern, 1929), 232.
4. John Wesley, *Sermons on Several Occasions*, volume 1 (London, 1829), 566.

5. Timothy George, "Unseen Footprints," *Preaching Today* audio, no. 290.

6. Adapted from Robert J. Morgan, *On This Day* (Nashville: Thomas Nelson, 1997), March 12.

7. Leonard Griffith, *God in Man's Experience: The Activity of God in the Psalms* (Waco, TX: Word Books, 1968), 59–60.

8. Charles H. Spurgeon, "The Treasury of David: Psalm 37," The Spurgeon Archive, www.spurgeon.org/treasury/ps037.htm.

9. From Leonard I. Sweet, *Strong in the Broken Places* (Akron, OH: University of Akron, 1995), 109.

10. Philip Yancey, *The Jesus I Never Knew* (Grand Rapids, MI: Zondervan, 1995), 275.

**CHAPTER 4   DEFEAT: THE FEAR OF FAILURE**

1. Robert A. Caro, *The Passage of Power*, vol. 4 of *The Years of Lyndon Johnson* (New York: Alfred A. Knopf, 2012), 16.

2. Ibid., 21.

3. From the Special Features segment of *The Fugitive*, © 1993 Warner Bros. Pictures.

4. J. Oswald Sanders, *Robust in Faith* (Chicago: Moody Press, 1965), 72.

5. William Sykes, *The Eternal Vision: The Ultimate Collection of Spiritual Quotations* (Peabody, MA: Hendrickson Publishers, 2003), 70.

6. Paul Laurence Dunbar, "Right's Security" in *Lyrics of Lowly Life* (New York: Dodd, Mead and Company, 1898), 179.

7. J. I. Packer, *Knowing God* (Downers Grove, IL: InterVarsity Press, 1973), 23.

**CHAPTER 5   DISCONNECTION: THE FEAR OF BEING ALONE**

1. Hal Niedzviecki, "Facebook in a Crowd," *New York Times*, October 24, 2008, www.nytimes.com/2008/10/26/magazine/26lives-t.html?_r=0.

2. Anne Hathaway, *Anne Hathaway Biography*, The Biography Channel, www .thebiographychannel.co.uk/biographies/anne-hathaway/quotes.html;jsessionid =A18297523C9AAAB6E9F6867A609ACBCD.

3. Quoted in Carl L. Adams, *Traveling Lighted Pathways* (Xulon Press, 2010), 138.

4. Quoted in R. A. Wise, *Wise Quotes of Wisdom* (Bloomington, IN: AuthorHouse, 2011), 252.

5. Walter Isaacson, *Kissinger: A Biography* (New York: Simon & Schuster, 2005), 145.

6. QuotationsBook, http://quotationsbook.com/quote/24232/.

7. Quoted in Billy Graham, *World Aflame* (New York: Pocket Books, 1965), 51.

8. Jib Fowles, *Starstruck* (Smithsonian Institution Press, 1992), 205.

9. Quoted in Debra Ollivier and Lauren Rosenblum, "Emilio Estevez on 'The Way': Actor Discusses New Movie, Life, Love, Faith and Micro-Farms," *The Huffington Post*, October 14, 2011, www.huffingtonpost.com/2011/10/14/emilio-estevez-the -way_n_1009852.html.

10. Jerry Adler, "Online and Bummed Out: One Study Says the Internet Can Be Alienating," *Newsweek*, September 14, 1998.

11. Nicholas Carr, *The Shallows: What the Internet Is Doing to Our Brains* (New York: W. W. Norton, 2010), 86.

12. Deborah Netburn, "Nomophobia""Fear of Being without Your Phone""Is on the Rise," *Los Angeles Times*, February 17, 2012, http://articles.latimes.com/2012/feb/17/business/la-fi-tn-nomophobia-on-the-rise-20120216.

13. Sherry Turkle, *Alone Together: Why We Expect More from Technology and Less from Each Other* (New York: Basic Books, 2011), 248.

14. Ibid., 249.

15. Peter Steiner, *The New Yorker*, July 5, 1993 (vol. LXIX, no. 20), 61.

16. Cited in Charles R. Swindoll, *The Tale of the Tardy Oxcart: And 1,501 Other Stories* (Nashville: Word Publishing, 1998), 352.

17. Erle Stanley Gardner, *The Case of the Drowsy Mosquito* (New York: William Morrow and Co., 1943), 179.

18. Atul Gawande, "Hellhole," *The New Yorker*, March 30, 2009, www.newyorker.com/reporting/2009/03/30/090330fa_fact_gawande.

19. John Phillips, *Exploring the Pastoral Epistles* (Grand Rapids, MI: Kregel Publications, 2004), 449–450.

20. Bobby Allyn, "More Singles Living Alone and Loving It, Despite the Economy," *The Tenneseean* (April 27, 2012), http://usatoday30.usatoday.com/news/nation/story/2012-05-02/living-alone/54585114/1.

21. James Joyner, "Record 28 Percent of American Households One Person Only," Outside the Beltway (February 1, 2012), www.outsidethebeltway.com/record-28-of-american-households-one-person-only.

22. R. Kent Hughes and Bryan Chapell, *1 and 2 Timothy and Titus,* Preaching the Word (Wheaton, IL: Crossway Books, 2000), 259–260.

23. Quoted in J. Oswald Sanders, *Spiritual Leadership* (Chicago: Moody Publishers, 1994), 121.

24. John R. W. Stott, *Guard the Gospel: The Message of 2 Timothy* (Downers Grove, IL: InterVarsity Press, 1997), 120.

25. Handley C. G. Moule, *The Second Epistle to Timothy* (London: Religious Tract Society, 1905), 158–159.

26. Dietrich Bonhoeffer, *Life Together* (New York: Harper, 1954), 99.

**CHAPTER 6   DISAPPROVAL: THE FEAR OF REJECTION**

1. Ed Welch, *When People Are Big and God Is Small* (Phillipsburg, NJ: P&R Publishing, 1997), 17.

2. Ibid., 14.

3. Andrée Seu, "Fear of Man," *World*, April 14, 1999, www.worldmag.com/1999/08/fear_of_man.

4. Charles H. Spurgeon, "In the Garden with Him," Sermon No. 2106, August 8, 1889, www.spurgeongems.org/vols34-36/chs2106.pdf.

5. Matthew Henry, *An Exposition of the New Testament* (London: William Mackenzie, 2009), 270.

6. Neil T. Anderson and Rich Miller, *Freedom from Fear: Overcoming Worry and Anxiety* (Eugene, OR: Harvest House Publishers, 1999), 25.

7. Ken Walker, "Time to Bow or Bow Out?" *Sports Spectrum*, September 1997, 22–25.

8. Charles Kuralt, *Charles Kuralt's America* (New York: Anchor Books, 1996), 220.

CHAPTER 7   DANGER: THE FEAR OF MAJOR TROUBLE

1. Sebastian Junger, *The Perfect Storm: A True Story of Men against the Sea* (New York: W. W. Norton & Company, 2009), 106.
2. William Hughes Mearns, "Antigonish," 1922.
3. Franklin D. Roosevelt, 37th Inaugural Ceremonies, March 4, 1933, www.bartleby .com/124/pres49.html.
4. Gary L. Thomas, "The Freedom of Surrender," *Discipleship Journal*, September/ October 1996, 52.
5. Craig Brian Larson and *Leadership Journal, 750 Engaging Illustrations for Preachers, Teachers, and Writers* (Grand Rapids, MI: Baker Books, 2007), 493.
6. James Paton, John Gibson Paton, *Missionary to the New Hebrides: An Autobiography*, volume 2 (London: Butler & Tanner, 1889), 192.
7. Ibid., 325.
8. Timothy Keller, *King's Cross* (New York: Dutton, 2011), 52.
9. Joni Eareckson Tada, *Hope . . . the Best of Things* (Wheaton, IL: Crossway Books, 2008), 16.
10. C. S. Lewis, *The Problem of Pain* (New York: Macmillan Publishing Company, Inc., 1973), 84.
11. Randy Alcorn, *If God Is Good* (Colorado Springs: Multnomah Books, 2009), 275.
12. Ibid., 275.
13. Lamar Williamson, *Mark: Interpretation, a Bible Commentary for Teaching and Preaching* (Atlanta: John Knox Press, 1983), 102.
14. Ruth A. Tucker, *From Jerusalem to Irian Jaya* (Grand Rapids, MI: Zondervan, 1983, 2004), 137.
15. C. S. Lewis, *A Grief Observed* (New York: Seabury Press, 1961), 9.
16. Charles Haddon Spurgeon, "Fearing and Trusting—Trusting and Not Fearing," *Sermons on the Psalms* (London: Marshall, Morgan & Scott, 1963).

CHAPTER 8   DEPRESSION: THE FEAR OF MENTAL BREAKDOWN

1. Barbara Kantrowitz, "The Fugitive," *Time*, September 27, 1993, 54–60; and Pam Lambert, "Alice Doesn't Live Here Anymore," People.com, October 4, 1993, www.people.com/people/archive/article/0,,20106382,00.html.
2. Kay Redfield Jamison, *An Unquiet Mind: A Memoir of Mood and Madness* (New York: Vintage Books, 1996), 112.
3. Ed Welch, *Depression: Looking Up from the Stubborn Darkness* (Winston-Salem, NC: Punch Press, 2004), 143.
4. J. B. Phillips, *The Price of Success* (Wheaton, IL: H. Shaw Publishers, 2000), 201.
5. William Styron, *Darkness Visible: A Memoir of Madness* (New York: Vintage Books, 1992), 84.
6. Dante Alighieri, *The Divine Comedy* (Oxford: Benediction Classics, 2001), 11.
7. "The Numbers Count: Mental Disorders in America," National Institute of Mental Health, www.nimh.nih.gov/health/publications/the-numbers-count -mental-disorders-in-america/index.shtml; Janice Lloyd, "CDC: Antidepressant Use Skyrockets 400% in Past 20 Years," *USA Today*, October 20, 2011, http:// usatoday30.usatoday.com/news/health/story/health/story/2011-10-19/CDC -Antidepressant-use-skyrockets-400-in-past-20-years/50826442/1.

8. Bret Stephens, "The Great Depression," *Wall Street Journal*, March 9, 2007.

9. J. Oswald Sanders, *A Spiritual Clinic* (Chicago: Moody Press, 1958), 113.

10. Charles Spurgeon, "Fear Not," The Spurgeon Archive, October 4, 1857, www .spurgeon.org/sermons/0156.htm.

11. Quoted in Steven J. Lawson, *Holman Old Testament Commentary: Job* (Nashville: Broadman & Holman Publishers, 2004), 39.

12. John Knox, *Writings of the Rev. John Knox* (Philadelphia: Presbyterian Board of Publication, 1842), 265.

13. John Bunyan, *The Works: Being Several Discourses upon Various Divine Subjects*, Volume 2 (London), 299.

14. Ray C. Stedman, *Let God Be God: Life-Changing Truths from the Book of Job* (Grand Rapids, MI: Discovery House Publishers, 2007), 51.

15. David B. Biebel and Harold G. Koenig, *New Light on Depression* (Grand Rapids, MI: Zondervan, 2004), 64.

16. William Barclay, *The Letters of James and Peter* (Philadelphia: Westminster Press, 1960), 147–148.

17. D. Martyn Lloyd-Jones, *Spiritual Depression: Its Causes and Cure* (Grand Rapids, MI: Eerdmans Printing Company, 1965), 18–19.

18. C. H. Spurgeon, "The Minister's Fainting Fits" from *Lectures to My Students* (Grand Rapids, MI: Zondervan Publishing House, 1970), 155, 156.

19. Mike Mason, *The Gospel according to Job* (Wheaton, IL: Crossway Books, 1994), 56.

20. Dan Phillips, "Battling Depression," March 15, 2011, http://teampyro.blogspot .com/2011/03/battling-depression.html.

21. John W. Yates, "Overcoming Discouragement," *Preaching Today*, number 42.

22. Mason, *The Gospel According to Job*, xii.

23. Welch, *Depression*, 249.

### CHAPTER 9   DEATH: THE FEAR OF DYING

1. Wayne Hale, "After Ten Years: Working on the Wrong Problem," January 13, 2013, http://waynehale.wordpress.com/2013/01/13/after-ten-years-working -on-the-wrong-problem.

2. Stephen White, "Revealed: NASA Chiefs Didn't Tell Columbia Space Shuttle Crew They Were about to Die," *Daily Record*, February 2, 2013, www.dailyrecord .co.uk/news/uk-world-news/nasa-knew-space-shuttle-columbia-1569567; Gina Sunseri, "Columbia Shuttle Crew Not Told of Possible Problem with Reentry," ABC News, January 31, 2012, http://abcnews.go.com/Technology/columbia -shuttle-crew-told-problem-reentry/story?id=18366185.

3. Eric Lax, *Woody Allen: A Biography* (New York: Da Capo Press, 1991), 26.

4. "Death, Dying and Beyond," Lebanon Valley College, www.lvc.edu/rel314 /euph.aspx.

5. Kevin J. Gardner, *Faith and Doubt of John Betjeman: An Anthology of Betjeman's Religious Verse* (New York: Continuum International Publishing Group, 2006), 77.

6. Philippe Ariès and Helen Weaver, *The Hour of Our Death: The Classic History of Western Attitudes toward Death over the Last One Thousand Years* (New York: Vintage Books, 1982).

7. Joseph Bayly, *The View from a Hearse* (Elgin, IL: David C. Cook Publishing Co., 1969), 11–12.

8. Eugene O'Kelly, *Chasing Daylight: How My Forthcoming Death Transformed My Life* (New York: McGraw-Hill, 2007), 17–18.

9. Dr. S. I. McMillen and Dr. David E. Stern, *None of These Diseases: The Bible's Health Secrets for the 21st Century* (Grand Rapids, MI: Fleming H. Revell, 2000), 228.

10. Ligon Duncan, *Fear Not!: Death and Afterlife from a Christian Perspective* (Tain, Scotland: Christian Focus, 2008), 24–25.

11. Philo, *Every Good Man Is Free*, 3:22.

12. Ruth Overholtzer, *From Then till Now* (Warrenton, MO: CEF Press, 1990), 130.

13. Nino Lo Bello, *The Incredible Book of Vatican Facts and Papal Curiosities* (New York: Barnes & Noble Books, 1998), 16.

14. The fifth verse of Watts's (untitled) hymn number 112, as found in collections of his hymns.

15. Larry Libby, *Somewhere Angels* (Sisters, OR: Multnomah Books, 1994), 41.

16. Rev. Peter J. Marshall, ed., *The Wartime Sermons of Dr. Peter Marshall* (Tulsa, OK: CrossStaff Publishing, 2005).

17. *Perfect Illustrations for Every Topic and Occasion*, compiled by the editors of PreachingToday.com (Carol Stream, IL: Tyndale House Publishers, Inc., 2002), 289.

18. Robert J. Morgan, *The Lord Is My Shepherd* (New York: Howard Books, 2013), 116–117.

19. James M. Campbell, D.D., *Heaven Opened* (New York: Revell, 1924), 178.

20. Michael P. Green, ed., *Illustrations for Biblical Preaching* (Grand Rapids, MI: Baker Book House, 1989), 91.

21. Corrie ten Boom, *He Cares, He Comforts* (Old Tappan, NJ: Fleming H. Revell Company, 1977), 89–90.

22. Franz Liszt, *Les Preludes: Symphonic Poem No. 3* (Van Nuys, CA: Alfred Music Publishing, 1985), 39.

23. C. S. Lewis, *The Last Battle* (New York: Macmillan, 1956), 210–211.

24. Charles L. Allen, *You Are Never Alone* (Old Tappan, NJ: Fleming H. Revell, 1978), 77–79.

### CHAPTER 10 DEITY: THE FEAR OF GOD

1. C. S. Lewis, *The Silver Chair* (New York: HarperCollins Publishers, 1981), 22–23.

2. Harold S. Kushner, *Conquering Fear: Living Boldly in an Uncertain World* (NY: Anchor Books, 2009), 166.

3. Charles Crismier, *The Secret of the Lord* (Richmond, VA: Elijah Books, 2011), 49.

4. A. W. Tozer, *The Knowledge of the Holy* (New York: Harper & Row, 1961), 78.

5. Dr. Dan B. Allender and Dr. Tremper Longman III, *The Cry of the Soul: How Our Emotions Reveal Our Deepest Questions about God* (Colorado Springs: NavPress, 1994), 100.

6. Peter Kreeft, "Perfect Fear Casts Out All "Luv,"" www.peterkreeft.com/topics /fear.htm.

7. Sinclair Ferguson, *Grow in Grace* (Colorado Springs: NavPress, 1984), 236–237.

8. A. W. Tozer, *Whatever Happened to Worship?* (Camp Hill, PA: Christian Publications, 1985), 36.

9. John Murray, *Principles of Conduct: Aspects of Biblical Ethics* (Grand Rapids, MI: William B. Eerdmans Publishing Co., 1957), 236–237.

10. Vance Havner, "Have You Lost the Wonder?" *The Alliance Weekly*, August 21, 1948, 532.

11. Ravi Zacharias, *Can Man Live Without God?* (Dallas: Word Publishing, 1994), 89.

12. Kreeft, "Perfect Fear Casts Out All "Luv,"" www.peterkreeft.com/topics /fear.htm.

13. Paul Thigpen, "Loving God, Fearing God: How Can We Do Both at the Same Time?" *Discipleship Journal*, July/August 2000, www.navpress.com /magazines/archives/article.aspx?id=10960.

14. C. S. Lewis, *The Lion, the Witch, and the Wardrobe* (London: Penguin Books, 1950), 75.

15. Martin Wells Knapp, *Revival Tornadoes: or, Life and Labors of Rev. Joseph H. Weber* (Boston: McDonald, Gill, & Co., 1890), 178.

16. Quoted by Edgar H. Lewellen in *Revival: God's Proven Method of Awakening His Church* (Maitland, FL: Xulon Press, 2005), 10.

17. Wesley L. Duewel, *Revival Fire* (Grand Rapids, MI: Zondervan, 1995), 139–141.

18. Ibid., 139–141.

19. John Piper, *The Pleasures of God* (Sisters, OR: Multnomah Books, 2000), 198–199.

## EPILOGUE

1. cndrewdrvr8, "I Fear: Life," The Experience Project, August 24, 2011, www .experienceproject.com/stories/Fear/1739001.

*stay connected to the teaching series of*

# DR. DAVID JEREMIAH

Publishing | Radio | Television | Online

# FURTHER YOUR STUDY OF THIS BOOK

## *What Are You Afraid Of?* Resource Materials

To enhance your study on this important topic, we recommend the correlating audio message album, study guide, and DVD messages from the *What Are You Afraid Of? Facing Down Your Fears with Faith* series.

### Audio Message Album

The material found in this book originated from messages presented by Dr. David Jeremiah at the Shadow Mountain Community Church where he serves as Senior Pastor. These ten messages are conveniently packaged in an accessible audio album.

### Audio Message Album

This 128-page study guide correlates with the *What Are You Afraid Of? Facing Down Your Fears with Faith* messages by David Jeremiah. Each lesson provides an outline, overview, and application questions for each topic.

### DVD Message Presentations

Watch Dr. Jeremiah deliver the *What Are You Afraid Of?* original messages in this special DVD collection.

*New York Times* Best Seller
# God Loves You!
### by Dr. David Jeremiah

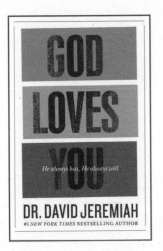

The knowledge that God loves us is the most profound truth in the universe. Experiencing this love has the potential to answer every question, solve every problem, and satisfy the deepest yearnings of the heart. So why are so many people who believe this still unable to fully utilize the power of God's love in their personal lives?

In this probing book, Dr. David Jeremiah reveals that not fully understanding and appreciating every dimension of God's love can lead to missed opportunities to experience His love. He explains how even the so-called negative dimensions of God's actions—hell, prohibitive commandments, pain and suffering in the world—can only be rightly understood by viewing them in light of God's unfathomable love for us.

*God Loves You* will enable you to know God in a way that will consciously connect you with the healing power of His grace so you can experience the life of love you were created to enjoy.

### *God Loves You—He Always Has. He Always Will.* uncovers the truth of God's extraordinary love:

- God loves you even when you don't love Him.
- God's love never quits. • God loved you before you were born.
- God loves you when He is correcting you.
- God wrote His love in red. • God's love will never let you go.

---

To order this book, call us at 1-800-947-1993 or visit us online at www.DavidJeremiah.org.

CP0698

# BOOKS WRITTEN BY DAVID JEREMIAH

Escape the Coming Night
Turning Toward Joy
The Handwriting on the Wall
Invasion of Other Gods
Angels—Who They Are and How They Help…What the Bible Reveals
The Joy of Encouragement
Prayer—The Great Adventure
God In You
Until Christ Returns
Stories of Hope
Slaying the Giants in Your Life
My Heart's Desire
Sanctuary
The Things That Matter
The Prayer Matrix
31 Days to Happiness—Searching for Heaven on Earth
When Your World Falls Apart
Life Wide Open
The Secret of the Light, Co-authored with Thomas Kinkade, J.
Turning Points
Discover Paradise
Captured by Grace
Grace Givers
Why the Nativity?
Signs of Life
Life-changing Moments with God
Hopeful Parenting
1 Minute a Day—Instant Inspiration for the Busy Life
Grandparenting—Faith That Survives Generations
In the Words of David Jeremiah
What in the World Is Going On?

CP0699

The Sovereign and the Suffering
The 12 Ways of Christmas
What To Do When You Don't Know What To Do
Living with Confidence in a Chaotic World
The Prophecy Answer Book
The Coming Economic Armageddon
Pathways, Your Daily Walk with God
What the Bible Says About Love, Marriage, and Sex
I Never Thought I'd See The Day
Journey, Your Daily Adventure with God
The Unchanging Word of God
God Loves You: He Always Has–He Always Will
Discovery, Experiencing God's Word Day by Day
What Are You Afraid Of?

To order these books, call us at 1-800-947-1993 or
visit us online at www.DavidJeremiah.org.

CP0699

# STAY CONNECTED

Take advantage of two great ways to let
Dr. David Jeremiah give you spiritual direction every day!
**Both are absolutely free!**

## ① *Turning Points* Magazine and Devotional

### *each magazine features:*

- Monthly study focus
- 48 pages of life-changing reading
- Relevant articles
- Special features
- Humor section
- Family section
- Devotional readings for each day of the month
- Bible study resource offers
- Live event schedule
- Radio & television information

FREE!

---

## Request your free subscription today!

**CALL:**   (800) 947-1993

**CLICK:**   DavidJeremiah.org/Magazine

CP0700

Today's
# TURNING POINT
*with* Dr. David Jeremiah

**Heaven Rules**

*The Most High is sovereign over all kingdoms on earth and gives them to anyone He wishes....*
**Daniel 4:17 (NIV)**

The last of the Major Prophets tells the story of a prophet and statesman named Daniel, who was among the exiles from Judah living in Babylon during the time when the nation of Judah no longer existed and the city of Jerusalem no longer stood. From all observable evidence, God's promises to Israel had failed. The Jewish people, it seemed, were finished, and with them God's redemptive plan for the earth.

Recommended Reading
Daniel 4:34-37

But not so fast! The theme of the Book of Daniel is that the Most High still rules over the affairs of history regardless of who seems to be in control of the governmental centers of earth. The first six chapters of Daniel tell six stories emphasizing God's sovereign control over history, and the last six chapters give predictions as to God's plan for the future.

Listen to Today's
Radio Message

In every epoch, God's purposes are not delayed nor His decrees thwarted. Amid today's chaos and even during the coming Great Tribulation, God is and will forever be in control. We can rest assured "Heaven rules" (Daniel 4:26).

*Apart from Christ, history is without final meaning, for real history is the history of redemption. History is His story.*
**J. Oswald Sanders**

Start your day off right! Find words of inspiration and spiritual motivation waiting for you on your computer every morning! You can receive a daily e-devotional from Dr. Jeremiah that will strengthen your walk with God and encourage you to live the authentic Christian life.

## Request your free e-devotional today!

**CLICK:**        DavidJeremiah.org/Devo